HELLO GOD!

A Daily Call To Faith and Worship.

D1276471

By

Henry Lamar Hunt

HLH Ministries
PO Box 463
Candler, Florida 32111

ISBN: 0-9700985-1-0
Library of Congress Control Number:
00-132419

HLH Ministries
PO Box 463
Candler, Florida 32111

Cover Photography
Copyright © 2000 by
Morris Press

Illustrations are by Elaine M. Schaaf,
Sumterville, Florida.

Printed in the United States by:
Morris Publishing
3212 East Highway 30
Kearney, NE 68847
1-800-650-7888

PREFACE

Hello God experiences? The sudden insight! Those "Oh, yeah, Lord, I get it" moments!

Hello God happenings are those times when you are battered by adversity, overwhelmed by trivia, or lost from meaning, and quite unexpectedly you see the hand of God. You learn. You grow.

Many of the devotions in this book were *Hello God* experiences for me. I hope and pray that each one of them will be the same for you. I pray that you will be struck by, and confronted with, the awesome reality of God's presence and His love and grace in your daily life.

My evangelical faith and ecumenical spirit shape these devotions. I don't believe that those values are antithetical. They have been tested overseas and at home, in every conceivable context, and during nearly 50 years of ministry.

In following God's will for my life I have lived a long series of adventures, notable experiences, with some hardships: a true *spiritual odyssey*. Through all of them I have known that the Lord Jesus was walking with me, that His love for me was unfailing, and His grace was powerful to save.

Interspersed though out the book are devotions that move around on the calendar. You will find Ash Wednesday between January and February. Holy Week devotions are at the end of March. Ascension and Pentecost Sunday are between April and May. Thanksgiving Day is before November. Advent and Hanukkah are between November and December. These are extra devotions that I hope you will use in addition to the regular, dated devotions.

Scripture verses are from the New King James Version of the Bible, except where otherwise indicated.

DEDICATION

To the men and women of the United States military and their families: especially to my children, Alan, Lisa, and Mark; all three of whom served their Country honorably on active duty.

To chaplains and chaplain assistants, unsung heroes; who accompany the troops in the jungle, across the desert, in the air, and on the sea. It has been a distinct pleasure for me to serve with these Unit Ministry Teams. I enjoyed, and was nourished by, professional relationships with folks from many denominations. This was particularly true of Catholic friends, with whom I shared many lonely hours in unaccompanied tours, in field exercises, and in combat.

To Shirley: wife, friend, lover, and alto singer; who set a standard for military spouses in assignments all over the United States, in Europe, and in Central America.

To my sister Betty Kilgore, and her husband Clifford, who took care of my parents while I was deployed around the world; and to Shirley's brother Maurice Turner, and his wife Ann, who did the same for Shirley's parents.

And to Jesus, my Lord and Savior; by whose mercy I am saved, and through whose grace I have been privileged to carry His Gospel.

ACKNOWLEDGEMENTS

A sincere thanks is extended to Bishop Joe A. Wilson of the Central Texas Conference of the United Methodist Church. My bishop. He took time to review this work and write a foreword. Bishop Wilson is a true pastor's pastor.

I am also grateful to my former teacher, and the Dean Emeritus of Erskine Theological Seminary, Doctor Randall T. Ruble. Waiting for him to read the book, write a foreword, and mail the foreword to me, took me back to when I waited apprehensively for his comments and grades on my class work. I was delighted that he took the time and made the effort to write a serious discourse.

Doctor Buckner Fanning, while shepherding the huge Trinity Baptist Church in San Antonio, Texas, is more than that, a pastor to the whole community. His remarks, from so busy a pastor, are most generous.

Miss Barbara Fairchild, beautiful in body and spirit, was gracious to review and recommend *Hello God*. This precious child of God, and her husband, Roy, live, entertain, and minister in Branson, Missouri.

My daughter, Lisa Keating, read the entire volume twice. She discovered many errors, both in typing and in content. She found places where a sentence or paragraph was either illogical or redundant. She helped me remember the times and events that fill the pages of *Hello God*.

Don Keating, a friend of over thirty years, taught me how to format, insert, and do a dozen little computer things, that helped to get this book to press. Don also gave the manuscript a thorough proofing.

Special thanks for proof reading and editorial assistance on the 2d printing to Barbara Wilson, gifted teacher, and wife of my pal Chaplain Tom Wilson.

FOREWORD

Hello God is a marvelous book of spiritual "vitamins" that will strengthen and enrich your days. Chaplain Lamar Hunt, a retired US Army Chaplain, has written a book of daily devotions that will provide you with inspiration and instruction for living a strong and victorious Christian life.

Hello God is rich in illustrative and sermon building material, a gold mine of resources for the busy pastor.

The reader will find *Hello God* to be true to the Scriptures and evangelical in doctrine. The devotions also reflect the writer's ecumenical spirit, a warm and embracing vivacity that served him well in thirty years of ministry on active duty to America's young people in uniform.

Pastor Buckner Fanning
Trinity Baptist Church
San Antonio, Texas

FOREWORD

This wonderful book will be a blessing to so many people. I'm so happy to have the chance to recommend *Hello God* to others. Many lives will be changed through this precious work. It's great!

I have come to know Chaplain Hunt through the annual Veterans Homecoming in Branson, Missouri. I have seen his heart for the Lord many times. I see that same heart written on paper and I am enriched by the experience. Thank you Chaplain Hunt for being so real.

Miss Barbara Fairchild
Branson, Missouri

FOREWORD

Chaplain Lamar Hunt writes these daily devotions from a unique perspective.

After serving nine years as a local church pastor and over thirty years as an Army Chaplain, achieving the rank of Colonel, he shares an understanding of faith that both refreshes and challenges each new day.

Chaplain Hunt has known combat, been decorated for valor, traveled in 35 countries and served as an Army Chaplain in Vietnam, Korea, Germany and Panama. He has shared the joy of family life through a long, happy marriage, which has produced three children and three grandchildren. Out of these rich life experiences, many of which are offered through brief insightful stories, he is able to introduce the reader to moments of inspiration and hope.

Grounded in a strong Christology, a firm belief in the Scriptures, an evangelical faith, and an ecumenical heart, he has produced a marvelous collection of daily readings that will "kick-start" every morning with wisdom saved from the journey of a Christian pilgrim.

Many of these devotions end with prayer and scripture that tie together the message for the day in a beautiful, woven pattern of thought. In *Hello God* the author has assembled a book that is truly a "faith odyssey," offering the sojourner a rare opportunity to drink daily from the refreshing waters of Christ-centered worship.

Joe A. Wilson, Bishop
Central Texas Conference
United Methodist Church

FOREWORD

Devotional literature belongs to the very essence of the Biblical tradition. The book of Psalms has often been called the book of worship with its strong accent upon the praise of God and memories of His mighty deeds. Literature written to enable believers to meditate and reflect upon God and the Holy Scriptures was among the first developed in the early church. It has continued to hold a prominent place in the life of God's people all through the years.

In this time of transition to the next century, the church is confronted anew with the question of the praise of God. As both the nation and world face tragedies, natural catastrophes, and crimes, of unparalleled magnitude, a new interest in the praise of God has been awakened. Earlier in this century, Karl Barth wrote, "Praise of God is the most endangered and the most dangerous undertaking of the church. Everyone can praise, even the heretic! Thus it must be that at certain times one speaks but little or not at all of the praise of God, that there are special times when it awakens with power and then is neither endangered nor dangerous" (Credo, p.124).

Hello God attempts to help us praise God and draw near to Him. Good devotional literature has clear characteristics, which bode well for its usefulness in the religious community. While it must be rooted in the Bible, it must also grow out of human experiences so that the great issues of life are addressed. Devotional literature intended for daily use must be concise enough to be read in a few minutes, and, above all else, it must be appealing and beneficial for the reader. Such literature has usually been produced by pastors or rabbis of local congregations who are involved in the spiritual struggles of those under their care. Sometimes an academic leader enters this arena. But it is rare for a military chaplain to offer a volume of devotional literature.

Henry Lamar Hunt, retired Colonel in the U.S. Army Chaplaincy and a former student of mine, explores in his contribution to this growing field of literature the nuances of what he describes as the "faith odyssey."

Gearing his reflections to the Christian year, Chaplain Hunt draws heavily from the Gospels and Epistles, but he does not neglect the Old Testament's rich witness, especially as found in the book of Psalms. Chaplain Hunt's long military career provides the context for many of his observations about life. He has lived all over the world and his rich range of experiences is used to explicate a short Biblical text for the day.

His observations range from natural occurrences and living quarters to events in the cycle of family life. Natural developments in his children form a bond with his own spiritual growth and maturity. Major happenings and persons in American history are often cited to make his point. Religious and civil holidays find a place in his reflections.

The style of *Hello God* is both simple and engaging. The anecdotal character of each devotion is cast in flowing, crisp sentences making for easy reading. The blending of the spiritual with the practical invites the reader to follow along a path by which Chaplain Hunt has found his way into the presence of God. The author demonstrates how a person may live a religious life in the world, not by turning one's back upon it, but by embracing it with all the opulent resources of the Christian faith. Anyone will be abundantly repaid for tracing Chaplain Hunt's footsteps as he looks deeply into the human soul and opens the way to the spirit of God.

Randall T. Ruble
Vice President and Dean Emeritus
Erskine Theological Seminary
Due West, South Carolina

January 1

Happy New Year.

John Newton wrote the great hymn, *Amazing Grace*. When he was transferred from a small country church to a large church in London he prayed for what he called "London Grace." He called it a grace strong enough to enable him to live a Christian life, even in London.

There was a man named Job. He was an upright, God-fearing, man of wealth and family. But that didn't make him immune to sorrow and suffering. Marauders killed his servants. His stock animals were lost in a fire. All of his children were killed in a tornado. Then, his whole body was covered with loathsome sores. His wife urged him to curse God and die.

Yet Job clung tenaciously to his hope in God, "...I know that my Redeemer lives and. in my flesh I shall see God" (Job 19:25,26).

Hello God!

Job found grace, "...The Lord blessed the latter days of Job more than his beginnings..." (Job 42:12).

When the children of Israel had been taken captive, away from their home country, they cried, "How shall we sing the Lord's song in a strange land?"

Israel found grace. So did Job. And John Newton. You can too!

His grace is there for you for wherever you are. Your particular need. Nothing is too hard for Him. Cling to Him. All year long. His grace will see you through painful nights and lonely days. The supply of His grace is unlimited.

There is New Year grace! Every day and every thing grace! Yours!

"...Grace *abounded* much more."
Romans 5:20

Walk me through this year, Lord. Bless me and make me a blessing, through Jesus Christ, my Lord. Amen

January 2

A little girl was leading her younger brother on a hike along a path up a hillside. He said, "This is a stupid path. It's nothing but rocks and bumps." "Silly, they are what you climb on," his sister replied.

There will be many rocks and bumps in your path in the coming year. Use them as stepping stones.

You may trip, but you won't have to stay down.

You may experience great pain, and sadness may darken your spirit. But don't despair. You have a friend. The Lord Jesus will be there to help you. He is never more than a prayer away.

You will see someone struggling along on his or her journey. Lend an uplifting and steadying hand. Be as good to others as God has been to you.

It won't be all rocks and bumps. You will enjoy the beauty in "ordinary" things: the sparkle in a friend's eye; the wet kiss of a baby; the fulfilling satisfaction of a maturing relationship; the nourishing instruction of a faith community; the joy of being alive.

Hello God!

Will You be with me this year, Lord? Can I count on Your presence and blessing in my life?

Father, I want to know Jesus Christ as Lord and Savior, and live out His claims on my life every day of the year. I want to always live by the Golden Rule. I want to be charitable to those in need, to do the right thing, and to temper all of my actions with mercy.

Bless me, O Lord: love me, save me, empower me, and sustain me. As I pray now I am thankful for Your many blessings of the past, the rich sustenance You provide in the present, and Your glorious promise for the future. Amen

"My times are in Your hand...make Your face shine upon Your servant...."
Psalm 31:15,16

January 3

Only one was under fifty years of age.

They were four chaplains, three National Guardsmen, and one Army Reservist, on their way to war in the Persian Gulf. I was responsible for their training and met them for a working breakfast.

They were filled with enthusiasm, eager to accompany their units into combat.

They reminded me of Caleb during Israel's wilderness wanderings. He and Joshua had urged Moses to go in and possess the land, even though the majority of their spy team disagreed. Moses accepted their minority report and Israel did possess the land.

Forty-five years later Caleb petitioned Joshua, who by then had succeeded Moses, for his rightful share of the land. Most of the best land had been divided among the twelve tribes.

"...I am as strong this day as I was on the day that Moses sent me...now, therefore, *give me this mountain....*" Caleb demanded (Joshua 14:11,12).

He was *85* years old! What a spirit.

What an attitude for a new year, and a new century.

"...Joshua blessed him, and gave Hebron to Caleb...because he wholly followed the Lord God of Israel."
Joshua 14:13

You only need one resolution for a new year or a new century: never stop until you are all that God wants you to be and have all that He wants you to have.

So are you ready? To claim your mountain? Well, then go get it. Amen

January 4

When our first grandchild was born Shirley flew to Texas to help out, leaving me, and our Yorkshire Terrier, alone in Fort McPherson, Georgia.

I was handling the grandfather bit quite well. Taking it pretty much in stride. Really cool. When friends asked how it felt to be a grandparent I answered that it was no big deal. Actually, it hadn't really dawned on me yet.

Well, it did dawn on me, with a vengeance, when I called my mother to report on the health of my daughter and grandson.

"Hi grandfather!" she said cheerily. "Good Lord," I thought, "I'm now the same as my mother." One day I was her boy and the next day I was a fellow grandparent.

In our fantasies we would be forever young. But people and events, over which we have no control, define our status.

I am known by many identifiers: Shirley's husband; Mark's dad; Jerry's friend; Joe's neighbor; Betty's brother; Ian's, Presley's, and Turner's grandfather; and others. But friends, family, and neighbors change.

However, one relationship never changes. If you are God's son or daughter now you carry that identity right with you, into eternity.

Today I hope that you will reflect on this wonderful connection. You may be poor in human terms but a child of the King, royalty, in the eyes of God.

Dear Lord, don't let me forget that You are my Father. Help me to act like a family member should. Amen

"Behold what manner of love the Father has bestowed on us, that we should be called children of God...."
1 John 3:1

January 5

"All I need now is an airplane."

That was my dear friend's remark after he gave me the grand tour of his new home.

He and his family had moved into their lake home. They have a pontoon boat, dock, and motor home. They are employed and blessed with good health.

Even though he is a good and charitable person his remark troubled me. Jesus taught that, "...One's life does not consist in the abundance of the things he possesses" (Luke 12:15).

How do you evaluate your life? Is it defined by what you have? We live in a culture that defines success and worth by material things. However, the Scriptures place value on giving, as opposed to having.

Another defining quality of our society is its unwillingness to postpone today's gratification for a better future good. We pray, "God, give me patience, now!"

I hope that you will re-assess your personal priorities. That you can realize that true riches are of the Spirit. And that they aren't measured by the things that you have.

If an airplane would make you happy; or a Town Car, or a home in a gated community, or $1,000 suits, you may have your values skewed.

Dear Lord, I am so blessed with things that it is embarrassing. Help me to see beyond the material. Help me to catch sight of the eternal, and to latch onto the things that will remain forever. Amen

"...Where your treasure is, there your heart will be also."
Matthew 6:21

January 6

On a cold, winter, morning a pastor's wife saw a boy selling newspapers on a corner. He was barefoot, and standing on a steam grate to keep his feet warm. She parked her car, took the boy into a shoe store, and bought him a pair of warm socks and new shoes.

The kid, in his excitement, rushed out of the store immediately. Then he stopped, and ran quickly back to thank her.

"Excuse me, ma'am," he said, "But may I ask you a question?"

"Of course, son, what is it?"

"Are you God's wife?"

"No, I am not God's wife," she answered. Then, after thinking a few moments she continued, "But I am one of His children."

"I knowed you must be some kin to Him," the boy asserted.

Hello God!

Today is Epiphany, the day that the church celebrates the revealing of Christ to the Gentiles, as represented by the visit of the Magi to the Christ Child. Pastors traditionally preach on missions and world evangelism on the Sunday nearest today.

We must also lay our gifts at His feet. Jesus ordered the church to preach the Gospel to the whole world. Every Christian must take part in that outreach. Today is the ideal time to review your stewardship and commit yourself to obeying the church's Great Commission.

Dear Lord, please don't let me go through this day without buying someone a pair of shoes. And help me to give my best in support of the Gospel at home and abroad. Amen

"...When they had opened their treasures, they presented gifts to Him: gold, frankincense, and myrrh."
Matthew 2:11

January 7

A country preacher's ministry became so successful that he was called to a big city church in New England.

The secretary at the new church was a recent immigrant. Even though she had studied hard and become fairly fluent in English she knew nothing of the regional accents. So when she typed the Sunday sermon from an audio dictation Holy Spirit came out "Holy Spurt."

The Christianity of some seems to be characterized more by spurts than Spirit. Great intentions wane with the passing weeks. Pledges and promises are not kept over time.

Are you a spurting Christian?

Do you remember the story of the race between the tortoise and the hare? The hare got off to a great start but soon began to play, circle, and take naps under shade trees. The tortoise shoved himself into a steady crawl, and kept going. Do you remember who won?

Jesus taught His disciples that their commitment ought to be like a king going to war. First he counts the cost, then commits for the duration of the battle. St. Paul wrote to Christians of his time: "You ran well. Who hindered you from obeying the truth?" (Galatians 5:7)

Are you hindered? A hindrance?

The secret is to keep going. Run if you can. Trot if you must. Crawl if you have to.

Grant it dear Lord, for me and for them. Streams, rivers! Not spurts. Amen

"Do you not know that those who run in a race all run, but one receives the prize? Run in such a way that you may obtain it."
1 Corinthians 9:24

January 8

I have lived in many beautiful places during over 30 years of active duty in the U. S. Army.

From my quarters in Fort Wadsworth, NY, I could watch the big ships transiting the Verazano Narrows. From my chapel at Fort Clayton, Panama, I could see all of the ships passing through the Panama Canal.

(Of course there were less pleasant places and views; and some months my "house" was nothing but a poncho liner under the open sky.)

Then I was assigned to the Presidio of San Francisco. The view was breathtaking. And again I heard the hauntingly beautiful sound of foghorns. I wondered if even Heaven could be so beautiful as the view from Upper Simonds Loop.

I like it here, on earth, in this nice house; with these wonderful conveniences, this good fishing lake, and these great sunsets.

It is not fashionable to speak much of Heaven anymore. All on my street live too well to need the idea of Heaven as a better place. (When I was younger, and poorer, Heaven was a frequent sermon topic.) However, if the Scriptures are to be trusted, and I certainly trust them, we are eternity bound human beings.

In prayer today let us reflect on our immortality, and the eternal destiny that we all face.

The highway of life forks into a wide thoroughfare leading to destruction and a narrow path leading to eternal blessing. Jesus taught us which road to take, and how to take it. Be sure that you are on the right one. Amen

"In my Father's house are many mansions...I go to prepare a place for you."
John 14:2

Lord, I have sung about Heaven and wanting to go there all of my life. Am I being dishonest with myself? Help me to see beyond the temporal. I don't want to be so earth bound that I am of no heavenly good. Amen

January 9

It was so funny, hearing our daughter give us instructions on how to care for our grandson. He was only a few months old and it was the first time that Shirley and I had kept him at our home while Lisa and her husband were out of town.

"Sissy, we raised three children," I said.

"But this is a precious child," she responded.

"You were precious, too," I insisted.

"This child is more precious than I was," Lisa remarked, with proud and protective maternal instincts showing.

"No, Sissy, this child is indeed very precious. But he is no more precious than you were," I concluded.

Did you ever wonder why God chose the parent-child relationship to define Himself? Christ came not just as a son, or even a well beloved son, but the "Only begotten Son."

History's greatest news (Gospel=Good News) is that God somehow, in some wonderfully incomprehensible way, loves us, and that He loved us enough to give His "more precious child" to die for us.

Don't we need to wake up to the reality of God's love?

Dear Lord, I don't understand how You could give Your son to die for me. I wasn't even born. And I'm no great prize. You know about my failures (it's easier to talk of failures than sins, Lord).

You know that I tend to run hot or cold, to promise more than I perform, and to talk faith better than walk it. However, since You do love me that much, and You said that You do; I am just going to accept Your love, and be blessed. Amen

"In this the love of God was manifested toward us, that God has sent His only begotten Son into the world, that we might live through Him"
1 John 4:10

January 10

Boy did she cut him down!

Shirley and I were eating dinner in Branson, Missouri, in May. The restaurant was filled with retired people who had come early to attend the music shows before the kids got out of school and the crowds increased.

The waitress talked to the man at the next table in a very patronizing tone. (And I must state here that she was not representative of the Branson folk.)

The old gentlemen had asked for coffee and when it wasn't forthcoming he asked again. The waitress called across the room and pointed to the man, "He wants a cup of coffee, and he needs it."

I was so embarrassed for him. He was pointed out and put down.

A saintly old priest used to whisper "Jesus" every time he passed someone on the road, to remind himself that the person was a unique creation of God.

I will assume that every person I meet is someone that God loves. What about you? And how will it affect your behavior?

My pastor once said that I effect everyone I touch, that I make them better or worse. I have problems with that because each person is responsible for his or her own growth. But the pastor had a point.

It is so easy to hurt someone: a thoughtless remark, a condescending attitude, or a careless deed. Words hurt just like sticks and stones.

Little wonder that the Psalmist prayed,

"Set a guard, O Lord, over my mouth; keep watch over the door of my lips."
Psalms 141:3

Dear Lord, I talk too much. Help me to apply the math guideline: since I have two ears and one mouth I must listen at least twice as much as I speak. Amen

January 11

Do you have any old habits lingering in your psyche? Festering in your soul?

Local chaplains and chaplain assistants at the Presidio of San Francisco were gathered for their monthly Unit Ministry Team (UMT) breakfast. When the chaplain host introduced the UMT members to the guest speaker he referred to the males by their rank and the lone female by her first name.

I glanced at her and she shrugged it off. Later, at his conclusion, the guest speaker's "Thank you fellows for coming this morning" drew another glance and another shrug.

Male chauvinism? Sexism? Well, I believe that both men would deny it. They consider themselves to be good, caring persons. So do I. Further, I don't believe that either of them would intentionally harbor a hurtful thought against anyone because of race, sex, religion, national origin, or any other cultural distinctive.

Then why the slip ups? I think that the incident shows how entrenched old habits are. So much so that we appear to discriminate even when we didn't intend to. And it shows how much farther we still have to go.

We work the big-ticket items, violence, drugs, etc. But we mustn't let the little things, the spiritual misdemeanors, grow in our hearts unchallenged.

Oh Lord, help me today to mind my habits. After I have spent so much effort to insure proper attitudes to people different from me I mustn't injure someone unintentionally.

Lord, I know how to be politically correct. I want to be spiritually correct, too. I am working hard on the big things. Help me with the little things that hang around to haunt me. Help me with,

"...The little foxes that spoil the vines...." Amen
Song of Solomon 2:15

January 12

Sweatpea, our Yorkshire Terrier, was Shirley's dog. We promised each other not to get another dog until we retired. Yet she bought him anyway.

Since she didn't get my permission to buy the dog I tried to act like it was her dog, not mine. So I resisted most urges to take care of him, only doing so when I stood to gain something from it.

One wet, cold, morning I was walking the dog. Sweatpea weighed only 3 lb., but he could apply 20 lb. of forward pressure to get to the bush, shrub, tree, or hydrant. I was trying to keep him as dry as possible. However, I became irritated with his constant straining to get to a certain leafy, wet, bush. So I dropped the leash, and he plunged into the wet bush.

Sweatpea backed out of the bush, soaking wet, and looked back at me. His expression was as though to say, "I was counting on you to hold me back."

There are many things that hold us back, constrain us, keep us straight.

Negative reinforcements, such as laws, and civil codes have their effect. The expectations that others have of us also influence our behavior. (I heard a fellow say that he would never cheat on his wife because she would kill him.)

But there is something much weightier.

They are the values that grow from a strong spiritual source, a solid Biblical base, that shape our lives and behavior.

Yet even religious laws aren't enough. There has to be a force stronger than legal and civil prohibitions. And there is.

"...The love of Christ constrains us..."
2 Corinthians 5:14

Lord, I know that living right; being good, and keeping the rules are all okay, even commendable. But I won't ever depend on what I am able to do for my salvation. I will do the best I can to please You, but I will trust only in Your grace. Amen

January 13

A dear friend unburdened her heart during dinner about the deep hurt she still feels from her relationship with her father. Her dad is a very successful pastor of a large church.

She had not even wanted to attend her parents' fiftieth wedding anniversary, and wouldn't have if her husband hadn't insisted on her going.

Her father spent his life caring for others, giving freely of himself, working day and night in pastoral ministry. But very early she began to feel peripheral to his life.

She and her siblings were expected to be model PKs (preacher's kids) and not get in the way.

The resentment grew and was intensified when she was newly married and really needed his help with a problem and he refused to give it.

The anger and hurt remains today as a canker on her soul.

Someone once wrote, "What does it profit a man if he gains the whole world and loses his own children?"

A famous American actor owned a whole South Pacific Island. He had great success and wealth. Imagine his grief over his son's being charged with murdering his sister's boyfriend.

If you ever want to feel good as a parent, read about David's problems with his children in 2 Samuel 13:37, "...David mourned for his son every day."

What a wonderful opportunity, but awesome responsibility, we have as parents, especially in these troublesome times.

Merciful Father, help me to love my children in deed, and not just in word. I need more patience, Lord. Let me be the kind of parent that they will want to be with their children. Amen.

"Fathers, do not embitter your children, or they will become discouraged."
Colossians 3:21 NIV

January 14

Are you strong enough to bend?

As you head south out of San Francisco on U.S. 1, just after passing the Cliff House on your right, you will see a great old tree on your left.

The tree's windward side has been virtually denuded of its greenery by the prevailing winds. Over the years, they have forced the tree to grow at a near horizontal, leeward, angle. It is a tree of awkward beauty that brings to mind a stubborn and persistent clinging to life.

I suppose that if trees had druthers they would all want to grow full, straight, and tall; or bushy, leafy.

Popular Country singer, Tanya Tucker, had a hit song entitled, *Strong Enough To Bend.* It is as good a sermon as some preachers can preach.

We often equate strength with an unbending resolve and fail to see that in some circumstances real strength is the ability to bend to change, so that life and growth can continue.

Being stubborn isn't the same as being strong.

Oh Lord, help me to clearly see the difference between the things that are so fundamentally right that there can be no compromise and those things that are more a projection of my own ego. When I should bend, help me to be strong enough to do so.

"Then *the Lord relented*, and did not bring on His people the disaster He had threatened."
Exodus 32:14 (NIV)

Don't try to hold on to your stubbornness by calling it sanctified determination. Or something just as silly. Deal honestly with the things that keep you from being all that you can be in Christ. Amen

January 15

Today is the birthday of Dr. Martin Luther King, Jr.

No other American has done more than this great American to eliminate social injustice. Born in 1929, he was ordained a minister at the age of 18 in his father's church, the Ebenezer Baptist Church, in Atlanta, Georgia.

Dr. King was a champion for equality and civil rights from his earliest ministry. While pastoring a church in Montgomery, Alabama, he led the boycott that caught the attention and captured the imagination of America. That event set into motion powerful forces that resulted in the march on Washington in 1963, and the passage of the Civil Rights Act in 1964.

I was in seminary when he made his moving *I Have a Dream* speech in Washington, D. C., in August, 1963.

His challenge to Americans was a source of great tension to me. I couldn't deny the rightness of his message. Yet the congregation that I was serving was staunchly segregationist. Part of me wanted to join the march, but another part was concerned with paying seminary bills while supporting a growing family.

Now, as I look back, I wish I had done more.

I wish that I had preached more than generic generalities on love, equality, justice, and brotherhood. It really was a time, and a cause, that the appropriate action could be nothing less than vocal and visible involvement.

I believe that many of my fellow clergypersons also failed to provide forceful leadership for human rights during that period. But God didn't fail. Neither did Dr. Martin Luther King, Jr. And America is a much better place for their faithfulness. God bless America.

So what about you? Is your heart free from prejudice?

"Have we not all one Father? Has not one God created us? Why do we deal treacherously with one another...?"
Malachi 2:10

January 16

Have you ever seen something in nature that you felt sure taught you a spiritual reality?

I learned something from a bird in a department store.

The bird was trapped and couldn't get back out of the store. He flew back and forth from one end of the building to the other, just under the ceiling. Occasionally he would alight on a sign hanging from the ceiling, then drop to a glass panel near the door. He never figured out how to escape.

The reason the bird couldn't fly out of the building was his bird (avian) instinct. Birds fly upward.

For him to escape the bird would have to fly levelly or even downward in order to exit through the open door. On each flight he jumped up and away, only to be stopped by the wall. Every effort by people to "shoo" him out of the door only seemed to add to his confusion.

Such sad irony. There was a frightened creature seeking escape and humans eager to help him. But there was no way to bridge the gap of understanding and communication between the species.

How similar to the human condition, and mankind's estrangement from God!

Oh Lord, you know that I trust you as my Savior. But I still feel sometimes that you are sending but I am not receiving your messages. Surely Your Holy Spirit is the connection that will allow me to hear. But even when I hear, Lord, I sometimes find myself failing to obey. Dear Lord, fill me with your Spirit so that I can know and do your will. Amen

"...The natural man does not receive the things of the Spirit of God, for they are foolishness to him; nor can he know them, because they are spiritually discerned."
1 Corinthians 2:14

January 17

I felt sorry for the poor creature. And tried to help it escape.

Because of the gulf between birds and humans we couldn't let the bird know that we wanted to help him escape. And he was terrified of our efforts to assist him. When he flew off his perch he flew upward, following avian instinct. Thus he hit glass wall above the doorway.

Another story comes to mind.

On a bitterly cold evening after a long period of below zero nights a pastor sat by his window watching a flock of birds, huddled, freezing, on the ice covered yard between his house and barn.

Wanting to help the birds avoid freezing to death he opened the barn door for them.

They were afraid to enter the barn. Next he put a light in the barn. Still no entry. Then, he threw corn in the entrance and into the barn. Still the same. Finally he tried to shoo them in and they flew away.

Back in the comfort of his living room chair he pondered the experience, wondering what it would have taken to get the birds into the warm barn. Then it hit him. The answer was *example*.

If he had been able to change himself into a bird just like those in his yard he could have joined the flock, walked into the barn, started eating corn, and they would have followed him and been saved from the killing cold.

"...Christ...suffered for us, leaving us an example, that you should follow His steps...."
1 Peter 2:21

Dear Lord, help me to always follow the example that Jesus set for me. And help me to be the kind of example that others need to follow. Amen

January 18

The kid's choir members at the Georgia Church were decked out in their finest. It was the first Sunday in May, Youth Sunday. It was a church without teenagers, just old folks and grandkids.

A pretty little girl in the middle of the front row stood out from the rest. Her voice strong and clear, she could be heard above all the others. She kept her eye on the director (who was also playing the piano), never missing a cue. Her articulation was precise. She exuded great confidence.

By all the common measurements--position in the choir, memorization of lines, attention to the director, and applause-- she was doing great. But there was one critical element that she missed, *she couldn't carry a tune.*

I have learned that a lot of people who want to join the choir really can't sing. And often they don't know it. I remember a soldier who claimed that he sang in a quartet back home. He not only could not carry a tune, he couldn't tell that he couldn't carry a tune. The choir director was furious at me for recruiting him.

We need others to tell us the things that we cannot see about ourselves. For we may not always be doing as well as we think. Feedback! Fellow Christians owe loving and objective feedback to one another. Yet, even that can't always be relied on. Friends aren't usually objective. They often are more concerned with helping us feel good than in giving possibly painful feedback.

The Scriptures are the mirror that reflects us back to ourselves as God sees us. How often do you check yourself out in that mirror?

"All Scripture is given by inspiration of God, and is profitable for doctrine, for reproof, for correction, for instruction in righteousness."
2 Timothy 3:16

Dear Lord, I may get out of tune today. Help me to obey the teaching of Holy Scripture and hear the advice of brothers and sisters in Christ when they tell me I am off key. Amen

January 19

You hear *family* in the strangest places.

I was enjoying a street fair in San Francisco on a warm and breezy last day of June? The crowds were colorful. One simply can't dress improperly in San Francisco. Anything goes. The sights and sounds linger in the memory.

Placards and enthusiasts urged the crowd to support the National Endowment of the Arts in their struggle with a Southern Senator, join in an AIDS march, keep San Francisco a nuclear free zone, and other initiatives that I cannot remember now.

The cuisine was rich and varied. I could have had sushi from a sidewalk vendor, plus Cajun, French, and numerous other specialties. The calamari was my choice.

We listened to soloists, folk and Andean musicians, rock groups, and a guy playing pretty good tunes on the top of a metal drum.

The juggler was the best act of the day. Taking up his position he began yelling to the passers by: "Come on over here. Gather in close. We're going to make a family."

Family? From a throng on Filmore street? Another valued idea prostituted, like the use of peace and democracy by totalitarian regimes?

We belong to several families, the most basic being our nuclear and extended families. The Army was my family for over thirty years. My home church and denomination are my spiritual families.

The most precious family connection is the one into which we come through faith in Christ the Savior. Be sure your are a member.

"...I bow my knees to the Father of our Lord Jesus Christ, from whom the whole *family in heaven and earth* is named."
Ephesians 3:14,15

January 20

Happy St. Sebastian Day.

For years I have planned my work with the help of the Ecumenical Daily Appointment Planner published by the Catholic Church. It is an excellent calendar for Christian workers whether clergy or lay. It tells me that today is St. Sebastian Day.

Protestants pay little attention to the Patron Saints. Catholic Christians, however, find great importance in them. St. Sebastian is the Patron Saint against the plague.

Not a great deal is known about St. Sebastian's life. I appreciate that he had been a soldier, like me.

He was a Roman soldier. He was shot by archers, but recovered. He was later beaten to death. He is honored in the ranks of Christian Martyrs. He was martyred for doing right, for living his life as he felt that Jesus wanted him to, for his faith in the Christ as Savior and Lord.

We in America enjoy great freedom in faith and worship. In many parts of the world one can still be slain for the mere fact that he or she is a Christian.

While American Christians are generally safe from violent persecution because of their faith, one still may pay a price for living the Christian life.

The price may be ridicule, ostracism, or a polite shunning. In an everybody-is-doing-it age, Christians must be careful to always do what's right.

Dear Lord, I am humbled when I read about earlier Christians such as Saint Sebastian. I have it so easy. Help me to always do the right thing, even when it costs. I don't want to be wishy washy, a spiritual wimp. Help me to be strong, to stand up when it is called for, and to speak up when I should. Amen

"Blessed are those who are persecuted for righteousness' sake, for theirs is the kingdom of heaven."
Matthew 5:10

January 21

During the year leading up to his death at the age of 93, Armand Hammer bought 12 new suits and 10 new pairs of pants.

I recently heard a speaker describe the difference in hope and optimism. Optimism, according to him, derives from the confidence a person has in his own abilities. Hope, on the other hand, is based on trust in God.

Faith can produce great optimism, as in St. Paul's assertion, "I can do all things through Christ who strengthens me" (Philippians 4:13). Faith also nurtures a profound hope, "Which is Christ in you, the hope of glory" (Colossians 1:27).

So the Word of God really is a two-edged sword. It can inform and strengthen your human potential. But it also can enhance your eternal connection, the hope that derives from confidence in God.

Mr. Hammer could buy a new wardrobe at age 93. And you can put your trust in an almighty and loving God.

Can we as Christians be confident amidst political scandal, economic uncertainty, and the threat of new and dangerous diseases?

Yes. We can remain confident of the basic goodness of our national character, in the strength of our institutions, and in the bedrock values of the American people.

Can we also hope? Yes. We can do so through a personal and living faith in a sovereign God and loving Savior.

Dear Lord, there are readers today who are at their wits' end. They have lost hope. Give them hope, Oh Lord; confidence in You. And me, too, Lord. Amen

"And now, Lord, what do I wait for? *My hope is in You.*"
Psalm 39:7

January 22

Do you smell good? A strange question for a daily devotion?

Many people are obsessed with how they smell. If you stroll down the aisle in the cosmetics section in any drug store you will see a huge array of products to keep you from smelling bad or to make you smell better. And if you don't duck you might get sprayed.

When we were stationed in a foreign country, where household help was plentiful and inexpensive, I encouraged Shirley to hire someone to help with the chores. Before the first visit of the cleaning lady she cleaned the house from top to bottom. When I kidded her about it she said she didn't want anyone to think that she didn't keep a clean house. She also washed the stinky clothes that the cleaning lady left at our house. (She also will get onto me for writing about this.)

All odors aren't bad. What can beat the odor of coffee perking, or bacon frying? What about a big sirloin on a charcoal grill in the back yard? Or roses sprinkled with dew? Or the purplish delight of lilacs on a calm Summer eve?

The apostle Paul taught that Christians are supposed to carry a good odor throughout the world.

Through our good deeds, our faithful witness, and our compassionate interaction with the needy, we demonstrate a Gospel pleasantly attractive.

So, I must always smell good. It is my spiritual duty.

"...Thanks be to God, who always leads us in triumph in Christ, and through us diffuses *the fragrance of His knowledge* in every place."
2 Corinthians 2:14

Dear Lord, I hope I don't stink spiritually. Keep me washed clean through the instruction of the Scriptures and the work of Your Spirit. Cover me with the fragrance of Your divine presence. I want to smell good Lord. Amen

January 23

Have you ever won a race?

While visiting Fort Ord, California, I took time to participate in the promotion of a chaplain friend. All of the important people were there: mom, dad, wife, children, friends, and fellow soldiers.

After thanking everyone, and to fill time while the photographer fiddled to get the camera working, the chaplain told of winning a trophy in a 10 kilometer run a couple of days before. He was one of only three people in the over fifty category and there were three prizes. He didn't say where he placed.

"All I had to do was begin and finish," he said.

If a journey of a thousand miles begins with a single step then it also ends with a single step.

Running a race and growing a garden are much alike.

I had a neighbor who began his garden early, while the threat of freezing weather still existed. He plowed, fertilized, planted, and bragged about the great garden he was going to have.

The others of us had less glorious beginnings, but we lasted longer. When the Bermuda grass really got to growing, and the birds, squirrels, and nematodes took their toll, my neighbor's enthusiasm waned. By August he had abandoned his dream garden, but I was still enjoying fresh vegetables, and Shirley was able to fill up the freezer.

Life is like a 10-kilometer run, and a garden. The key to both is perseverance. It is not just how great is your beginning. It is also how well you continue. And of course, whether you finish the task.

"...He who endures to the end will be saved."
Matthew 10:22

I'm running with you, Jesus. Help me to keep up. Amen

January 24

It isn't always easy to keep going.

When the commander approached the city he found it burned. Families had been taken captive. There was talk of insurrection, of his actually being attacked personally. He did three things in rapid succession.

First, he dealt with his own attitude. He had been greatly distressed at the carnage, but knew that he must set the example in attitude as well as in action.

Next, he prayed. He drew strength from his faith. He sought God's will, specifically, as to what he should do.

Then, he attacked.

This story could depict many great commanders that I have served while on active duty in the Army. Men and women of great human feeling, who knew the vital importance of attitude and esprit; commanders who prayed, who evidenced a deep spiritually, who sought God's blessings with truly humble hearts; aggressive commanders who knew that a well conducted offensive saves lives.

But this story comes out of the Bible. It is from the annals of General David, later king of all Israel. He set the great example for soldiers, and civilians, too. It isn't only soldiers who must maintain a great attitude, be men and women of prayer, have humble hearts, and be proactive.

I pray that you fit that description. If you don't, get started.

"...David was greatly distressed...David encouraged himself in the Lord his God...David inquired at the Lord...David pursued...."
1 Samuel 30:6-10 (KJV)

Lord, like King David I need an attitude adjustment. I am looking deeply into my heart and soul today. I am praying. Encourage me, Lord. Nudge me. Help me to keep up the spiritual pursuit. Amen

January 25

Preachers like big words.
We toss them around as though they were known by all.
I have often suspected that some of my peers fill their sermons
with big, in-house words, in order to impress their hearers. And
that may be sour grapes, for I have never been gifted in the use
of grand vocabulary.

Nonetheless, I choose a big word for today: justification.
To get its meaning I will create a scenario.

Suppose you think that I stole your lawnmower. You
take me to court. Suppose that I am convicted, but pardoned,
because of my job and reputation. I still won't be able to show
my face in the neighborhood. Even if there is a mistrial,
because of insufficient evidence, I still must live with a cloud
over my head.

But suppose that I am acquitted. I am found not guilty.
Then it will not be just as though it never happened. It really
never happened.

Did you get it? *It never happened.* Even justification
seems like a word too small to convey such a giant reality.

That is the essence of the great Scriptural doctrine of
justification. God's great redemptive act through Christ does
not just bring us forgiveness and pardon, as wonderful as those
realities are; it pronounces us just.

Those bad things never happened.
That's the meaning of justification.

**"He was delivered over to death for our sins and was
raised to life for our justification."**
Romans 4:25

Lord, I can understand forgiveness and pardon. And I
know the meaning of acquittal. But my mind boggles at
justification. What grace! What love! What a wonderful
Savior! Thank you again. Amen

January 26

What a sight!

The band had played. The troops in formation were sharp. The spectators were enjoying a great military spectacle, a retirement ceremony.

The winds at the Presidio of San Francisco must always be reckoned with. On that June afternoon, they were fierce.

Three soldiers struggled to keep their colors in a proper upright position. But the Army Flag, with its many streamers, was too heavy to be controlled easily. Strong gusts would force the Staff Sergeant (male) off his stance and he would have to reposition himself, leaning more to his right, into the wind. Then I noticed what the Sergeant (female) to his left, holding the Sixth Army flag, was doing. With each heavy gust she would push her hips slightly but firmly to her right to support the Staff Sergeant.

I chuckled quietly. I have always believed that women have a rightful place in the Army. But I never saw that fact illustrated so creatively.

We all need someone to lean on. A great song, "Lean on Me," became a popular movie.

David expressed his great hope in God (Psalms 23) when he asserted that when he came to the "...Valley of the shadow of death...You are with me."

"Leaning, leaning
Safe and secure from all alarm;
Leaning, leaning,
Leaning on the everlasting arms."

(Elisha Hoffman)

"Trust in the Lord with all your heart, and lean not on your own understanding"
Proverbs 3: 5

Dear Lord, when the winds of life threaten to blow me over, help me to stand. Straight. Amen.

January 27

The car ahead had two bumper stickers. One said, "If you are going in the wrong direction God allows U-turns." The other one said, "Don't follow me, I'm lost, too."

(Where else but in San Francisco?)

Do you ever feel that way? Your role requires you to lead, guide, mentor, supervise, instruct, pastor, or train. Yet, as a person, spouse, parent, or sibling, you are no different from the others. You have to help people get their lives straight but are sometimes plagued with a profound awareness of your own limitations.

Abraham: Lord, are you kidding? You know that I am too old to found a nation.

Moses: Lord, haven't you heard me talk? Do you really want a stutterer to lead your people?

Mary: Lord, I'm a virgin. How in the world am I going to have a son?

Jesus: Oh Father, is there any other way? Must I be crucified?

You are never weaker than when you pretend strength. And you are never stronger than when you admit your weakness.

If you need to make a U-turn you can. Christ stands at the intersection of your life. He is the way to go, the truth to tell, and the life to live. Amen

"And He said to me, 'My grace is sufficient for you, for *My strength is made perfect in weakness*'...."
2 Corinthians 12:9

Heavenly Father, I am sometimes better at displaying bumper stickers than living out my faith. I am counting on You for help, dear Lord. Amen

January 28

You have heard about having a monkey on your back? Well, this is a story about an old man traveling with a child and a donkey.

When they passed a certain village the man was leading the donkey and the child following behind. The villagers called him a fool for not riding so he climbed onto the donkey's back.

In the next village the people said he was mean for making the child walk, so he got off and put the child on. In the next village they taunted the child for laziness because he was making the old man walk. So they both road the donkey.

In the next village they criticized the travelers for overworking the donkey. The man was last seen carrying the donkey down the road.

Are you carrying any donkeys around?

Old grudges? Ancient hurts? Unreasonable expectations you have of yourself? Or that you have allowed others to put on you? Doubts? Fears? Worries? Worry is interest paid in advance of something that probably won't even happen anyway.

Today is a good day to dump the donkeys. Each morning you have a fresh sheet upon which you can write the rest of your life.

If you need forgiveness ask God for it. If your heart is broken He is the mender of hearts. If you are fearful remember that the Scriptures teach that God's love casts out fear. And God does love you. Amen

Do like the blind man, who,

"...Throwing aside his garment (*donkeys*?), he came to Jesus."
Mark 10:50

Dear Lord, I have enough on my back already. Just living out my faith. Help me to dump the monkeys and the donkeys. Amen

January 29

Sisyphean. I thought that I had made up the word. In fact, at military training events I claimed credit for making up the word, and others gave me credit for it.

Then one day I heard another person use the term. So I looked, and sure enough, there it was in the Dictionary.

Sisyphean is an adjectival construction of the Greek noun, Sisyphus. He was the cruel king of Corinth. As punishment for some deed he was condemned forever to roll a huge stone up a hill in Hades only to have it roll back down when it neared the top.

Sisyphean tasks are those that we have to keep doing over and over.

The concept is okay in the military, where even a high level of proficiency, honed like a sharpened steel blade, quickly loses its edge.

But you ought not to have to learn spiritual lessons over and over again.

I once heard a preacher say that God could do so much more for me if He didn't have to do the same things over and over. What an incredible waste of time and energy. After all of these years of being a Christian I find myself having to learn the lessons of humility, honesty, charity, and forgiveness over and over again.

Are you about ready to join me in a prayer of deliverance from sisypheanism?

Dear Lord, please save me from sisypheanism of the soul. I want to be a faster learner. And I want to retain what I learn from and about you. Increase my capacity. I am tired of climbing that hill. Thank you, Lord. Amen

"You have been going around this mountain...long enough...."
Deuteronomy 2:3 (RSV)

January 30

One of the most tragic failings is shortsightedness.

When George Washington Carver showed up at the little schoolhouse he was greeted with, "What do you want, boy?" He answered that he wanted to learn about the sun and moon, about writing and arithmetic, about plants and animals, and butterflies.

Later, as a brilliant scientist, Doctor Carver experimented with new ways to do things. Once he held a peanut in his hand and prayed that the great creator would show him why He made it.

At Tuskegee he did marvelous things with the peanut. He extracted milk; and made cereals, butter, and vinegar. From the peanut he also manufactured soaps, face creams, paints, oils, shampoo, and axle grease. The results of his research greatly aided the nation during dark times.

Doctor Carver had an eye to see. Where others saw the lowly peanut as a pleasant food he sought its greater benefit. When the vision of others was fixated on poverty and suffering, his mind was searching for solutions.

Do you have an eye to see? Beyond your own little space? Beyond your misfortunes and complaints? We miss out on so much because we can't see beyond the difficulties, the storm clouds, the handicaps, and the threatening future.

Heavenly Father, please don't let me fail because of my own limited outlook and meager faith. Stretch me. Enlarge my vision. Increase my scope. Don't let me rest in a comfortable mediocrity.

Don't let me see only peanuts when You have something much better in mind for me. Help me to be more than I am, to be all that I can be in You. Amen

"Where there is no vision, the people perish...."
Proverbs 29:18 (KJV)

January 31

This old sixth grade teacher has a grammar lesson for today. To prepare for class you may read the 23rd Psalm.

The psalmist begins by speaking in the third person, "The Lord is my shepherd." He uses the words *He*, and *Him*. When it is green pastures and still waters He is sitting out there, on the hillside, in sight, watching over the flock.

The third person continues during times of refreshing when the soul is restored and down peaceful paths of righteousness.

Then comes a dramatic change in *person*. Before the psalmist is the threatening valley of the shadow of death. He glances to the hillside but the shepherd is no longer there, not *out* there, that is. He turns, and there the shepherd is, *beside* him. The pronoun changes from He to *Thou*, from the third person to the second person, and stays that way throughout the rest of the Psalm. The Lord, out there, became the Lord beside him.

Get it? The Lord is not out there. He is the Lord beside you. Sense His presence. Feel His warmth. Hear His whisper.

This is a joyous truth for Christians.

My dad was confined to a wheel chair for several years, and finally to bed. In the few weeks before his death a calmness settled over him. He wasn't morbid at all. Rather, he spoke of dying with confidence and peace. He talked of going to be with the Lord. Death no longer frightened him.

In my career I have traveled a lot; alone, in airplanes, and in automobiles. I can't say that I always enjoyed it. But there is one trip that I won't have to make alone. Can you say Amen?

"...THOU art with me...."
Psalm 23:4 (KJV)

Lord, I sometimes can't see You over there, watching over me, because I am looking down at my feet. Help me to life up my eyes to the hills. Amen

Ash Wednesday

Soon it will be Ash Wednesday. The color on the altar will be purple, the color of penitence.

Many of us will find our way to an Ash Wednesday service. The minister or priest will rub ashes on our forehead and utter, "Remember that thou art dust, and to dust thou shalt return."

Thus begins the season of Lent, a period of 40 days preceding Easter not counting the 6 Sundays. The name is derived from the old English lenckten, meaning, the "spring."

As a time of abstinence, almsgiving, and acts of devotion, Lent is intended to serve as a preparation for the Easter festival.

Lent is a blessed season for millions of Christians who look inward, examine their lives, evaluate their behavior, and seek to draw nearer to God. Millions will sacrifice, abstain from, some cherished thing for the period of lent. It is a time for prayers and fasting.

Lent never meant much to me until I became an Army Chaplain. As a Protestant living among and working with Catholics through over 30 years of active duty, I have grown to appreciate the observance of Lent.

Some might say that I have become more *catholic*.

May this day bring a new spiritual beginning for you. And may the Lenten Season be a time of real personal and spiritual growth. Your Easter will then be more joyous.

Dear Lord, during this period of Lent help me to comprehend the sacrifice of Christ more than I ever have. Help me to draw closer to You than I have ever been. And may I know You better, oh Lord and Savior, than I ever have. Amen

"Now therefore, says the Lord, turn to Me with all your heart; with fasting, with weeping, and with mourning. So rend your heart, and not your garments. Return to the Lord your God, for He is gracious and merciful, slow to anger, and of great kindness."
Joel 2:12,13

February 1

One Memorial Day I attended a patriotic service at a large cemetery in Sacramento, California. Chaplain Don Crowley, the California State Chaplain, was the speaker. His text was the 23rd Psalm.

Don found something in the text that I had never noticed in all my years of preaching. He pointed out that it says the good shepherd leads you *through* the valley of the shadow of death. He doesn't leave you at the entrance, nor abandon you part way through, or wait for you on the other side.

I had preached from the Shepherd's Psalm many times, but had missed this simple, yet profound, fact.

There is a great blessing here, wisdom too. God is not a quitter. People change. Friends forsake. A family member leaves. God is always there. He is there on the hillside when things are going well. He is beside you when things get scary. And he will still be with you all of the way through whatever your valley is.

As a counselor I have seen many goals unrealized, relationships broken, and dreams shattered. The fault is not with God. He is there, even through the darkest stretches of life's pursuits. In fact, He promised to never forsake us.

Today your resolve may be battered by adversity or your will leached by a flood of trivia. Tragic news may come to trouble your soul. I hope none of this happens. But just in case it does, today, or next year, you can make it. You could almost make it on your own. So with the presence and blessing of the Lord you can't fail. Write it down!

Dear Lord, it is dark in the valley. I am afraid to go there alone. I am glad that you promised to go through it with me. All of the way through it. Here's my hand, Lord. Amen

"Surely goodness and mercy shall follow me all the days of my life...."
                                   Psalm 23:6

February 2

"I yam what I yam!" Do you remember Popeye's trademark phrase? It implies, at least to me, that he was quite proud of himself, and gave himself credit for becoming what he had become.

It is okay to have pride in oneself, providing it is not a smug or false pride. A good self-image is part of a healthy self. It is also okay to own the hard work and discipline that leads to one's reaching cherished goals. Just as it is true that one must take responsibility for his or her actions when they lead to failure.

There is a danger, however, from taking this approach too far.

No one ever really succeeds alone. Without hardworking parents that provided a home for me I would never have been able to attend the Bible College across town. Without a congregation that was willing to allow me to go to seminary while serving as their pastor I would never have become a chaplain. Without a seminary dean that was willing to provide a fifty- percent scholarship for me I would not have been able to stay in school. Without a good woman who loved and supported me, kept our home, raised our kids, and endured the hardships of military life I would never have had a career in the Army. See my point. No one ever really travels alone.

This story gets passed around. A turtle was sitting on a fence post. He said to the other creatures: "I didn't get up here by myself."

We too often overlook the wonderful grace of God in our lives. A piece of schrapnel hit my back flat, instead of on its jagged edge, and I was spared a serious injury. Of all the others He could have called, He called me! I never walked alone.

"...By the grace of God I am what I am...I labored more abundantly than they all, yet not I, but the grace of God which was in me."
1 Corinthians 15:10

Thank you, Lord, for letting me be me. Amen

February 3

Happy Four Chaplains Day.

It was on this day in 1943 that the *USS Dorchester* sank into the icy waters of the North Atlantic from a German U-boat's torpedo that crashed into its engine room. Hundreds of soldiers died immediately below deck.

There were four chaplains aboard the Dorchester: George L. Fox and Clark V. Poling were Protestants, Alexander D. Goode was Jewish, and John P. Washington was Roman Catholic. According to the testimony of survivors, the four chaplains gave encouragement to the frightened men while helping to distribute life jackets and assisting the men into lifeboats.

When there were no more life jackets the chaplains removed theirs, and gave them to terrified young men. They didn't ask whether the recipients were Protestant, Catholic, or Jewish.

John Ladd, an eyewitness to the chaplains' heroic sacrifice, commented, "It was the finest thing I have ever seen or hope to see this side of heaven."

At the dedication of the Chapel of the Four Chaplains in 1951, President Harry S. Truman said, "That day they preached the most powerful sermon of their lives."

Today I hope that you will thank God for chaplains in the military, prisons, hospitals, and similar institutions. And that you will pray God's richest blessings upon their ministries. Pray especially for military chaplains and chaplain assistants who accompany troops into combat.

"Greater love has no one than this, than to lay down one's life for his friends."
John 15:13

Lord, I get so sick of petty parochialism. Help me to see beyond the differences between my fellow Christians and me, and lay firm hold on what unites us: Your Love, Lord, and the task that You have given all of us as Christians. Amen

February 4

What a stupid question! Is this man mean, or what? I might have thought that if I had been standing near Jesus and had heard his question to the paralyzed man at the pool of Bethesda. He asked a crippled man if he wanted to be well.

To our touchy feely sensitivities the question seems blunt, even cruel. We talk around difficult subjects. Like my visit to a pastor friend after his heart attack. I talked about this and that until I realized what I was doing. When I finally said that I was worried about him, he said that he was scared to death. Then we had a real conversation, and prayed together.

Jesus didn't take a poll of the onlookers, "Now how do you feel about it, brother Jacob, sister Elizabeth? Do you think I should heal this man or not?" No. His question was always personal.

Jesus didn't go around doing things to people without checking it out with them first.

His approach to the paralyzed man showed compassion. He was really asking, "Can you handle what I can do for you? Are you ready for the changes that being well will bring?" Changes in your lifestyle? Leaving this place where you have been 38 years? Getting a job? It is a timely question. Are you ready for what God can do for you?

When you pray for the Spirit are you afraid you might get carried away? If you pray to be used by God are you willing to go to a mission field? Or across the street to share your faith with a neighbor?

Jesus is asking you if you are ready for what He can do for you.

"...Wilt thou be made whole?
John 5:6 (KJV)

Yes, Lord, I want to be made whole. Heal me Savior. I want to be well spiritually, emotionally, and physically. Thank you Great Physician. Amen

February 5

When my youngest son, Mark, reached driving age he wanted a truck. So I found a nice old one for sale.

The truck ran okay and was worth the $500 that I agreed to pay the soldier. I reasoned that if Mark got a dent in it no one would notice. Also, it would provide more protection in an accident than a small car. Sure enough, he did roll the truck and sure enough, he came out unscathed.

I met the seller at the tag agency. We filled out the papers and as I was about to step to the counter to pay the tax, he whispered under his breath for me to step aside for a moment. Then he said, "We usually write down a smaller amount for the price of the sale to save on taxes. So I wrote down $100 even though you will actually give me $500."

I was quite taken back. And for the first few moments I was thinking of what I could do to save him embarrassment. Then I realized that what he needed from me was honesty, not protection. There was no way I was going to falsify the paper and I saw no way to save his feelings.

So, I put my arm on his shoulder and said, "Look, son, I try to live honestly. And to me this is lying and cheating. Even though it might seem a small thing to you, and even, as you said, your buddies all do it, I don't." Now he really was embarrassed. I lined through the $100 and wrote in $500, and paid Caesar his due.

I can't remember the joke, but the punch line is "Madam, we have already established *what* you are. We are now haggling about the *price*.

"He who is faithful in what is least is faithful also in much; and he who is unjust in what is least is unjust also in much."
Luke 16:10

Lord, it is the little things that get me. I do all right on the big issues. I would never commit murder. But I can hold a mean grudge. Bless me, Lord. Help me to be faithful in all things, big and small. Amen

February 6

God bless Boy Scouts. A Sunday near this date will probably be designated Boy Scout Sunday in your church. I hope that you will give it your support.

When British Army commander Colonel Robert Baden-Powell was unhappy with the attitude of his troops he published, "Aids to Scouting" (1899), a military textbook. The book was later adapted for the training of boys in British schools.

Baden-Powell conducted the first Boy Scout camp in 1907, and the next year he published "Scouting For Boys." The book contained the Scout's Oath, "Be Prepared," and the qualities that Boy Scouts should have. They are listed below with appropriate Scriptural verses.

OBEDIENCE: "...If you will indeed obey my voice...you shall be a special treasure to me...." Exodus 19:5

HONOR: "A good name is to be chosen rather than great riches" Proverbs 22:1

THRIFT: "...Let each one of you lay something aside, storing up as he may prosper..." 1 Corinthians 16:2

WILLINGNESS TO HELP OTHERS: "...Whoever has this world's goods, and sees his brother in need, yet shuts up his heart from him, how does the love of God abide in him?" 1 John 3:17

Dear Lord, I pray for all boys. Keep them from the many evils that fill the airwaves, the streets, and the communities. Give them strong homes, loving parents to nurture and teach them. And help all adults to give their best support in helping young boys become good men.

Thank You, Lord, for my two sons, Alan and Mark, and my two grandsons, Ian and Turner. Bless them abundantly. Help them to know You as Lord and Savior. Keep them in the hollow of Your hand. Amen

"...Exhort the young men to be sober-minded."
Titus 2:6

February 7

Is something wrong only if you get caught?

A shocking 90% of Naval Academy midshipmen thought so according to a church magazine that quoted a major American newspaper's survey.

The "it's only wrong if you get caught attitude" is pervasive in our society: perpetrators of large savings and loan scandals are unrepentant; convicted inside-traders show no contrition; a gang member being tried for the brutal murder of a female jogger says, "It was fun."

When Ted Koppel spoke at Duke University a few years ago he decried popular slogans such as "it's okay to shoot drugs if you use a clean needle," and "have sex with whomever you wish but always wear a condom." He concluded his rousing speech by reminding the audience that what Moses received on Mount Sinai were not ten suggestions.

What happened to the sense of right and wrong?

Are a sports hero's sexual exploits acceptable as long as he wins games? Is it okay for a President of the United States to have sex with numerous women as long as the economy is good? Is it all right for an executive to demand sexual favors from his or her employee as long as the employee is rewarded financially?

It is still a sin to cheat, steal, kill, and commit adultery.

And all of the other behaviors so marked by the Bible are still sin. And sin still has consequences. You can't sow to the flesh and expect a crop failure.

Oh Lord, renew my sense of right and wrong. And help me to have the courage to do the right and to not do the wrong. Amen

"Do not be deceived, God is not mocked; for whatever a man sows, that he will also reap."
Galatians 6:7

"An honest man's the noblest work of God." Burns

February 8

A man fresh from the old country got a job on a railroad work crew. On payday he was required to sign his name to verify receipt of his pay. He made an X. They fired him because he could neither read nor write.

With the money he was paid he bought a bolt of cloth and sold it, house to house, by the yard. With that money he bought two bolts, then four. Before long he had his own store. He became a millionaire. Just think, if he had not been fired he might have made it to crew chief or foreman.

How we react to disappointments is critically important.

The night before his wedding Joseph Scriven's fiancee was killed. He joined the Army and was selected for officer training. Just before graduation he took seriously ill and was unable to graduate. He fell in love again but, once again, his fiancee became ill and died. Lesser souls would have crawled into a corner and brooded. He wrote, "What A Friend We Have In Jesus."

Through his steadfastness, Joseph rose to great power in Egypt. He had been sold into slavery by his brothers. Even though he was a slave, his character and abilities drew the attention of powerful people in the Egyptian government and he was promoted to great authority.

Then Pharaoh's wife developed a sexual interest in him and he refused her advances. She lied to her husband and Joseph was thrown into a dungeon. His talents came again to the attention of the Pharaoh, who made him Prime Minister of Egypt. Later, in the midst of severe famine he was able to save his family from starvation.

Demas couldn't take the heat. He abandoned Paul and the missionary journey (2 Timothy 4:10). Had he stayed he might have written a New Testament Book. Instead, he is known as a quitter. Boy babies aren't named after him.

"...Let us not grow weary while doing good, for in due season we shall reap, if we do not lose heart."
Galatians 6:9

Don't even think of giving up. Amen

February 9

What would be worth dying for?

A newspaper columnist had asked that question of six persons at random on a San Francisco street. The answers given and number of times were: human/minority rights=3; peace=2; environment, beliefs, and oil=1.

None of those interviewed answered country, faith, family, or friends.

I never doubted that my Dad and Mom would have risked their lives for me. And I would do the same for my own children, as would most parents.

Once in a combat experience our medic was blinded by napalm. I ran out to him and led him to safety. I remember feeling very exposed, afraid. I don't remember thinking about country, patriotism, family, democracy, or even the Army. I just wanted to get him out of there as quickly as possible, and not get either of us killed.

If I had known for certain that I would have had to die to save him, I doubt that I would have gone out after him. Maybe most heroism is reaction, based upon proper training, and a good attitude toward one's buddies. My limited experience doesn't qualify me to answer that question.

But in the case of our Lord's sacrifice of Himself for sinners it was not reactive but deliberate. He came into the world with a mission. He didn't just stumble into a situation that resulted in His crucifixion. God had a plan.

Dear Lord, I thank You that You were willing to sacrifice Yourself for me. I can never be worthy of what You did. But I am sincerely grateful. I want to be as responsive to the needs of others as You have been to me. I want to be as selfless as You expect me to be. But it isn't easy, Lord. I like my comfort and security. Help me to put others first. And help me to be a true witness to others of Your great salvation.

"...When we were still without strength, in due time Christ died for the ungodly...."
Romans 5:6

February 10

How long will you be remembered?

I was looking down at the sidewalk one morning and noticed the imprint of a leaf imbedded in the concrete. Not a fully intact leaf. Just the skeleton outline of one.

Sometimes the littlest thing will set my imagination to spinning. It did so then, causing me to think of the impression I make on people and how they will remember me.

At Fort McPherson we shared a large duplex on Staff Row with the FORSCOM Command Sergeant Major. When the engineers poured a connector between the walks leading to our back doors and the street we decided to leave our marks for posterity.

Into the wet concrete on his side he pressed his Command Sergeant Major insignia of rank, and wrote his name, and "hoo-ah"; an expression that troops shout to indicate esprit. I put my name, branch insignia, a cross, and the symbol of my rank. We hoped that in a hundred years or so, people would see the symbols and wonder about us.

Some folks will be remembered in infamy. Tokyo Rose was an American who broadcast Japanese propaganda to American troops trying to demoralize them during WWII. Ask your Dad or Uncle what he thinks about her.

The convicted American soldier that sold secrets to the Soviets and got a lot of Americans killed in Viet Nam must be painfully aware of his legacy.

Famous people are remembered long after their deaths. But the average person is forgotten in one or two generations.

It is more important how you are remembered than how long.

"A good name is to be chosen rather than great riches...."
Proverbs 22:1

Dear Lord, as long as You remember me I will be satisfied. Amen

February 11

God spoke to me through a dove.

Never had I struggled so much with a decision. I knew what I wanted to do and felt that it was God's will for me. But if I did it I would risk losing friends and alienating family. It would be a huge leap of faith.

There was an Olympic size swimming pool at the motel where I was staying in San Antonio, Texas. I was there on temporary duty. I had an appointment with the bishop in Dallas the following week. It was decision time. As I was walking across the motel grounds to the meeting room I saw the dove.

Texas was in the midst of a terrible drought.

The dove was trying to get a drink from the pool. He walked the length of the pool, stopping every few feet to bend down, to see if he could reach the water. He must have bent over to try to drink 20 times. I waited. What would he do? All of a sudden he jumped into the pool. Then, after he got himself a drink, he flew away. It was the strangest thing I had ever seen a dove do. Then I began to hear a message from the Holy Spirit, resonating deep inside my soul.

I realized that I had procrastinated long enough. There are times for waiting, soul searching, and contemplating. But there comes a time when you have to jump. Standing there beside the pool I made my decision. I decided to jump. And I have never regretted it.

What about you? Are you waiting beside your pool? Is there a class that needs teaching? A relationship that needs mending? A child that needs an adult? Someone who needs a friend? A call to a ministry?

Listen to the Holy Spirit's urgings. Then jump! Amen

"...He saw a man named Matthew sitting at the tax office. And He said to him, 'Follow Me.' And he arose (jumped?) and followed Him."
Matthew 9:9

Hello God!

February 12

Happy Abraham Lincoln's birthday. Mr. Lincoln will remain for all time one of our great presidents. A few brief snapshots will illustrate his own personal struggle and growth.

16 June 1858: "A house divided against itself cannot stand. I believe this government cannot endure permanently, half slave and half free."

22 August 1862: "If I could save The Union without freeing any slave, I would do it; if I could save it by freeing some and leaving others alone, I would also do that." (He continued by stating that his personal wish was "that all men everywhere could be free.")

4 April 1864: "I claim not to have controlled events, but confess plainly that events have controlled me."

4 March 1865: "With malice toward none...to bind up the nation's wounds..."

People still debate why President Lincoln issued the Emancipation Proclamation. Was it his own personal values that forced him to do so or was it practical and political considerations that nudged him into the action?

I have my own theory: Lincoln grew.

The capability to grow is the great human distinction. It is a spiritual quality that separates us from all other creatures. A leopard can't change its spots, but people can change their attitudes and behavior. On Lincoln's birthday I urge you to evaluate your need for growth: personally, spiritually, and relationally.

Then we can sing John Newton's great words:

Amazing grace how sweet the sound, that saved a wretch like me,

I once was lost but now I'm found, was blind but now I see.

"...There is neither slave nor free...for you are all one in Christ Jesus."

Galatians 3:28

February 13

Are tears words to God?

Hezekiah had been a good king, ever mindful that the God of Israel had placed him on the throne and blessed his rule. God had given him many victories. The people loved and respected him.

But he became ill and was at the point of death.

Word came from the prophet that he was going to die. Then he turned his face to the wall and prayed, and wept bitterly. Hezekiah's tears moved the heart of God. He sent word that He had heard Hezekiah's prayers and seen his tears, and that he would be given 15 more years to live.

Tears touched the heart of Jesus.

As He approached the village of Nain He was met by a funeral procession. A young man, an only son, was lying a corpse. His mother walked beside him, weeping. Not talking. Just tears.

Jesus heard the tears. They were eloquent: "Oh, my son, my darling boy! What will I ever do? Oh, dear God, take me too. How can I go on?" Jesus, moved with compassion, stopped the procession. "Weep not," He told her. Then he raised her son from the dead.

Jesus wept. At the tomb of his dear friend, Lazarus, no words could express the deep emotions that Jesus felt. So He cried.

Tears are powerful prayers. In great revivals people are sometimes so overwhelmed by their sense of sin that they weep. Have you ever been so burdened that your prayers were more broken sobs than eloquent petitions? Perhaps Paul had such in mind when he wrote to the Romans,

"...The Spirit also helps in our weaknesses...the Spirit Himself makes intercession for us with *groanings* which cannot be uttered."
Romans 8:26

"Oh eyes, no eyes, but fountains fraught with tears..."
Thomas Kid

February 14

Happy Valentine's Day. Our modern celebration of the day derives from several sources.

One tradition says that the Roman Emperor Claudius II, in the third century, forbade young men to marry. He thought that single men made better soldiers. (Sound familiar?) A Priest named Valentine disobeyed the emperor's order and secretly married young couples.

Another story says that Valentine befriended children. When he was imprisoned for refusing to worship the Roman gods, the children missed him so that they tossed loving notes through the bars of his cell window.

Many stories agree that Valentine was executed on 14 February A.D. 269. In A.D. 496, the Pope named 14 February as St. Valentine's Day.

In Norman French, a language spoken in Normandy during The Middle Ages, the word "galantine" meant gallant or lover. Its resemblance to Valentine added to the mystique of St. Valentine being a special saint for lovers.

By the fifteenth century, the English were sending love letters on this date. By the 1700s, men were pinning their lovers' names on their sleeves giving rise to the saying "Wearing his heart on his sleeve."

It is appropriate, on this day, to give a special thanks to God for those who love you and whose love you are happy to return.

I like Valentine's Day. Even though it has become very commercial, its roots are spiritual. Be sure and tell that special person that you love her, or him.

"Then Isaac...took Rebecca, and she became his wife, and *he loved her*...."
Genesis 24:67

Dear Lord, bless young lovers. Help them to understand the moral imperative that marriage is the proper and Biblical context for family. Bless the older folks, too. Give them good health and prosperity. Keep their love young, strong and resilient. Amen

February 15

All who teach our young people deserve our support and prayers.

A teacher, on recess duty, went to investigate a disturbance on the playground. A boy was on the ground, crying, and clutching his abdomen. The teacher asked what was wrong. A little girl, with tears rolling down her cheeks, answered, "We all got a pain in Jimmy's stomach."

Empathy is defined as identification with and understanding of another's situation, feelings, and motives.

Two very public events call the meaning of empathy to mind. One was the merciless beating of a citizen by uniformed policemen in a large American city.

The other was the conduct of American servicemen and women in the Gulf War.

Did the policemen experience a perverse satisfaction from their primitive behavior? For sure the American military evidenced no personal satisfaction from the suffering that resulted from their actions. They had a job to do and they did it, without malice, and in a highly professional and technically proficient manner.

Nations at war have acted historically to dehumanize their enemies, calling them gooks, infidels, krauts, and so forth. But in the process of dehumanizing others we dehumanize ourselves.

Dear Lord, bless our young servicemen and women. Don't let them become divided by racism, or religious, or cultural prejudice. Keep their hearts honest and free of hate. Teach them to love their fellow humans, and You, oh great and mighty Father. And all of the rest of us too. Amen

"But I say to you, love your enemies, bless those who curse you, do good to those who hate you, and pray for those who spitefully use you and persecute you."
Matthew 5:44

February 16

My family experienced hard times in the late thirties.

Although I was just a little scutter I still remember Dad's ingenuity in feeding a family while getting only occasional work with the WPA. We usually ate what we grew or what Dad killed with his 22-caliber rifle. And we trapped quail (illegally, I am sure).

One morning, on the way to the pepper field, we stopped to check the traps. Our only catch was a red bird. (It was years before I knew that they were cardinals.) He was so pretty that I just had to have him. So I persuaded Dad to let me keep him. But his pecking me really hurt. So I put my sandwich in my back pocket and put the bird in the brown paper bag.

When we arrived at the pepper field I was careful to place the bag in a shade. At noon I couldn't wait to see my bird. He had suffocated!

That red bird stayed in my memory. In counseling cases, and in experiences with my own family, I remembered the lesson of the red bird: it is possible to cling too tightly.

There was a great Country song a few years ago, *Give Me Wings*. In sum its message was, "Let me fly so that I can choose, on my own, to stay."

Parents need to learn that. Married couples too. You can hold on so tightly that you suffocate the other person. And what sort of relationship is it if it is coerced?

God set the example. He allowed us to choose to accept his love.

Dear Lord, help me to always allow others the freedom that you have given me, through Jesus Christ my Lord, Amen

"...See, I have set before you an open door...."
Revelation 3:8

February 17

My wife, Shirley, and I were traveling through Central Florida on a trip to say goodbye to family and friends. We were heading to our next assignment at the Presidio of San Francisco.

She commented on the beauty of the Phlox, flowers that bank the roadside and blanket the meadows in spring. They are pink, purple, white, and various shades in between.

Phlox were nothing to me. I played in fields of them as a kid, and staked out the milk cow to feed in them.

Later, when traveling around the world in the Army, I was struck by the great beauty of the Texas Bluebonnets, and Holland's Tulips.

But Phlox were just Phlox. Until Shirley helped me to see their beauty.

Do you fail to see the hand of God in the routine things of your life?

Hello God!

Are you attracted by some distant or special thing while overlooking the grandeur all around you?

Bluebonnets and Tulips are beautiful. But so are Phlox.

If you are tempted by the exotic doings of some new cult perhaps you have failed to see the simple beauty in Jesus, the Savior.

Are you at wits end over the rebellious anger of a son or daughter? Disappointed at the shortcomings of a spouse? Bone-wearied by a debilitating disease? Sad at the loss of a friend? A job?

Your day may seem dark but you are surrounded by splendor. Pry open your spiritual eyes. See the magnificence around you.

Know that God loves you.

"...*Consider* the lilies of the field...."
Matthew 6:28

Okay Lord. I get the message. I have counseled others to stop and smell the roses, but often have overlooked the phlox. I won't keep doing that. Amen

February 18

Picture a classy lady about 80 years old. She was immaculately dressed, and well made up. She was participating in an event for senior citizens at the community center.

Across the room sat a handsome gentleman about 82. He also was immaculately dressed. His full head of hair was silver. The cut of his jaw was firm. He was lean and strong for his age. He obviously was a virile male in good health. He walked over to her.

"Excuse me, lady, but you have been staring at me all morning."

"Oh, please forgive me. You are right. I have been staring at you. It's just that you look so much like my fifth husband.

"Dear lady, how many husbands have you had?"

"Four."

You are never too old to plan ahead. Say it differently: you will never reach an age when it is not appropriate to ask, "What's ahead?"

The prophet Joel was the visionary who, while defining the reasons for Israel's calamities, foretold a glorious redemption:

"...It shall come to pass afterward that I will pour out My Spirit on all flesh; your sons and your daughters shall prophesy, *your old men* (and ladies*?) shall see visions.*"

Joel 2:28

What's next for you? Are you still dreaming of new challenges?

How about your spiritual life? Anything new happening to you? What are your plans for spiritual growth this year? Next year?

"...Get yourself a new heart and a new spirit...turn and live!"

Ezekiel 18:31,32

What must a Christian do about beggars?

It is a question that I struggle with. I know that many of them are professional hustlers. I also worry about efforts to politicize the homeless for seemingly sectarian reasons. So, I began to find myself walking on by.

But the teachings of Jesus troubled me. He seemed to be calling on me to give without regard to how dishonest or deceitful the beggar might be.

It all came to a head on a San Francisco street.

An elderly gentleman, trim, gray beard, coat and tie, but emaciated looking, was positioned at the corner of Union and Laguna. I avoided eye contact. When I walked by he said, "God bless you." That hooked me. I went back and gave my change (nearly a dollar). As I walked on I wondered what he could buy for change. I had not given him enough money for beer.

As I passed the Bakery at Buchanan and Union a street person, dressed in dirty rags, emerged with a hunk of bread. It was about as large a piece as could be purchased with change.

It dawned on me that people sometimes beg to buy bread.

So, here is what I have decided. And it isn't always easy for me to keep my commitment.

Unless it is obvious to me that the person begging is a scam artist I will give. I thank God that I can afford it.

I will leave the charlatan to God. I would rather give to an occasional laggard than fail to help someone who is hungry.

"Give to him who asks you, and from him who wants to borrow from you do not turn away."
Matthew 5:42

Lord, You tell me to be charitable to the poor and needy. Okay. I will do it. And I will trust You to keep the books. Amen

February 20

I have first hand knowledge about guns in church.

Back in the dark ages (I was nineteen years old) I preached a revival meeting in Northwest Alabama. It was a very rural area, and folks didn't yet have television. Revival meetings were social events for the entire community. Hundreds attended the meetings. They came by car and by horse drawn wagons.

Many of the men stayed outside during the services. When I asked why I was told that they were bootleggers and that it would be inappropriate for them to come inside. However, the ushers always went outside with the offering plates. It's a good thing that they did, too. The bootleggers were the most generous givers.

One night a bully came to the meeting and sat on the back row.

He sent a kid to tell me that he was going to kill me. As I looked at him he opened his shirt, and pointed to a holstered 45 caliber pistol. When I told the pastor that the man said he was going to kill me he exclaimed, "My God, Brother Hunt, he'll do it too. Let's kneel and pray."

"Kneel and pray?" I thought, "How about run and escape!"

When we arose from prayer he whispered to one of the sisters of the church. She promptly slipped out of the side door. In a few minutes her husband pulled up to the side door in a huge, expensive, car. I eased out of the door and into the car, and was driven to their house.

I spent the night, safely, in the home of the county's biggest bootlegger.

Why not? God can use whatever resource He chooses to take care of us. If He decides to use a bootlegger to save a young evangelist who am I to complain?

"Surely the wrath of men shall praise you...."
Psalm 76:10

February 21

To hear the voice of God we sometimes need to turn down the volume.

Elijah, on the run from wicked Jezebel, desperately needed to hear from God. He listened through a fierce wind, a mighty earthquake, and a scorching fire. Nothing.

As he waited quietly God spoke, in "A still small voice" (I Kings 19:12)

Hello God!

I once conducted an entire worship service in whispers. I had to assure the company commander that I could conduct a service without drawing fire from a large, dug in, North Vietnamese force. They were about two hundred yards across a creek from us. Every sound or movement had drawn fire.

About 15 of us crawled our heads together into as close a circle as we could get. I conducted a full service: prayers, a sermon, and communion. All in whispers. I had copies of a hymn in my rucksack. We whispered all four verses and the chorus to "Blessed Assurance." It remains the most memorable service I ever conducted.

Each year technology adds to the rush and clamor of daily life. If you want to hear God's voice you will have to listen carefully. He often speaks in whispers.

The fires, winds, and jolts of human experience may buffet you today. That's the way life is. But there is a voice of God for you. Find a quiet moment, collect your thoughts, and listen. It may be a whisper, but you will know He is there.

"Be still, and know that I am God....
Psalms 46: 10

Lord, You know that I like to keep moving. I don't like to sit still. Can't You talk to me while I am doing something else? Forgive me Lord. I know better. Help me to be still so that I can know. Amen

February 22

Happy George Washington's Birthday. Our first president was born on this date in 1732.

Let's honor him, and seek the blessings of God on our Country, by praying together extracts from his

Prayer for the Nation:

Almighty God, we make our earnest prayer that Thou wilt keep the United States in Thy holy protection; that Thou wilt incline the hearts of the citizens to cultivate a spirit of subordination and obedience to government, and entertain a brotherly affection and love for one another and for their fellow citizens of the United States at large.

And finally, that Thou wilt most graciously be pleased to dispose us all to do justice, to love mercy, and to demean ourselves with that charity, humility, and pacific temper of mind which were the characteristics of the Divine Author of our blessed religion, and without an humble imitation of whose example in these things we can never hope to be a happy nation.

Grant our supplications we beseech Thee, through Jesus Christ our Lord. Amen.

(Written at Newburg, June 8, 1783, and sent to the Governors of all the States.)

We live in an age where political rhetoric includes the meanest things about politicians. There seems to be no boundaries. Sex life and/or orientation is fair game.

As a Christian you have a duty to pray for political leaders. How can you do that honestly while spouting the vilest hatred for a mayor, governor, representative, senator, or a president?

"...I exhort...that...prayers...be made for all...in authority...."

1 Timothy 2:1,2

February 23

Jesus enjoyed His friends.

Perhaps His best friends were the siblings Lazarus, Martha, and Mary. They lived in the bedroom community of Bethany, on the Jerico Road, just east of Jerusalem. Weary travelers loved to stop overnight at Bethany to rest and refresh themselves before going on to the Holy City.

Jesus often stayed at their home in Bethany. Martha fussed over Him, cooked His favorite foods, and insisted that He relax and enjoy Himself. Mary was an intellectual, a stimulating conversationalist. Lazarus and Jesus were buddies.

Lazarus became deathly ill. The sisters immediately sent a runner for Jesus. But Jesus didn't come. Lazarus died. Still no Jesus. The sisters paced the floor, repeating that their brother wouldn't have died if Jesus had been there. When Jesus finally arrived they scolded Him for not coming sooner. Lazarus had been dead for four days.

Jesus knew of Lazarus' illness and could have rushed to his bedside. He chose not to "for the glory of God" (John 11:4).

It was a *deliberate delay*.

God doesn't have to meet your deadlines. In fact He may delay the answer to work a greater good in your life.

Listen to your praying. Does it sound more like you are giving God an order than seeking His will and submitting to it? He will work, but in His own time, for His glory, and your good. Amen

"...It is not for you to know times or seasons which the Father has put in His own authority."
Acts 1:7

Dear Lord, I know that I am impatient. And I understand that my impatience indicates a lack of confidence in You. Your responsiveness, timeliness. Help me, for I am a person of little faith. Amen

February 24

Giving up singing?

A newspaper article stated that a famous singer had "repented" and given up singing. I remember how well he sang *Morning Has Broken,* a truly great song.

Leaders in his religion considered his singing to be sinful. I don't mean to be critical of another religion, but that is so sad to me. I can't imagine a life without singing.

One day, while stationed in Panama, I was really depressed. I decided to take a walk, get out of the office. An "ugly bird" (a name I gave them because they are really ugly) drew my attention. He was sitting on a limb overhanging the sidewalk. He was singing for all of his might.

As a songwriter I know the numbers of musical notes. For example, do is 1, re is 2, mi is 3, and so forth. I wrote down the various numbers that he sang. To my utter amazement I discovered that he had used all of the seven basic notes of the music scale.

Franz Lehar needed no more notes than the bird to write the main movement of Volglalied, a classic popular the world over.

I had a delightful spiritual experience on that sidewalk. I started singing. By the time I got back to the office my mood had lifted.

Singing is the gate of the soul. Through singing flows joy, sorrow, grief, anger; any emotion.

But you say that you can't carry a tune? Well, don't worry.

The Psalmist has a way for you,

"Make a joyful *noise* unto God...."
Psalm 66:1 (KJV)

Thank you Lord for letting me learn to play musical instruments. I pray that You will help me to always put You first, and that I will use the gifts that You have given me for Your glory. Amen.

February 25

My best buddy, Bob, an Italian American from Brooklyn, taught me how to eat pizza. You take a single slice, pinch the crust together so that it can't leak on your shirt, and eat it, starting at the tip.

Then why was I trying to eat pizza with a plastic knife and fork on a Sunday Afternoon in the Presidio of San Francisco? It was the dress blue uniform. There is no anonymity in the Post Exchange Snack Bar, especially when you are a senior officer in a dress up uniform with shining brass.

As a senior officer I knew that I must always set the example of propriety. But pizza with a knife and fork!

As a Christian you have a responsibility to present Christ to the world in the best possible light. What does being a Christian mean if it doesn't mean that in some way you should represent Him?

"If you were arrested for being a Christian would there be enough evidence to convict you?" someone asked.

As a Christian you are always open for inspection. Granted, the standards that people use can be quite arbitrary. And critics are not usually motivated by generosity, nor even by a mature understanding of Biblical norms.

Yet, if what you do speaks so loudly that people won't hear what you say, you must always know that people are watching.

Lord, I don't like this spotlight, but I know my responsibility. By what I do and say let my life reflect You as the world deserves to see you. Amen

"...*Put on* the Lord Jesus Christ, and make no provision for the flesh, to fulfill its lusts."
Romans 13:14

Nice suit!

February 26

The Dean of Women drew back sharply, lifted her hands in a defensive position, trembled, and shrieked, "Brother Hunt, you make me cringe! You mustn't touch the women!"

That happened in my first week of Bible College. I apparently had touched her shoulder with my left hand while shaking her right hand. Her response left me embarrassed and rattled. I'm sure that I shook hands from a front leaning position for years. I still think she was out of line.

Jesus touched when He didn't have to. Although He sometimes healed by a simple verbal command, He often seemed to go out of His way to make physical contact: clay and spittle on blind eyes, fingers in deaf ears, and jostling in a rowdy crowd.

The best example of the ministry of touching is the case of the lonely leper. It was a capital offense to touch a leper. Neither could a person get closer than precise limits set by strict religious law. Lepers were required to stay downwind from people to avoid the possibility of infecting them. They had to shout, "leper," and wear distinguishing marks on their bodies. At the risk of His life, *Jesus touched the leper.*

The leprosy departed with the verbal command. Then why the touch? The leper had been completely de-humanized. Jesus' touch was a merciful act, a *re-humanization of the leper.*

Studies have shown that infants require a lot of human touching to be normal and strong. Someone even documented the number of hugs that an adult needs to stay healthy.

Don't let the Dean of Women scare you, too. Reach out and touch someone today.

"...Jesus, moved with compassion, put out His hand and *touched*...him...."
Mark 1:41

Thank you, Lord, for touching me. Help me to touch others. Amen

What would you think if your doctor stuck his fingers in your ears, spat, then touched the spittle to your tongue? That's what Jesus did to heal a deaf man.

Jesus always deals with us from where we are.

The ancients believed that spittle had curative powers. Jesus was using a familiar method, one that the man knew and trusted. Had he gone into a discourse about germs, chemicals, science and applied medicine it would have been a waste of the man's time. What the man needed was to have his faith built up. He needed help in believing that he could be healed.

In His approach to healing the blind man, Jesus chose a very personal method. No form letters, no recorded messages.

I remember a particular trip to the doctor. He happened to be a personal friend and we were both members of the same post commander's staff. During almost my entire visit he was turned away from me, writing, fiddling with things. I finally said, "Scotty, dad gum it, look at me when we talk."

The Christian religion is not founded upon a science, but a relationship. It is one of a loving and seeking Savior who accepts imperfect people into his embrace and makes them better.

Just as I am, without one plea
But that Thy blood was shed for me
And that Thou biddest me come to Thee
O Lamb of God, I come, I come.

"Immediately his ears were opened, and the impediment of his tongue was loosed, and he spoke plainly."
Mark 7:35

You can use any technique You wish, Jesus. Just let me know Your saving grace, and feel your healing power. Amen

Prisons and hospitals depress me. Because of that I have always sought troop assignments over specialized ministry. So, whenever I visit either place, I usually go with a list of specific persons to visit. And I don't loiter.

On the occasion in mind I was zipping down the stockade corridor, with singleness of purpose, when an inmate called out, "Chaplain!" I stopped.

"Sir, will you forgive me?" he asked.

"Only God can forgive sins," I responded, in good Protestant orthodoxy.

"I know that, Chaplain," he pleaded, "but I am so ashamed of myself, and so sorry for the terrible things I have done. It would mean a lot to me to hear someone say that he forgives me."

"Then reach through the bars."

I took his hands in mine. Then, looking him squarely in the eyes, I said, "I forgive you." Tears, and a big smile, thanked me.

Strange behavior for a Protestant Chaplain? Well, yes. I fear that we Protestants have over reacted to perceived abuses by our Catholic brothers and sisters. And in doing so we have overlooked a powerful promise.

Perhaps the greatest gift you can give a fellow human is forgiveness. Perhaps the meanest sin is to withhold it.

Today, forgive a son or daughter; a spouse, parent, sibling, friend, or an enemy. In so doing you are also forgiven.

"...Receive the Holy Spirit. If you forgive the sins of any, they are forgiven them..."
John 20:22,23

Lord, You know that forgiving is just about the hardest thing that you require of me. I would rather hold a grudge, get even. Help me, Lord. Amen

A good self-image is one thing, but let's not get carried away.

Alexander the Great once found his philosopher friend, Diogenes, standing in a field, looking intently at a large pile of bones. When asked what he was doing the old man replied, "I am searching for the bones of your father, Philip, but I cannot seem to distinguish them from the bones of the slaves."

Alexander got the point: everyone is equal in death. From the greatest to the least, from the most beautiful to the most ordinary; death is the universal equalizer.

In the church at Rome some of the members were apparently boasting of their superior gifts. Perhaps the more glamorous ones, like prophecy, or tongues. (Read about in Romans 12:3) Paul instructed them that a person should not "Think of himself more highly than he ought to think...as God has dealt to each one a measure of faith."

St. Augustine wrote, "It was pride that changed angels into devils; it is humility that makes men as angels."

It is said that Caesar had a slave ride beside him in his chariot to repeat, "Remember, Caesar, you are just a man."

Pride is a deadly sin. Like a pill that dissolves and its essence spreads throughout the glass, pride is a poison that permeates the soul.

Think of an unruly child trying to grab hold of your leg and you putting your hand on his head to keep him away. Then read the following text.

"God *resists* the proud, but gives grace to the humble."
1 Peter 5:5

Lord, I don't want to feel Your hand on my head, holding me back from You. I confess my pride, Oh Lord, and pray for Your grace. Amen

March 1

Growth can be painful.

My buddy, Dan, who is also a retired soldier, earns extra money by putting the data on gravestones. I go out with him occasionally to do "gofer" chores.

He was asked to smooth out the top of a headstone that had not been finished properly by the supplier. The top was about four feet long and seven inches wide and solid granite.

First Dan attacked the headstone with a grindstone. After a few minutes it became apparent that the grindstone was not going to be enough to get the job done. Next he used a small jackhammer with chisel attached to flake off the big pieces. Finally he was able to use the grindstone to finish the job.

During this process I was thinking that if God is concerned about who I am and what I can be He surely is at work in my life. And since He is at work in my life there may be times when He uses the jackhammer. What a frightening thought. There may also be times that I must face the grindstone.

Ira Stanphill wrote a great song, *He Washed My Eyes With Tears That I Might See.* In the song he developed the truth that we don't always get what we want, and what we want isn't always best for us. Further, real growth and maturity as a Christian often come through painful experiences. I knew Ira, and even preached in his church when I was in Bible school. What a great person, pastor, and songwriter.

Dear Lord, When I need chiseling or grinding, help me to see that You are working in my behalf. And to believe that what I am able to become through Your grace will make anything else seem insignificant. Amen

"...The vessel that He made of clay was marred...so He made it again into another vessel, as it seemed good to the potter to make."
Jeremiah 18:4

March 2

One evening as Shirley and I were eating supper she said, "There's a bird in the fireplace."

"What?" I asked. "How long has he been there?"

"Since yesterday. I meant to tell you last night but forgot."

Sure enough, there was a beautiful bluebird trapped behind the wire grate. He must have fallen down the chimney.

He was terrified of my efforts to free him. He escaped into the house and kept crashing into the picture window in the dining room. I finally caught him with my minnow net and released him at the front door.

As he flew away he not only didn't look back to thank me for my saving his life but probably thought that he had escaped sure death through his own efforts.

What a great parable of our relationship with God. He may be working to save us but we may think that He is trying to kill us.

I tried out for my home church and prayed earnestly to be called as its pastor. I had grown up in the church. I knew the community. I believed that I could lead them to numerical and spiritual growth.

They called someone else! I was crushed.

A few months later I received a call to a church in another state, just ten miles from a fine seminary. If I had been called to my home church I would have settled into a ministry that was wrong for me.

I would have never been able to attend seminary, and I would never have been able to enjoy over thirty years of Active Duty as an Army Chaplain, a ministry that I now know was God's will for me all along.

"...As the heavens are higher than the earth, so are My ways higher than your ways, and My thoughts than your thoughts."
Isaiah 55:9

March 3

What does your praying sound like?

Many folks try to sound like a preacher when they pray. *Too professional.* Some seem to pray to be heard by the audience more than to God. *Too social.* I have crafted prayers (get the verb) that in retrospect seemed to be aimed more at the historical record. *Too calculating.* Most of the commanders I had in the Army hated prayers that were written out and read. *Too canned.*

Your praying should sound like you.

When our first child, Alan, was still learning to talk we started out on a trip. As we were driving away he reminded us that we hadn't prayed. So I asked him to say the prayer. "Oh Dod, don't wet us have a weck.," he prayed.

Another great prayer came from a chaplain assistant. One of our companies had been ambushed on the Korean Demilitarized Zone. We were racing to the site in an open jeep during a monsoon's torrential downpour. Mike burst out with, "Oh God, don't let them get us too."

I am not saying that you shouldn't be reverent in your praying. I am saying that you should be yourself.

Jesus charged you to pray always and not faint (Luke 18:1). That will be impossible as long as you try to sound like pious, professional, other-bodies.

It will be easier for you to pray effectively when you understand prayer as your own personal conversation with God. Even though he may be a great person of faith, don't try to sound like your pastor. Pray like you talk, doing so with due respect for the Lord.

"...When you pray do not use vain repetitions as the heathen do, for they think that they will be heard for their many words."
Matthew 6:7

Lord, teach me to pray. Again. Amen

March 4

He was old, tired, and sick.

The missionary had served 50 years in a primitive country. His children had died early from the plagues of that distant land. Just recently he had buried his wife and long time companion. Now he was returning home to his own country. Alone.

Aboard the same ship was a popular governor. He was returning from a big game hunt. Bands played as the politician's trunks and trophies were taken ashore. Then the governor spoke to a cheering crowd.

There was no one to welcome the missionary. He rented a cheap room to rest and ponder his next moves. He was so overcome by emotion that he fell across the rickety bed.

"Lord," he sobbed, "I have given my whole life to your service. I have buried my family in a foreign land. Crowds came to greet a politician, but no one came to welcome me home."

Then he heard a voice that he had learned to recognize long ago, a voice that came from deep within his spirit. The voice said, "My son, you aren't home yet."

Hello God!

When is the last time that you thought of Heaven? Have the comforts of the modern world dimmed your vision of eternity? It's easy to be so engrossed in the now that you forget the next.

Yet the joys and sorrows of *now* pale in comparison with the grandeur of *then*. As a child of God you have a great destiny. A grand welcome awaits the follower of Jesus, when he gets home. Amen

"...I will come again and receive you to Myself; that where I am, there you may be also."
John 14:3

Lord, bless all that travel so far and sacrifice so much for Your glorious Gospel. Amen

March 5

I have vivid memories of people handling snakes in church.

Once a man came into the church, where my family attended until I was about 10 years old, and announced that he had caught a six-foot rattlesnake. He asked the pastor if he believed the Scripture about handling snakes. The pastor said that he believed every word of the Bible. He told the man to bring the snake. And that if he didn't handle the snake in three nights he would quit preaching and put up his Bible.

By the third night there were hundreds gathered at that little country church.

When he felt ready the pastor kicked open the box containing the snake and handled it. He wasn't bitten. Another brother handled the snake and was bitten, but suffered no ill effect. I remember seeing the two fang marks on his hand with drops of blood hardened on the skin.

Some scholars explain that the Scripture reference to handling snakes is spurious, a later addition to Mark's manuscript. That the text is unreliable.

Others go into the Greek construction to explain that the original text does not say what it seems to say in English. Thus they can ignore a difficult passage while claiming a strong view of the Scriptures.

Well, I have seen snakes handled, and I've studied Greek.

To me the passage has powerful validity. It commands us to take on the things that crawl, rattle, and bite. To take up our problems and handle them. To face them squarely, and not run away from them.

Is there something critically important in your life that you are afraid to deal with? Letting it simmer? It won't go away. *Take up your serpent(s).*

"...In My name...they will take up serpents...."
Mark 16:17, 18

Lord, You know that I don't like snakes. But I do want to deal courageously and wisely with the things that hinder me. I will take up my serpents. Amen

March 6

Their arrogance troubled me.

They were two famous television personalities (a man and a woman). If I mentioned their names you would recognize them immediately. They were discussing *white lies* on their nationally broadcast news magazine.

They agreed that it was okay to tell a white lie if it was for the other person's good.

Now it is commendable to be concerned for the other person's good.

That is what love is in its Biblical meaning. Loving is not having a warm fuzzy feeling about someone. It is acting, unselfishly, in the other person's interest. Love in the Scriptures is action, not feeling.

Then why was I concerned? Because I don't like having someone making decisions for me. For when someone withholds information from me for my good, however well intended, he or she exercises power over me. They deny me the possibility to take responsibility for myself.

I prefer to have the facts and be responsible for my own actions in response to the information.

The problem some have with truth is that they think that it has to be told in brutal exactness. For example, "My, what an ugly baby you have." St. Paul's exhortation to the Ephesians gives the key, "Speaking the truth in love...."

So what does love demand from us as Christians? Certainly not taking responsibility away from someone by withholding the truth from them *for their own good.*

Our Christian responsibility is to tell the truth in love.

"...You shall know the truth, and the truth shall make you free."
John 8:32

Lord, the preacher said that truth isn't something, but Someone. Sweet Jesus, living Truth of God, help me to fully embrace You as Lord, Savior, and Guide. Let my conversation and behavior be pleasing to You. Amen

March 7

Many things were decided for me.

I am thankful to be the son of Henry Edward Hunt and Nettie Marie Jordan Hunt. And I would choose them now as parents if I had the option, but I never had that option. My name was chosen for me.

Being a citizen of the United States of America is one of history's greatest blessings. I would never give up my citizenship. But I didn't choose it. I was born a citizen.

Being a male was chosen for me. I choose daily what I will do with my maleness: whether I will be a true man, an honorable human being. I have choice in those subheadings, but gender was something over which I had no choice.

The greatest choice of any human being is in his relationship to God.

At this point people dance around a lot. With some it is easy, do nothing at all. Others are content to live in a perpetual limbo of indecision. Others postpone any decision, promising to do so later. Still others respond with a token response, offering up a part of themselves, but shying away from anything nearing full commitment.

Holman Hunt's painting of the Light of the World shows Christ outside a door. Someone noted that there was no latchstring. The artist exclaimed, "The latchstring is on the inside." You must decide if Christ is invited into your life as Lord and Savior. Parents cannot ultimately make that decision for you, although they can influence it.

A critic of Winston Churchill said that one could love him or hate him but no one could ignore him. It is more so with Jesus Christ.

"...What then shall I do with Jesus who is called Christ...?"
Matthew 27:22

Here is what I will do Lord. I will swing wider the door to my heart and beg You to come inside with more of Your power and presence. Here goes Lord. Do it now. Amen

March 8

"Hey, listen up. Has anyone seen Jesus?

Jesus was only twelve years old when He accompanied His parents to the Holy City for the Feast of Passover. He had been captivated by the sights and sounds of the place.

When it came time to leave He "Lingered behind in Jerusalem" (Luke 2:43).

Joseph and Mary journeyed a whole day before noticing that Jesus was not in the group of travelers. But when they discovered that He was missing they acted immediately. They did a quick U-turn and headed back to where they had last seen Him.

Have you lost the presence of Jesus?

Did it happen when you moved out of the neighborhood, and away from your home church? And you just never got around to finding another place of worship?

Did it happen when you had a "relationship" with someone other than your spouse? And your feeling of guilt became a self-imposed wall between you and the Lord?

Did it happen as you busied yourself taking care of your family? Getting ahead? Making money?

Or did you just drift away? Failing to keep a daily devotional schedule? Easing back on your stewardship? Starting to miss church?

Then one day you looked around and didn't see Him.

Do like Joseph and Mary. Return to where you left Him. He will be glad to see you. His arms are outstretched. Go. Amen

"...They will return to the Lord, and He will be entreated by them and heal them."
Isaiah 19:22

Lord, I pray today for those who have lost the sense of Your presence in their lives. Help them to be honest enough to admit their falling away and the courage to return to You. You are still there Lord. Waiting. Arms open. And thank You for it. Amen

March 9

A wealthy and eccentric old man was faced with choosing an heir. His only relatives were three nephews.

He called the three together and said, "Here's a ten dollar bill for each of you. The one who can buy something with it that fills this large room will be my heir." He gave them until sunset to finish their quest.

They searched the city over and at sunset returned to their uncle.

One brought a huge bale of straw and scattered it around, but it scarcely covered the floor. The second youth brought two bags of feathers. They cluttered the air, but didn't really fill the room.

The third youth looked sad, and said, "I gave five dollars to a hungry woman and more to some children. With what was left I bought this candle and matches." He then lit the candle and light filled the whole room. He became the heir.

Remember the parable that Jesus told of the man who distributed his capital to his servants for them to invest?

One who was given five talents gained five more. Likewise for the one given two talents. But the servant who was given only one talent was afraid to risk it. So he buried it for safe keeping. While the first two received generous praise the fearful servant was severely punished.

What are you doing with your talent(s)? Are you bringing glory to God? To the furtherance of His kingdom? Don't be afraid. Use it. Or lose it. Let it grow. Amen

"...Whoever has, to him more will be given; but whoever does not have, even what he has will be taken away from him."
Mark 4:25

Lord, my instinct is to grab the shovel and bury the gift so that I won't lose it. You have taught me better. I am trying to learn. Help me. Amen

March 10

God bless golfers.

I don't play golf. But I do know more than the guy who shot a hole in one and was trying to figure out how to have it mounted.

Actually I played a lot of golf during seminary. And even up to that fateful day that the Post Chaplain at Fort Benning asked me to play with him. He was a "full bull" colonel and I was just a green first lieutenant. Needless to say I was pleased to be so honored. A bit nervous, too.

On the second "T" I hit a line drive off a pine tree and onto the shin of the Post Chaplain. I thought that it was so funny, him hopping around and cussing, since he was normally a quiet, undemonstrative man. I laughed. But he didn't. As I apologized for laughing at him it was hard to keep from giggling. He never asked me to play again. And I haven't played since. I have decided to play mandolin. It's safer.

I can't say for sure that God is concerned about your golf score. But I do know that He cares for you. He follows your good times and bad. Whether you are talented or untalented, rich or poor, handsome or plain, He loves you.

So today, be kind to a golfer, or a mandolin player; a brick mason, a janitor, a tailor, or a housewife. And know that God loves you and them.

God cares about the times that you stand at a loved one's casket or say goodbye to a wayward child. But He also cares about the little things in your life, too. Amen

"...The very hairs of your head are all numbered...."
Luke 12:7

Lord, it boggles my mind to think that You love me. And You loved me before I ever knew to love You. And You loved me enough to allow Jesus to die as my Savior. Really boggling. But thank You anyway. Amen

March 11

There were teardrops on every page and I could hear the catch in Frank's voice at every mention of his son's name.

An old friend, Army Chaplain Frank Deese, sent me a copy of his personal and painful reflections on the death of his son, Charles. Charles was the oldest son of Frank and his wife Gaynelle.

Charlie had worked for me as a Chaplain Assistant in Kaiserslautern, Germany. He was a great soldier and a most careful and respectful son. Frank took great pride in Charlie. We all loved Charlie's great wit and respected his remarkable talents.

A youthful driver ran a stop sign, hit Charlie's car broadside on the driver's side, and killed him instantly.

With Charlie's death, Frank was crushed (as were all of Charlie's family and friends). Weeks later he wrote:

> *The stabbing pain still comes at times, but it is met by the knowledge of what it means to participate in the reality of the resurrection. My faith has been tested to the core. The rafters of my theology have trembled. I touched bottom, but I am happy to report that THE BOTTOM IS SOLID!*

The air is crisp and invigorating on the mountaintops. We all love the lofty views from our successes.

But sometimes life walks us through the darkest valleys. Sometimes we experience great loss. Sometimes we bounce off spiritual bottoms. That's possible because, as Frank wrote, *the bottom is solid.*

"...For Christ's sake, I delight in weaknesses...in hardships...in difficulties. For when I am weak, then I am strong."
2 Corinthians 12:10

This is hard for me to understand, Lord, but I am trusting You. Amen

March 12

Thank Heaven For Little Girls is a song made famous by Maurice Chevalier.

After the success of the Boy Scout movement in Great Britain, people started to see the need for a similar organization for girls. And like Boy Scouting before it, the Girl Scout movement also crossed the Atlantic.

The Girl Scout movement was organized on March 9, 1912, by Juliette Gordon of Savannah, Georgia. Congress eventually passed a law giving a special charter of incorporation to the Girl Scouts of America. Membership in the United States is around three million, making the Girl Scouts the world's largest voluntary organization for girls.

Girl Scout activities include arts and crafts, nature walks, and community service projects. Much of the group's funding comes from the annual sale of Girl Scout cookies.

On a Sunday near this date your church will probably feature Girl Scouts. Churches are a favorite meeting place for Scouts. We as Christians should give our best support to Scouting: financial, moral, and in volunteering our services.

Dear Lord, I thank You for my own daughter. She is a woman now, with children of her own, but I still think of her as my little girl.

Bless all of the young girls of America, Lord. Help them to avoid the evils so prevalent in our society. Let them grow in spirit as well as body. And help us, as individuals and as a society, to do all that we can to make that possible. Amen.

"Let no one despise your youth, but be an example to the believers in word, in conduct, in love, in spirit, in faith, in purity."

1 Timothy 4:12

March 13

It's the gospel truth!

How many times have you heard someone say that? Often as though it were to emphasize that what they were saying was a true truth, a more truthful than normal truth? Get it? A lot of people seem to believe that the word gospel means truth.

Well, the gospel of Jesus Christ is true, but the word gospel doesn't mean truth. The word gospel means good news.

Here's an example. Suppose you are waiting anxiously outside the operating room. Your beloved daughter is in there. There has been a horrible accident. She was taken by air evacuation to this hospital. The doctor comes out of the operating room and says, "I am sorry, we did our best. She didn't make it." Now that may be the truth but it surely isn't gospel.

Now suppose that the doctor comes out of the operating room and says, "Your daughter made it through the emergency operation fine. After a few weeks she will be all right." That statement may be the truth, and it is also gospel. That is, it is good news.

And you ask, "What is the good news?"

The good news is that the Son of God came into the world, identified with sinful mankind, took upon himself our sins, suffered a cruel death on a cross, was buried, was raised from the dead, and remains our Savior. He is sitting at the right hand of God making intercession for us. He will come again in glory to establish His rule over the earth.

The preceding paragraph surely does not exhaust the definition of gospel. But it does state the core of the good news.

"The beginning of the Gospel (*Good News*) of Jesus Christ, the Son of God."

Mark 1:1

March 14

Was the mighty prophet suffering from *post miracle syndrome*?

Elijah had gone against the wicked king Ahab and prophesied that there would be a debilitating drought. Sure enough, it had happened. God had sustained Elijah throughout the drought by sending ravens to bring him food. Then he had challenged the 450 prophets of Baal to a public showdown. Israel would know once and for all which god was the true God.

Read the story in 1Kings 18 and 19.

They prepared two sacrifices, one for the god Baal and one for the God of Israel. The one that answered by fire would be seen as the true God. The prophets of Baal prayed, cried, and cut themselves for hours. Nothing happened. Then Elijah prayed that the God of Abraham, Isaac, and Jacob would consume the sacrifice. Fire came from heaven and consumed the offering, the wood on which it lay, the stones around it, and the water in the trench encircling the altar. The people all acknowledged the true God.

Now fast-forward a day or two.

Queen Jezebel has sent word that she will have Elijah killed as the prophets of Baal were. Elijah is hiding in the wilderness, whining, and complaining. He prays for God to just take his life. Then in deep depression, and weary from running, he falls asleep under a broom tree.

An angel awakens him and gives him food. Elijah regains his strength, and makes his way to a high mountain, to a cave, to hear from God. Do you get it? *God saved Elijah from his self-destructive mood.* He saw that Elijah's greatest danger came not from Jezebel, but from Elijah, himself.

Dear Lord, when I am down, save me from my moods. Amen.

"...Arise and eat, because the journey is too great for you."

1 Kings 19:7

March 15

Jesus doesn't make it easy!

And let me say up front that this devotion whacks me more than anybody else. I heard a preacher say that when he pointed one finger at someone else that left three fingers and a thumb pointing back at him.

So, what does it mean to *deny* oneself?

The word, deny, in the English text comes from the Greek word, *arnasastho*, which means *disown*. "...Whoever denies Me before men, him I will also deny before my Father...." (Matthew 10:33).

The word also carries the meaning of *renounce*. The grace of God teaches us that "...Denying ungodliness and worldly lusts, we should live soberly, righteously, and godly, in this present age." (Titus 2:12)

The word also means *refuse*. "By faith Moses, when he became of age, refused to be called the son of Pharaoh's daughter." (Hebrews 11:24)

Thus the claims of Christ cover the page. He must come before my personal, my ego, considerations. He must come before my physical comforts. And he must come before any cherished social or political advantages.

Dear Lord, don't You know that I am living in an age of creature comforts? Don't You know how much I need to be liked? Surely You understand my need for financial security. No? Okay, Lord, I admit to all. Forgive me. Help me to be the person after Your heart, to put You where You insist on being, and deserve to be, first in my life. Amen.

"...If any man desires come after Me, let him deny himself...."

Luke 9:23

March 16

"Let's have a show of hands." How many times have you said that or heard it said?

You know, what we do with our hands says a lot about us: our commitment to God; and our dedication to Christian service

It doesn't help to just wring our hands, clucking, "tsk, tsk," and murmuring, "too bad."

The Old Testament character, Lot, cried and bewailed the evil in Sodom but did little or nothing about it. On the other hand, Noah heard from God that a mighty flood was coming and built an ark, thus saving his family from death.

Some people simply hold their hands out, palms upward, while shrugging their shoulders, as if to say, "It's not my fault. What can I do about it?" They don't have an opinion about controversial subjects. They won't risk becoming involved in anything that might incur disapproval. Their motto is, "on the one hand I believe this, but on the other hand I believe that, too."

Some people simply put their hands in their pockets, and withhold their cooperation. They look the other way, in a kind of see no evil, know no evil response.

Some people hold their hands in front of their chests, palms outward, disclaiming responsibility. It isn't my problem. I didn't do it or cause it. Therefore, it is none of my responsibility.

Too many times we are out of the net, away without leave, when there is a service to be done for Christ: the sick, the needy, fighting pornography, carrying the gospel to the whole world.

We can and must do better.

"Whatever your hand finds to do, do it with all your might...."
Ecclesiastes. 9:10

Lord, my hands are too soft. Not enough calluses from real work in the Kingdom. It is easier being a thinker than a worker. Give me a kick if I need it Lord. Amen

March 17

Did you ever thank God for not answering a prayer?

A former Chief of Army Chaplains, Major General Norris Einertson, spoke of the unanticipated problems of answered prayer.

For years we prayed about the situation in Eastern Europe. With shocking suddenness the walls came down. The mighty USSR separated into several smaller entities, each one with different problems. Our prayers were answered. But new struggles arose. New programs were required.

A friend was urged to cancel his marriage the following Sunday because his fiancee's religious connection was incompatible with his. He couldn't bring himself to cancel. So he prayed that if the marriage was not right for him God would let something happen. On the Friday night before the wedding was scheduled to happen he had a wreck. He married the girl two days later, on crutches.

You had better be careful about what you pray for because you might get it. You must be prepared to deal with the unexpected. Perhaps that is why Jesus taught His disciples to pray for God's will to be done.

So, don't pray as a spoiled child, just for what pleases you. Pray as a mature adult that God, in His wisdom and by His mighty power, will work His will in the world and in your life.

Oh Lord, I sometimes don't know what I should pray for. So pray in and through me, by Your Spirit, so that Your will may be done in my live. And when the answer comes help me to see Your wisdom and love in the answer You give. Amen

"...Whatever things you ask when you pray, believe that you receive them, and you will have them."
Mark 11:24

March 18

What does it take to be a man? (Ladies, please allow an emphasis on being a man in today's devotion. I pray that it will also be beneficial to you.)

"Men That Are Turnoffs?" was the question posed by the newspaper article. Some of the answers were interesting, to say the least.

A 40-year-old woman responded, "Nerds, men in suits. No tattoos or pierced ears, and they don't like heavy metal. My dude has 71 tatoos and a pierced nipple. As soon as he showed me his chest he was my man."

A 34 year old woman said, "I like men who aren't afraid to show their emotions. Who can be sensitive and not worry about their ego not being intact."

You can't answer the question about masculinity culturally, because cultures vary. Nor can physical size be the criterion, for some of history's greatest leaders have been frail or diminutive. Social class doesn't hold, for second and third generation progeny often demean their ancestors.

It's easier to state what masculinity isn't than what it is.

However, I believe that manliness must flow from a deep and abiding spiritual strength. I have seen such strength in men who wore it quietly, and who were disdainful of others who wore their spirituality on their sleeves.

Heavenly Father, it is difficult to be a man when society has so many different definitions of manhood. Help me to be the kind of man that will be pleasing to You, and will bring spiritual blessing to my family. Let my life reflect Your image to the world.

And Lord, I pray for my sons and grandsons. Help me, and them, to know what it means to be a real man and have the guts to be so.

In the name of Your Son, the Lord Jesus Christ. Amen

"So God created man in *His own image*...."
Genesis 1:27

March 19

I walked into our house that morning and informed Shirley that I was depressed.

"What's wrong?" she asked.

"The doctor says that I might have glaucoma in my left eye. With all of the trouble I have with my vision I don't need another problem," I whined.

Then I checked my e-mail and learned that my best buddy has malignant cancer. He has a golf ball sized growth on his kidney and the cancer is already in the bone marrow of his right leg. I felt ashamed of my complaining. The last word of his e-mail message was *pray*.

I have been praying for his wife for two years. She has had several operations for heart and heart related maladies. I even went to her bedside and anointed her with oil. Still, she hasn't regained complete wellness. Now her husband has cancer. I love those two people just like family.

How am I to pray more than I have been? Here's what I am doing. Since I detest wearing rings I started wearing a ring today to remind me to pray for my two dear friends. As annoyed as I will be because of the ring their names will be constantly on my lips. Now, what about you?

Does your arthritis keep you off your knees? Are you so busy that you have trouble finding sufficient time for prayer and meditation? Do you fall asleep when you pray lying down?

If your conscience tells you that you need to pray more you might think of a creative way to do so. A piece of string around a finger? A button on a lapel or blouse? A notice on the refrigerator? Do something. Pray!

Perhaps we should all begin our prayers with,

"Lord, teach us to pray..."
Luke 11:1

Lord, teach *me* to pray. Amen

March 20

How many friends do you have?

Friends, now, not acquaintances, associates, or peers. Don't count people who hang around because they need something from you or those you cultivate because you need something from them.

Compare your address book with one you used 20 years ago. How many names have remained in the book, and how many others are just memories? And the friends you now claim, do they mean enough to you to cause you to stop for a visit when you travel through their town?

Richard E. Byrd wrote "Alone" after being stranded for three months all by himself at a station near the South Pole. He concluded that friendship is the most important thing in life.

True friends are the kind that last a lifetime and like you as you are, persons with whom you can be completely yourself, and whose company you always enjoy. I believe that if a person has four or five friends like that she is rich.

The scriptures place a high value on friendship: "A friend loves at all Times" (Proverbs 17:17); "...There is a friend who sticks closer than a brother" (Proverbs 18:24).

Don't judge a person by his or her relatives. Rather judge a person by his or her friends. Friends are chosen, not given.

At one point in their relationship Jesus told His disciples that He called them no longer servants but friends (John 15:15). The most blessed friendship of all is with Christ the Savior. Are you Jesus' friend?

What a friend we have in Jesus,
All our sins and griefs to bear;
What a privilege to carry,
Everything to God in prayer.

"You are my friends if you do whatever I command you."

John 15:14

March 21

Words can be deadly.

The late U.S. Rep. Claude Pepper (D-FL) told how George A. Smathers used speech in the effort to unseat him from the Senate seat that he then held. To stir the passions of uneducated people he used words they would not understand in a way that implied great evil.

Here's how Mr. Pepper paraphrased the victor's speech :

"Are you aware that Claude Pepper is known all over Washington as a shameless *introvert*? Not only that, but this man is reliably reported to practice *nepotism* with his sister-in-law and he has a sister who was once a *thespian* in wicked New York? Worst of all, it is an established fact that Mr. Pepper, before his marriage, habitually practiced *celibacy*."

Words can kill or heal.

The wise man wrote, "A word fitly spoken is like apples of gold in settings of silver" (Proverbs 25:11).

When Job had suffered great personal tragedy and grief his "friends" came to comfort him. However, their words were flaming barbs of accusation. So much so that he shouted, "How long will you...break me in pieces with words?" (Job 19:2)

We've all said things that we shouldn't have. I know that I have. Still, there are the pleasant memories; those times when I was able to provide a timely word, an encouragement, good advice, that helped someone on her way.

Lord, talk is cheap. I don't want to be blabbering when I should be listening. Nor do I want to keep quiet when it is time to take a stand. My problem is that I don't always know the difference. Bless me, Lord. I'm hanging in there. Amen

"Let the words of my mouth... be acceptable in Your sight...."

Psalms 19:14

March 22

How do you like being alone?

Jacques Cousteau and two friends were scuba diving deep in an underground lake. Mr. Cousteau's air connection was damaged somehow and he was unable to breathe through it. His two companions took turns sharing their oxygen tanks with him. Thus a tragedy was averted.

Later, when asked what he had learned from the experience, Mr. Cousteau answered that when you are all alone you are in bad company.

Aloneness affects different people differently. Some seem to enjoy it, even thrive on it. I hate it. I turn into a world class pumpkin when I am alone.

While Shirley was preparing to visit our daughter and grandson I went around mumbling about how empty the big old house would be. I even fibbed about how I sometimes wish we had a smaller place.

I suppose I was really trying to get her to stay home. What a wimp!

Being alone reminds me of the ultimate aloneness, dying. For even if the deathbed is surrounded by family no one can make that giant step with you. You step into eternity alone. Right?

WRONG! Here the Scriptures give us great news. And it is the Christian's glorious hope. Someone will be with us. Here's my hand, Lord.

Dear Lord, I don't like feeling alone. And I have felt that way even in crowds. Let me always know and remember that You are with me, in all of life's joys and sorrows. Amen

"You are near, O Lord."
Psalm 119:151

Amen!

March 23

Did you ever play hide and seek?

When I was a kid I enjoyed visiting my aunt who lived on a farm near Frostproof, Florida. It was a wonderful place for a kid. There were animals, freshly plowed acres, strawberries, and a host of exciting flora and fauna. It was also a great place to play hide and seek.

One day I thought of the perfect hiding place. Between barns and other farm buildings was a huge haystack. Two or three inches of hay covered the ground all around it. I lay down and covered myself with hay, smug in the conviction that my cousins would never find me.

A few minutes passed and I heard (felt) an animal walking toward me. I remembered that there had been a huge mare munching on the grass nearby. She almost stepped on me, missing my leg only by inches. I was terrified. If I jumped up she might kick out at me in fear and hurt me. But if I did nothing and she stepped on me I would be also be hurt. What to do? I did nothing., except hold my breath and hope that she would ease on by. She did.

So much for a perfect hiding place.

Are you playing hide and seek with God? He is always seeking. Are you hiding? Some try to hide in the darkness of evil behavior. But the darkness is light to God. Some try to hide in the glare of good works. Good works are good. But one is saved by grace, through faith in the Lord Jesus Christ. Not by good works.

You can't hide from God!

"If I say, 'surely the darkness shall fall on me,' even the night shall be light about me; indeed, the darkness shall not hide (me) from you."
Psalm 139:11,12

Lord, help me to be open with You, to not try to hide anything from You. It is futile anyway. Amen

March 24

Suneidesus. How about a fancy word to set you to thinking this morning: The word means *a knowing with*. It is the Greek word for conscience.

Do you remember when some cars and trucks were equipped with governors? Devices that made it impossible to exceed certain speeds? I have always thought of the conscience in that light, but I really don't know exactly what a conscience is.

While the Scriptures don't define conscience they do enumerate a variety of types: good (I Peter 3:21), pure (I Timothy 3:9), evil (Hebrews 10:22), weak (I Corinthians 8:7), and seared (I Timothy 4:2).

Our first president referred to the human conscience as "that little spark of celestial fire." Perhaps conscience is that spark of divinity in mankind that survived the fall.

The scary part is that the conscience is fragile. It can become calloused, polluted, "defiled" (Titus 1:15).

When I was first thinking about writing on conscience the news media were preoccupied with a jerk that killed seventeen people (and ate parts of them?) over several years. I wonder if he felt bad the first time, and if it became easier in subsequent killings?

Oh Lord, help me to keep a sensitive conscience; to nurture it, to instruct it in the Scriptures. Please don't let me ignore that inward faculty to know what is right and wrong. I'm serious, Lord. This is important business. Don't let me go on in behavior that will muffle the inner voice. Zap me if I need it. Amen.

"...I myself always strive to have a conscience without offense toward God and man."
Acts 24:16

How is your conscience? Are you doing anything to defile it? Is it clear? If not you have work to do. Me too.

March 25

When Charles II was crowned King of England he was stripped to his waist, then anointed on his head, chest, back, shoulders, and elbows.

Some people are weak in the knees. Some have a weak back. But weak in the *elbows*!

I really get steamed when some complainer says *"They* ought to start a youth group," or "They should clean the chapel," or "Why don't *they* do something about the neighborhood," or "It looks like *they* could do something about the homeless." *They.* Never *me* nor *I.*

To pay the bills at Bible School I always had at least two, sometimes three, jobs at a time. One of them was church janitor. One day, while sweeping the rooms of the Sunday School building, I came upon Mrs. (we called her *Mother*) Wooliver standing before a box of rags.

"Whatever are you doing, Mother Wooliver?"

"I am making bandages to send to missionaries in India to use in treating the lepers, Brother Hunt."

Her legs and ankles were swollen. She stopped often to massage her arms and hands. I am still inspired by her attitude of humble service. There were no photographers. No mention would be made of her efforts from the pulpit in next Sunday's services. She would never see the people that her work would bless. (But in heaven some of them might look her up and hug her neck.)

Lord, please anoint my elbows. And my hands. And feet. My mind and heart, too. And those of every reader of this devotion.. Grease us good, Lord, the whole bunch of us. Amen

"...Lord, not my feet only, but also my hands and my head."

John 13:9

What do you do when it's hard to believe?

A lady: "Chaplain I'm losing my cool, yelling at my family. I call on Jesus but it is like He is not there. I sometimes wonder what's the use trying to pray."

The Psalmist: "How long, O Lord? Will You forget me forever? How long will You hide Your face from me?" (Psalm 13:1)

Jesus: "My God, My God, why have You forsaken me?" (Mark 15:34)

Don't panic, you are in good company. Don't toss the baby out with the bath water. Just because you struggle with one point of doctrine doesn't mean that you must reject the whole package.

If you *consider the alternative* you may decide that believing is easier than not believing. Are you ready to accept that there is nothing beyond what we can see or feel?

Finally, don't forget to *leave a place for mystery*. God's ways are as different from ours as the heavens are different from the earth.

It may be that the reason some never seem to struggle with their faith is that it is so shallow, so peripheral to their life, that it doesn't really matter. A true faith is one that grapples with great issues, one that grows from struggle. So keep at it.

The best example to emulate is the man whose son was seriously ill and the deciples couldn't heal him.

The man, to Jesus: "...If You can do anything, have compassion on us and help us."

Jesus: "...If you can believe, all things are possible to him who believes."

The man, with tears, to Jesus:

"...Lord, I believe; help my unbelief."
Mark 9:22-24

What a great prayer. Don't you think that we should pray it more often?

March 27

I arrived in Vietnam with only a small suitcase of personal items. They promptly loaded me down with two duffel bags full of gear and uniforms, then sent me to live in the jungle.

The First Cavalry Division was *airmobile* in those days. That meant that we traveled only by helicopters, or on foot. I quickly realized that I had to lighten my load. Everything had to fit into, or on, my rucksack.

On my web gear I hung my sleeping equipment which was a rubber mattress that was rolled up in a poncho liner that was rolled up in a poncho. I also attached my protective (gas) mask, ammo pouch (for my New Testaments and crosses), and all of the water containers possible. In the rucksack I carried soap; razor, razor blades (foam shave was too heavy and bulky); toothbrush, toothpaste; selected C rations; and clean socks. (I gave up on underwear early. When you get rained on every day and have to go for days without a bath or change of clothes the less you wear the better.) The other things in my rucksack were my loose-leaf Bible that contained sermon notes for a year and the elements for Holy Communion.

What am I getting at? Excess baggage! No one could have *humped* the stuff they issued me. And you probably are overloaded too.

What excess baggage are you carrying? Spiritually? Old hurts and bad habits clutter your spirit and poison your relationships. Just as your home needs the occasional cleaning your soul needs to be refreshed and washed clean. Get rid of the junk. Make room for good stuff.

You can grow today by dropping just one thing that weighs you down and retards your spiritual progress. Lighten up.

"...I consider everything a loss compared to the surpassing greatness of knowing Christ Jesus my Lord...I consider them rubbish, that I may gain Christ."
Philippians 3:8 (NIV)

March 28

Cannibalism is one of human history's most severe taboos.

Critics accuse Christians of cannibalism. And the words of Jesus, taken literally, and not understood in the context of faith, give ammunition for their attacks.

The synoptic gospels--Matthew, Mark, and Luke--describe the institution of the Lord's Supper. The Gospel of John gives the sacrament's *meaning*. (There is no actual account of Jesus serving the bread and wine in the Gospel of John.)

The meaning is rich indeed: *Internalize*. In the temple system of animal sacrifices only token pieces were burned. Priests and worshippers feasted on the rest of the sacrifice. Since God was believed to be present in the meal they were feeding upon, taking into their bodies, the deity.

So, Jesus is saying that we must take him into the very core of our being. Not theoretically, not peripherally, not academically, and not just theologically. But *really*. The word is Lord. In the Communion, through faith, I feast with and on the sacrifice, my Lord Jesus Christ.

There is no room in the Christian religion for the mantle-piece God. The one that you take down on Sunday Morning and put back after Church. The one whose claims are not felt in your daily living. The true God of heaven and earth will not accept a once a week relationship.

I love Rudyard Kipling and still have the two volume set. I have taken the set with me in military moves around the world, planning to read them some day, slowly and deliciously. But as of yet I have only snacked on them occasionally. They are part of the *collection* of my life, but they are not yet at the *core* of it. Jesus will not be merely a part of your collection. He will only be Lord!

"He who eats my flesh and drinks my blood abides in Me, and I in him."

John 6:56

March 29

It is amazing how things change over time.

Shirley and I were with friends enjoying the view of San Antonio from the observation deck of the Tower of the Americas. The tower stretches skyward like an eloquent sentinel, and announces the city's beauty like a huge exclamation point. If you are there, facing westward at sunset, it can be a truly breathtaking experience.

I asked my friend to point out the Alamo, because nothing else so defines the city's history and character. To my surprise it was hardly visible from that height. It was almost hidden from view by larger, more modern, buildings.

What a mighty fortress the Alamo was in 1836. It dominated the skyline. It took 4,000 of Santa Anna's troops to capture it from 189 defenders. Now it is dwarfed by buildings of commerce and industry. The once mighty bastion is now a shrine.

Time rushes on.

Values shift.

Things that once mattered the most are now less significant. Once cherished goals were abandoned somewhere along the highway of life. People who were once forever friends are now just people we used to know. Old adversaries come to be viewed with benign fondness.

Where does it end?

Where it began! With God. Some things survive life's shiftings. Some things are permanent, eternal. Amen

"And now abide faith, hope, love, these three; and the greatest of these is love."
1 Corinthians 13:13

Lord, let me give prayerful attention to the things that abide. Amen

Friends were very protective of their hemophilic son, careful to keep him from the usual childhood cuts and scratches. Finally, at age 15, internal bleeding caused his death.

Gene was an Army Chaplain and a great preacher. Whenever I was on duty near him I always went to hear him preach. It was three weeks after his son's funeral. Gene's text was 1 Kings 17:7-16, the story of the widow of Zarepath. It was one of the most moving sermons I have ever heard. I wept as I listened.

The widow and her son were caught up in a severe famine and down to their last meal, literally. The prophet Elijah asked her to feed him first, but promised God's blessing, "The barrel of meal shall not waste, neither shall the cruse of oil fail, according to the word of the Lord...." (v.14 KJV)

The title of Gene's sermon was, *Dipping From the Bottom of the Barrel.* As he described the widow's testing it was evident to me that he was also speaking of himself and his wife, Grace, at their profound grief and sustaining faith through the loss of their son.

There is power at the bottom of the barrel!

It is God's power! It has to be, there is nothing else. It is power that derives from God's faithfulness, and flows through a stubborn and persistent faith. It is power to keep dipping until the rains come again, until the fields again flourish with grain, until the famine ends. Until the pain subsides.

Are you at the bottom of your barrel, too?

Do you feel spiritually impoverished, leached of will and resolve? Has doubt sapped your faith and dimmed your hope?

You can dip! From the bottom of the barrel! Because His grace and power are always in bountiful supply.

"I can do all things through Christ who strengthens me."

Philippians 4:13

March 31

Jesus asked a question that to the modern mind seems "dumb."

He asked a sick man if he wanted to be well. (Read about it in John 5.)

Next Jesus commanded an "impossible" thing. Jesus told a man lying lame, paralyzed, crippled for 38 years, to rise, take up his bed, and walk.

It was impossible to the crippled man, but it wasn't impossible with God. For when God commands an action he provides the capability. Take a look at the meaning of the command.

Rise! Lift yourself up. Use what energy you have. I am telling you that you can. Seize the moment. Up!

Take up your bed! Don't leave yourself a loophole. Don't expect a relapse. Clean up your area and don't count on needing it again.

Walk! Get going right now. Leave this depressing place. Get into a new area, new friends; change your lifestyle. Get out of here.

A family member quit smoking. He left a pack of cigarettes on the mantel to prove to himself and others that he could stick with it. But every time he passed the mantel he craved the nicotine. Finally he started smoking again, and continued until his death. His first cigarette came from the pack on the mantel.

Is the Holy Spirit talking to you today about your need to do something?

Have you cluttered up your soul with excuses for not being closer to God? More effective in your spiritual life? More powerful in your witness?

Then pull yourself up from lethargic sameness, pack up the excuse bed, and get going. Amen

"Rise, take up your bed, and walk."

John 5:8

Palm Sunday

Soon it will be Holy Week. It begins with Palm Sunday. You may know it as Passion Sunday.

The crowd that met Jesus at Bethany was seething in tumultuous excitement. The word that Lazarus had been raised from the dead had spread like wildfire. Now the man that raised Lazarus from the dead was coming into Bethany (a suburb of Jerusalem), riding on a donkey.

The Hebrew prophet, Zechariah, (9:9) had prophesied that the Messiah would come to Jerusalem riding on a donkey.

So the people were welcoming their king! Now they would be freed from Roman rule. No more taxes to Caesar. No more foreign laws that conflicted with their religious beliefs and practices.

They cast their garments before Him, and strewed palm branches in His path. They cried, "Hosanna," and shouted praise to God. Jesus said that if the crowd were forced to be quiet the rocks would cry out.

But it was too good to be true. Here is a chronology of what happened next, as remembered by the four gospel writers:

Luke said that Jesus wept over the city.

Mark wrote that He denounced their barrenness.

Matthew recalled that He cleansed their temple.

John remembered that He received inquiring Gentiles.

By Thursday the crowd had forsaken Jesus. People that had shouted "Hosanna" were crying for His crucifixion.

But let's not get into that yet. There will be time enough to weep. Today, let us simply join in the Hosannas and lift up our voices in praise to Jesus Christ, the Son of God, the Savior.

The King is coming! Amen

"...Blessed is the king that comes in the name of the Lord."

Luke 19:38

Holy Thursday

Holy Thursday was a busy day for our Lord. Many of the Palm Sunday crowd had fallen back, frightened by rumors that the authorities were seeking to capture and kill Jesus.

The joy of that Passover meal with His disciples was tempered by the presence of a traitor at the table. He served everyone, even Judas.

Take this bread. It is my body, broken for you. And this wine. It is the New Testament in my blood. It will be a while before I eat and drink this meal with you again, but we will eat and drink together again, in the Kingdom.

In the Garden of Gethsemane He prayed until His sweat was as drops of blood. *Is there another way, Father? Can I avoid this cup of suffering? Your will be done.*

Then He was taken to a kangaroo court where He was beaten with a Cat of Nine Tails (a rawhide whip with glass and bone embedded in its strands). There He was mocked, scorned, and spat upon. A crown of thorns was crushed onto His head.

How did He spend the rest of the night? The record doesn't tell us. The Son of Man "had no place to lay His head." What were His thoughts? Was the sense of abandonment by the Father already creeping into His spirit? Did He get any sleep at all? Are you kidding? Really!

Holy Thursday is rich in symbol and substance for Christians. But it also brought a warning. One of His closest disciples, Peter, denied Him. One betrayed Him.

"...We esteemed Him stricken, smitten by God, and afflicted."

Isaiah 53:4

Hello God?

Look at this bruised and bleeding man. Can anyone doubt that He was truly human? A real person? Yet He was God incarnate. The creeds affirm that the living Jesus was truly God and truly man. I believe them. I rejoice.

Hallelujah!

Good Friday

What's good about Good Friday?

Is it good like the cool June day in 1215 AD, when King John signed the Magna Carta? Or September 22, 1862, when President Lincoln signed the Emancipation Proclamation? Or June 6, 1944, when the Allies went ashore at Normandy? Or May 17, 1954, when the Supreme Court gave its historic ruling on segregation?

What's good about Good Friday?

Not the nails in His hands and feet. Not the thorned crown piercing his head. Nor the festering stripes, the stinking spit, or the sagging weight of viscera that shut off His breathing. Neither the open wound in His side. Never the shame of His nakedness before friends and family. Mother!

As Churchill said after Rommell was routed in North Africa, it was "Not the beginning of the end, but the end of the beginning."

Good Friday made Easter *possible*, for "Without shedding of blood there is no remission" of sin (Hebrews 9:22). On the cross Jesus took upon Himself the sins of the world, yours, and mine and became our substitute.

Good Friday made Easter *inevitable*! Good Friday is not good because of what happened to Jesus, at least not in human terms, but because of what happened to us.

On Good Friday Jesus paid a price for us that we would never have been able to pay for ourselves. To risk a trite phrase, He was *there* for us.

Hello God!

Let this Good Friday be good for you. Reflect soberly on God's awesome gift, and Christ's great love for you, and recommit your life and service to Him.

"...He was wounded for our transgressions, He was bruised for our iniquities...."

Isaiah 53:5

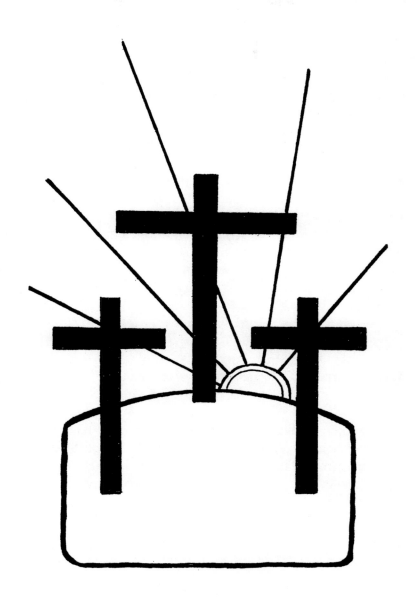

Holy Saturday

We followed Jesus through Holy Thursday.

We were shocked when His disciples abandoned Him. We flinched with each of the thirty-nine stripes beaten into His back with a cat of nine tails. We couldn't believe our ears when we heard Peter deny that he knew the Lord. It was a dark night.

Then we observed Him on Good Friday.

We saw nothing good about it. He looked so pitiful with His face and shoulders caked with blood from the crown of thorns. They must have pounded the thorns into His head with a stick. We gasped when He stumbled under the load of the cross. We shuddered with each clank of the hammer driving the nails through His hands and feet.

We wept with Mary. How much can a mother bear? That was her baby hanging there.

We saw the soldiers take Him down from the cross. We followed at a distance as they took him to Joseph's tomb.

Our hearts are broken.

And now it is Saturday. What does tomorrow hold?

"...He was cut off from the land of the living; for the transgressions of My people He was stricken."
Isaiah 53:8

Father, my heart breaks at the suffering of the Savior. Tears wash my face. I am choked from speaking. Sadness grips my spirit. They killed Jesus, my Lord. They buried Him. What's next, dear Father? I await the dawn. Amen

Easter Sunday

Happy Easter! Christ is risen! The Lord is risen indeed. Easter is a great victory.

First, it is a victory over *doubt*.

Thomas was not present at the disciples' gathering on Easter night and missed the appearance of Jesus. He was present a week later. It was Thomas, too honest to participate in a fraud, and too let down to believe another wild rumor, who said, "unless I...can place my finger in the mark of the nails...and in His side I will not believe" (John 20:25). Jesus dealt with Thomas, not treating him as a smarty, but gently, helping him to believe, to gain victory over his doubt.

The resurrection was also a victory over *defeat*.

At the successful landing of the Allies at Normandy the end of World War II was determined. Unfortunately, fighting would continue and many thousands more would die, but the end had become inevitable. So it was with the resurrection. The struggle between good and evil, Christ and Satan, would continue. But the result had been made certain. Victory. Victory for Jesus Christ, and us.

Finally, and most wonderfully, the resurrection was a victory over *death*.

It is a victory because we, too, will be raised from the dead. It is a victory because the mystery has been removed. Death is no longer a deep, dark, forbidding, mystery. Jesus kicked open the door of death and let the light in. Not only Jesus was raised on that first Easter. We, too, have been raised to spiritual life. The resurrection declares for the believer that the future has already begun. Celebrate your victory today.

More will come on Easter in the days ahead. The resurrection is too much for one devotion.

"God hath both raised up the Lord, and will also raise up us by His own power."
1 Corinthians 6:14

April 1

Happy April Fools Day. I want to tell you about one of the great fools in the Bible.

He had been a renowned warrior, the commander in chief of King Saul's army. Even David, the people's favorite to succeed Saul, had held him in high esteem. Then the lure of power enticed Abner to get involved with palace intrigue. (You can read all about it in 2 Samuel 3.)

Instead of welcoming and supporting David, the one anointed king by the prophet Samuel, Abner proclaimed a surviving son of Saul to be king. Civil war broke out between the two factions. In one battle Abner killed the brother of Joab, David's main general.

Abner fled to Hebron, one of the ancient Cities of Refuge.

Any person who had killed another could take refuge in Hebron, and be safe as long as he stayed inside the city. Abner seemed incapable of understanding the seriousness of his situation. Adding insult to injury, Abner further infuriated David's followers by taking one of Saul's concubines to himself. By that day's custom the concubines of a dead king became the property of the new king.

Abner could not abide living a cloistered life. Hebron was small and cramped his style.

So Abner left Hebron and plunged back into the political scene. He was soon enticed into a meeting with Joab who killed him to avenge his brother's death. David disclaimed responsibility for Abner's death and sang a lament over him.

"Should Abner die as a fool dies? Your hands were not bound, nor your feet put into fetters; As a man falls before wicked men, so you fell."
2 Samuel 3:33,34

He is a fool who abandons what is safe and sure to seek power and pleasure. As a believer you are safe in Jesus. Relax. Take it easy. You are blessed. Don't be a fool on April Fools Day. Amen

April 2

This is a strange story, but it is true.

I was chugging along in my 1947 Nash, in a driving rainstorm, on the way to the Bible College where I was a student. The windshield wiper was broken. Hadn't worked in months. I was in low spirits. At that time I was working three jobs: part-time shoe salesman, weekend night watchman, and church janitor. I was feeling sorry for myself big time!

"Lord, You could make it easier for me if You would," I whined. "You send other students large checks in the mail. I know because they get up and testify about it in chapel. Sometimes they sound more like bragging to me. When I pray for financial help I just get another job. It just isn't fair. Some of them aren't even studying for the ministry like I am. I must not have as much faith as they have."

"I am going to test it. I am going to pray that this windshield wiper works. Then I am going to turn it on. Then I will know if I have any faith."

Well, I prayed for God to make the wiper work. Then I flipped the switch. The wiper moved, an *inch*. It hadn't moved at all in several months of my driving the car and flipping the switch.

I was thrilled! My prayer had moved the wiper. Then I was humbled. I only had enough faith to move a wiper an inch. Forget moving mountains.

God must have chuckled at my youthful impertinence. That *little* faith brought me through 12 years of civilian ministry and 30 years of active duty in the Army. It has sustained me until this writing.

Thank you Lord, for giving me the measure of faith. Thank you for being with me all of these years. I look forward to continuing the journey of faith. Bless my readers as you bless me. Amen

"...If you have faith as a mustard seed, you will say to this mountain, 'move from here to there,' and it will move...."
Matthew 17:20

April 3

Occasionally I run across cute things that children pray. Here are a few examples:

"Dear God, did You mean for the giraffe to look like that or was it an accident?"

"Dear God, if You watch me in church Sunday I'll show You my new shoes."

"Dear God, thank You for the baby brother, but what I prayed for was a puppy."

Jesus' most profound statement about what He expects from us is stated in the simplest terms. He said that we are to be like children.

Children are trusting.

Children are forgiving.

Children are easily moved to tears or laughter.

Children are believing.

Children are innocent.

Children have empathy.

Children are imaginative.

Children are obedient (at least until they become spoiled rotten).

Children know how to receive and give love, purely, completely, without conditions.

Children have the capacity to grow. That is what childlike means to me. Did you grow today? Yesterday?

Dear Lord, I have become so set in my ways. I am not as trusting, forgiving, and believing as I used to be. Too often I have not been obedient to Your word and will. I am spoiled. Instead of eagerly serving others I often sit back and am offended because they don't put my interests first. Help me to love, purely, and completely, without conditions. Amen.

"...Whoever humbles himself as this little child is the greatest in the kingdom of heaven."
Matthew 18:4

April 4

The worst class I ever sat through was an English composition class at the college where I received my undergraduate degree. And it was a church related school, too. Even worse, I had to pay for the class.

The professor was angry at the so-called puritanical influences on societal norms and mores. He seemed to hate the church and all that it stood for.

His teaching style was to refer to current media articles and discuss them in class. He ridiculed the ones that reflected moral values and behavior and championed those that were risqué, even pornographic. I can still hear his caustic pronunciation of the word puritanical.

His pet theory was that God was away, out there somewhere, and therefore not personal. So anyone that claimed a personal relation with Christ was a deluded puritanical.

According to him, when God created the world and universe He set the system up with such precision that He didn't have to run it. Didn't the reliability of the tides and the rotation of celestial bodies prove his point? He would go on ad infinitum with examples of nature's predictability, and how it proved his point. He seemed to need for God to be *out there*.

Here's what got me the low grade. "Professor, your arguments don't necessarily prove your hypothesis. Granted that God set things up to run well, but not so that He could go away. Maybe He did it so that He could move in close to His children, and be among them. At least, that is my faith."

He stuttered and became red in the face. In his mind I had disrupted the class and ruined his day. And he got even. He graded my exam. But he was wrong. Not just in his philosophical views of God. He was wrong to try to impose those ideas on his students in an English composition class.

"...The Kingdom of God is in the midst of you."
Luke 17:21 (RSV)

April 5

While sitting in the backyard swing I noticed a caterpillar on a limb near me.

I began the conversation.

"You are an odd looking thing. Your legs are small, and funny. And you have so many."

"It's a rough life," the caterpillar responded.

I wanted to ask him about distance and space, and his perceptions, but thought that such concepts might be beyond his intellectual capacity.

So I asked him how he got around.

"With great difficulty," he said. "It takes me forty forevers to travel the length of this limb."

The next afternoon I was back in the swing when a beautiful butterfly lit on the same limb.

He began the exchange.

"Good to see you again."

"Again," I exclaimed. "Have we talked before?"

"Sure, yesterday. I was a caterpillar then."

"Well, mercy," I said. "How are things different now?"

"As different as night and day," the caterpillar, oops the butterfly, responded. "Yesterday I had to strain and stretch to move an inch. Today I can fly with the greatest of ease."

Hello God!

At that point I ceased talking to myself.

"That's it, isn't it Lord? Today I am earthbound, with a corruptible body. But tomorrow, in the resurrection, I will be changed, made completely different, like You. But it will still be me, without the physical limitations I now have."

From somewhere out there, or was it in there, I heard a quiet *Amen.*

"...Certainly we...shall be in the likeness of His resurrection."
Romans 6:5

April 6

"Don't let the world around you squeeze you into its own mold." Romans 12:2 (Philip's Paraphrase)

Isn't it amazing how quickly things change. Words take on new meaning. Values shift. Structures of social behavior crumble.

I grew up knowing that bad is bad. But it isn't necessarily so now.

"Isn't that a *good* rock group?"

"Yeah, man, they are really *bad*."

A man fell among thieves who beat and robbed him, leaving him bleeding, and unconscious, lying in the gutter. Along came two sociologists (I have a master's degree in the field) who looked upon him lying there.

One of the sociologists said to the other one, "Isn't that sad. The man who did that needs our help."

The perpetrator is too often viewed as the victim while the victim is often blamed. It is truly confusing.

Are you being squeezed into the world's mold?

Has the drumbeat of deviance caused you to question your values about sex? Are political arguments causing you to question your convictions about the unborn? Are you reaching a point where nothing seems to be certain?

Is there an anchor to which you can cling while the winds and tides of life are buffeting? Can you keep your head while all around are losing theirs? Is there any thing at all that is sure? Certain? And unchanging?

I am glad that you asked.

"...I am the Lord, I do not change...."
Malachi 3:6

Lord, You know me. I prefer to go along to get along. It is easier that way. Less hassle. And I like to be popular. You know, don't rock the boat, don't call attention to myself. I know that's cowardly, Lord. And I am going to work on it. Help me to live my life honestly, courageously, and true to Your word and will. Amen

April 7

I was channel surfing late one night, trying to stay awake when I decided to check out the Christian Broadcasting Network.

There I saw a chubby lad with a cherubic face, all dressed up for the interview with sweater, tie, and hat. He was upbeat and articulate, and very happy to talk about the Christian work in which he was engaged.

It took me a few minutes to discover that he was blind, and longer still to understand that he had other, severe, health problems.

Question from the talk show host,

"How do you manage to keep such a positive attitude with all of your problems?"

Answer, "I can find *two things wonderful* for every problem I've got."

More, "There's always a good side if you'll let yourself see it."

Still more, "Why would you need God if you were up all of the time?"

Tears clouded my eyes and a choke squeezed my throat. I tried to remember all the things I had complained about that day. That led me to remembering all of the things I had to be thankful about.

Oh Lord, help me to keep a positive attitude, and be sincerely thankful for Your many wonderful blessings. Let me always express that gratitude in true devotion to You, and in humble service to others. Amen.

"Not that I have already attained, or am already perfected; but *I press on*, that I may lay hold of that for which Christ Jesus has also laid hold of me."

Philippians 3:12

April 8

I sat and watched a great American retire from Active Duty. He is one of the very best Army Chaplains that I have ever known.

He was a star lineman for his university's football team. He won championships as a boxer in the heavy weight division. However, physical prowess is not what marked him to his friends. His infectious smile coupled with an uproarious laughter and keen spiritual sensitivities are his trademarks.

His military ribbons go off the back of his left shoulder and other medals cover his blouse. Someone read a portion from the narrative of his Silver Star Award. The writer of the narrative wears the Congressional Medal of Honor. My friend's great courage is a matter of record.

This big, strong, hero is the most caring chaplain I ever met. His ecumenical spirit and pastoral skills are legendary. I met him early in my career, and selected him as a mentor and friend, although he is not much older than I.

He is a spiritual giant. More than anything else he is true to his faith, never missing a chance to witness for his Lord. A senior Army officer once told me that my friend led him to Christ while they were jogging.

I hope that Connie Walker is not embarrassed by these remarks. His retirement was the chaplaincy's loss, but the lucky civilians who will share his ministry will be blessed.

What is your relationship with your pastor? Do you support him or her, in prayer? Financially? A good pastor is a blessing from God.

"He, Himself, gave some to be apostles, some prophets, some evangelists, and *some pastors....* "
Ephesians 4:11

Dear Lord, I acknowledge the great contribution that pastors have made in my life: Albert Rowan, J. Foy Johnson, E. T. Corbin, and others. Thank you for them, Lord, and bless all pastors and their families. Amen

April 9

Isn't it wonderful when you receive a *grace,* an unexpected and timely encouragement? Something that stands up directly in front of you and gets your attention.

One morning I was waiting for the doctor, dreading what he was about to do to me (run a camera down my throat and into my stomach). The fasting had heightened my anxiety. Also, I have a very healthy gag reflex.

I was annoyed by the show on the waiting room television. The speaker was oohing and aahing about the scenes of snow on Mt. Diablo. I wondered how he would sound with a hose down his throat. How could they put such drivel on television. Didn't they know that people had some sense? Wasn't it bad enough to be facing a scary procedure without also having to suffer banal gibberish?

There was an old devotional magazine on the table. I can't remember its name, but I do remember that I began to read it.

There was a brief article about a potential family disaster that turned out all right. The words did have a soothing effect on my troubled mind and did help me to regain a better perspective. I can't remember the name of the article, nor the name of its author, but I can remember the article's basic message. I will state it for you to the best of my memory.

There are two rules for dealing with stress:
> 1. Don't sweat the small stuff;
> 2. Remember, it's all small stuff.

Don't let the little things overwhelm you. Learn how to fluff them off. There are enough big things anyway. And God is with you in both the little and large experiences of life.

"Who is the man that serves the Lord...he himself shall dwell in prosperity."
Psalms 25:12,13

Dear Lord, I pray for my readers, especially those who will be in stressful situations today. Help them to count their blessings instead of their hassles. Amen

April 10

Who is in your corner?

Marvis Frazier, the son of Smoking Joe Frazier, was fighting a tall, rangy boxer. Like his Dad, Marvis is short and stocky. And like his Dad, he had to get inside in order to have a chance against a taller opponent.

Smoking Joe was in his son's corner. Marvis didn't do well in the first round. Back in his corner he asked his Dad how he was doing. Smoking Joe told him he was doing just fine, then gave him some pointers to improve his performance.

That scene was repeated round after round. "How am I doing, Dad?" "You are doing okay, Son, but you need to work on...."

At the end of a very rough fight Marvis was declared the winner.

Many believed that his win was in large part because of who was in his corner. Marvis' opponent was really fighting two Fraziers.

You will find yourself in the *ring* today. Your adversary may be trying to destroy your marriage, get your kids strung out on drugs, cost you your job, or a dozen other tricks. It is important that you know who you have backing you.

Jesus is in your corner.

Are you aware of just how blessed you are as a Christian? God is on your side because you have chosen Jesus to be your Lord and Savior. You and Jesus are a majority. The Christian is never outnumbered.

Hello God!

"...If God is for us, who can be against us?"
Romans 8:31

Lord, if You are in my corner I can't lose. Thank You. Amen

(The story about Marvis Frazier was told to me by Bernie Windmiller, a great American, soldier, and Army Chaplain.)

April 11

You met my buddy Dan in an earlier devotion.

Dan is retired Army like me. He earns extra money by etching information on headstones in cemeteries. He has all the equipment: a sandblaster, grind stone, small jackhammer, and much more. On this particular occasion I was along as his "gofer."

We were working on the headstone of a man but noticed that there was a stone with the same last name beside it. It didn't take much to figure out that they were father and son. The son was about twenty-five years of age and the father was about forty-five.

A strikingly beautiful young woman drove up to where we were working and placed a single red rose in the vase at the young man's headstone. She lingered a while, appearing to be ill at ease, then finally drove away. However she came back shortly and placed a sixteen-ounce can of Lone Star beer at the headstone, then left.

Upon a closer look, Dan and I noticed that in front of the young man's headstone was a marker of poured concrete in the shape of the state of Texas. Three items: a symbol of Texas, a red rose, and a large can of beer. Were those the things he valued most? And what about her? Or did those symbols simply bring to her mind cherished memories?

What about you? What do you value? And how do you mark or manifest your values?

Someone once asked, "If you were accused of being a Christian would there be enough evidence to convict you."

Jesus spoke often and powerfully about how we value things. He gave little value to the outward expression of piety so evident in His time but taught us to value heavenly things.

"Do not lay up for yourselves treasures on earth, where moth and rust destroy...but lay up for yourselves treasures in heaven...." Matthew 6:19,20

Dear Lord, don't let me major in minor things. Amen

April 12

Eighty five thousand people! And it wasn't even a homecoming game.

I was in the stands in the "Swamp" the Saturday that the University of Florida played Arkansas. Alligators versus Razorbacks. Gators versus Hogs. The Gators won 59-7.

Alumni and their families filled the stands. And what fans they are. If Texas A & M's fans are the "Twelfth Man" then Florida's fans must equate to at least the "Thirteenth Man."

When the visiting team had the ball the marquees flashed, "Noise," then, "Loud," then "Get wild," and similar encouragements to the fans. They responded by making so much noise that Arkansas had difficulty calling plays.

At signals from the Florida band the fans shouted, "Go Gators," and did the alligator chomp (waving their arms in a scissors-like action).

I let my imagination play.

What if this game were an acting out of a grander scenario? Symbolic of something played on earth but watched in Heaven? What if we Christians are on the playing field now as we live out our faith. Who is our competition? What are the rules of the game?

And who are in the stands? Abraham? Peter? Mary? Martha? St. Francis? Billy Sunday? Pastor Rowan? Mom and Dad? Jesus? The list must include the millions of Christians who have already crossed over.

Oh Lord, if I am on the playing field you must be my coach. Call the right plays for me. Help me to concentrate on each play and execute it faithfully.

I can hear the encouragement from the stands. I am on the right team. I am going to score. I know it, Lord. Thank You. Amen.

"...Since we are surrounded by so great a cloud of witnesses...let us run with endurance the race that is set before us...." Hebrews 12:1

April 13

A sacrament in a gasthaus?

There were four of us chaplains having dinner in Frankfurt, Germany. We were Episcopalian, Assemblies of God, Baptist, and Methodist. Jim, the Episcopalian, took the brotchen, broke it, passed pieces to each of us, and said, "Our Lord said, 'this is my body which is broken for you.' " We ate the bread.

He repeated the words of institution with the wine. There followed a quietness, a sense of the presence of Jesus at our table.

Hello God!

The Gospels of Matthew, Mark, and Luke record the actual meal that we know as the Lord's Supper. John doesn't. He records the Passover Meal (chapter 13) at which Jesus instituted the sacrament. I believe that it is in chapter 6 where John gives its meaning.

John's treatment of the sacrament followed the feeding of the 5,000.

So we learn of the *sacramental potential of every meal.* John elevated the sacrament, and deepened its meaning. It isn't just supposed to be an occasional thing, done with appropriate ceremony in a group worship experience, but an ongoing experience. A daily communing with Jesus.

I can't remember the entire message on the plaque that my mother had hanging on the wall when I was a kid. But one line said that Christ is "The unseen guest at every meal."

So the Christian never dines alone. When Jesus is invited to any meal in prayer, He comes to the table.

It is Jesus who speaks to us: *As the Bread of Life that graces every meal, I am present to make every meal a sacrament.*

So always pray before each meal. And expect a special guest. Amen

"This is the bread which came down from heaven...."
John 6:58

April 14

Our Lord apparently loved birds. I wonder if He didn't sometimes sit and observe them. We know that He talked about them.

There is a clear outline of a dove on the glass. The feathers of both wings are spread out as though the bird saw its mistake at the last second and tried to pull up. The wings were spread wide. It is so real that an artist could have painted it.

The big picture window in our game room faces west. Almost regularly doves fly in, over the pool, and try to fly through the (glass) opening in the wall. We see them dead on the roof when we look out of our bedroom window. Occasionally we actually hear the collision.

Have you ever been absolutely sure that the path you had chosen was right, only to have it end in disaster for you?

Abraham's nephew, Lot, was given the choice. (Read about it in Genesis 13.) Their two camps had grown too big. From a high vantage point Lot surveyed the rugged hill country and then the fertile Jordan valley. He chose the valley, and "Pitched his tent even as far as Sodom." It was a choice that ended in disaster. He lost his wife and home, and suffered disgrace in a shameful orgy with his two daughters in a cave.

A young girl goes off to the big city. Times get hard and she reasons that she can go beyond the bounds of decent and legal behavior for just a little while. Just long enough to get on her feet. She never planned to end up on the street, but there she is.

A young man was convinced that the drug made him more alert by sharpening his senses. He knew that he could stop anytime he chose. What he didn't understand was that the drug diminished his ability to make sensible choices. The drugs seemed to open a way, but like the dove, he crashed.

"There is a way that seems right to a man, but its end is the way of death."

Proverbs 16:25

April 15

Happy income tax day. If possible!

There is not a great deal about taxes in the Bible. However, the Biblical writers don't avoid the subject. Read about a real brouhaha in Israel's history in 1 Kings 12.

When the people petitioned the king to ease their tax burden, King Rehoboam told the people: "My father made your yoke heavy, but I will add to your yoke; my father chastised you with whips, but I will chastise you with scorpions."

As a result of his intransigence there was great strife among the people. Finally, an invading king from Egypt ended his reign.

We can even be thankful for one taxation. Through Caesar's gathering of the people of the realm we know of the visit by Joseph and Mary to Bethlehem where Mary had her baby and named Him Jesus. (Luke 2)

On taxation Jesus displayed a sense of humor.

When His disciples complained that the tax collectors were after them and they had no money Jesus sent them to catch a fish and find a coin in its mouth to pay the tax. (Matthew 17:24-27)   Strange stuff. Tax collectors were held in lowest regard in the New Testament. (Matthew 18:17)

So, do you feel like you have been chastised with scorpions? Do you view taxation and government in general as an intrusion? If so, what does Scripture require of you? It requires you to be a good citizen.

The power to vote is the power to participate in government. We must be good stewards of that privilege. We don't have to like taxes but we do have to practice good citizenship.

"Render to Caesar the things that are Caesar's and to God the things that are God's"
Mark 12:17

Lord, I thank You for the good things that government has done to make our society better. Amen

April 16

The winter of 1777-1778 was a time of severe testing for George Washington's rag tag army of 11,000 men.

While the British sat out the winter in the comfort of Philadelphia, Washington's troops were camped at Valley Forge. The bitter cold killed 3,000 of them. Most of the others were sick with various diseases.

If anyone ever had a reason to despair, Washington and his citizen soldiers did. But they didn't give up. By spring they were sufficiently disciplined to rout the British in June.

When God allows you to be tested, it is not to see how much you can bear. It is not to fit you into a *strength* category. Rather, testing is to insure that you are strong enough to face the blows that come into everyone's life.

This truth is born out in a verse from the Old Testament. "Behold I have refined thee, but not with silver: I have chosen thee in the furnace of affliction." (Isaiah 48:10 KJV)

We aren't made stronger from our successes, from the glittering silver experiences. In fact, success can blind our eyes to needed improvement.

It is in the furnace of affliction that we get a spiritual reality check. We are chosen by how we react in the furnace. Not by how we handle good times.

Dear Lord, I know that I will be tested. Help me to learn from the testing what I need to know and do to serve You better. And give me the strength and determination to do it. Amen

"Prove me, O Lord, and try me; test my heart and my mind."
Psalms 26:2 (RSV)

Don't despair friend, if you feel that God is testing you. Maybe it's like school: you have to pass the exams before you can be promoted.
Don't drop out of school.

April 17

By now you have surely figured out that I like birds.

I am a "watcher" in the sense that I observe and learn from them. And I do believe that there have been times that I have heard the voice of God through birds. However, I am not a member of any organized bird watching.

Shirley and I got to noticing the mocking bird caring for her two chicks. She was a hard working mother, solicitous of their well being.

Then one day there was only one baby bird left. (There were several cats on the street where we were living.) While the mother bird had been industrious before, she now became doting, hovering, over the lone offspring.

Once we watched her trying to nudge the baby out of the middle of the alley behind our house. Later, I saw her flying to the top of a large pecan tree with food in her beak. The little rascal was a high flyer but mother was still feeding him.

Did you ever notice how much we see God in nature? If the Scriptures are the written word of God, and I firmly believe that they are, then nature is the illustrated word of God.

Nature demonstrates the mighty power of God in its winds, fires, earthquakes, and storms. It also shows His capacity to create, to grow, to produce. Nature shows another side of God's nature: His caring, protecting, and nurturing attributes.

I hope that you can be especially mindful today of God's great love for you. He knows you by name.

Lord, I like having You take care of me. I am as spoiled as that little bird was. But I know that I am now an adult. I want to please you. Help me to be the caregiver. Many have never heard your Gospel. I want to do all that I can to get the message of Your love and salvation out to all of the world. Amen.

"As an eagle stirs up its nest, hovers over its young... so the Lord alone led him...."
Deuteronomy 32:11,12

April 18

A porter, walking through the train, noticed a suitcase sitting in the aisle beside a passenger. He asked the man to move it.

When the porter came through again the suitcase was still there. Again he asked the man to move the suitcase. On his next walk through the suitcase was still there.

"Look, Mister. If that suitcase is still there the next time I come through I am going to throw it out the window," the porter growled. When he came back it was still there. He threw it out the window.

"I told you I would throw it out!" The porter shouted.

"Taint mine," the rider responded.

Ownership!

There was a great song a few years back whose theme was this land belongs to you and me.

Change the words to church, community, country, or street. The question is, "Whose is it?" Is it theirs? Yours? Ours? The great cop-out is to assume that somebody else will do it.

Jesus calls on each of us to take ownership.

It is your church in which to work. Your pastor to support. Your community to lead to Christ the Savior. Your world to care for.

Oh Lord, don't let me slip into the convenient attitude of dodging responsibility. And not just for my personal behavior. I know that I can make a difference in how others conduct themselves if I try. Don't let me cop out. Amen.

"Each one has received a gift, minister it to one another, as good stewards of the manifold grace of God."
1 Peter 4:10

April 19

Wrecks don't happen in slow motion.

In the movies a fast moving scene will shift into slow motion for emphasis; for dramatic effect, I suppose, or so that you can see every detail. Life doesn't slow to a drag when you are being attacked by a hoodlum, when your child is wandering into the street, or when you are racing to the hospital with an injured spouse.

In real life the action flashes at high speed.

I was stopped, the second vehicle back, waiting for the traffic light to change. In about one second I saw (and/or sensed) the following: the car was about ten feet behind me; it was going to hit me (at 35-40 miles per hour according to the policeman); something was wrong with the driver. I learned later that she had been driving erratically, and was probably unconscious when she hit me, due to a diabetic condition.

The accident reminded me that bad things can happen in a split second. Of course, good things can happen suddenly too.

What about you and your faith? Are you in a right relationship with Christ? Are you ready? If He called for you today would you need a few minutes to prepare yourself?

When they wrote about the end time events, the writers of Holy Scripture used fast action images to urge the readers to maintain a state of constant readiness.

It is smart to keep your faith current? As my wonderful old pastor preached, are you paid up? Prayed up? And ready to go up?

"...The Son of Man in His day will be *like the lightning*, which flashes and lights up the sky from one end to the other."
Luke 17:24 NIV

Heavenly Father, thank You for keeping me alive and well. Bless me, and all of the readers, with Your bountiful grace and protection. Amen

April 20

DNA: *A polymeric chromosomal constituent of living cell nuclei, having two long chains of alternating phosphate and dexyribose units twisted into a double helix,* etc., etc. Did you get that?

Scientists say that there are thousands of *markers* in each cell of the genetic makeup of every human. Your DNA is unique from all other persons. DNA testing is now accepted by the courts as the absolutely reliable way to prove a person's identity.

The sweet singer of Israel asked, "What is man that You are mindful of him." (Psalms 8:4) Well, King David, it is like this. See, there is this stuff called DNA. And a person's body is made up of chemicals and minerals, and, well, it is too complicated to explain.

And if we could explain it we would still be missing the mark. The answer to David's question is in the heart of God. For reasons known to Him God loves every human being.

Although a single cell in your body is more complex than the most advanced computer, that isn't the reason God loves you. You are more than chemicals. The breath of God is in you. You are a living soul, created in the image of God.

If scientists can count the thousands of identifiers in each person's cell, why should anyone have difficulty accepting that God numbers the hairs on his or her head? And that He loves each and every human being?

What creatures we are! A complex mix of elements, but more importantly, we are made in the image of God. Living souls!

Now I know, dear Lord, that I am indeed special to You. Thank You. Amen

"I will praise You, for I am fearfully and wonderfully made...."
Psalm 139:14

April 21

Do you have any *holy habits*?

There are lots of addictions. Some are enslaved by alcohol. Others spend all that they can earn or steal on drugs. Millions must have a tobacco fix. I believe that caffeine is addictive because a family member gets a headache if she misses her morning coffee. I had a deputy that began each day with a Coca Cola for breakfast.

Habits aren't necessarily destructive.

I always begin shaving on the right side of my face. My morning routine is put the coffee on, get the newspaper, and then read it while watching the morning news on television. Later, my wife and I do our morning walk, always the same route.

The late Bishop Cushman compared holy habits to the *spasm* variety. He said that one layman with the former was worth more than a hundred with the latter. A spasm layman makes promises, even begins a good program or project, then fails to follow through.

So, what are your holy habits?

Do you read your Bible regularly? Do you have a devotional time each day? Are you regular in church attendance? Is your financial giving comprehensive and systematic? If you aren't employed are you a regular volunteer at some good charitable program?

Dear Lord, I have responded too often to Your word and will in spasms. I am always starting good things that I don't finish. I want to be reliable and trustworthy. Help me to *habitually* do what you expect of me. Make me a person of holy habits. Amen

"So He came to Nazareth, where He had been brought up. And *as His custom was*, He went into the synagogue on the Sabbath day, and stood up to read."
Luke 4:16

Did Jesus go to Hell? I am not being flippant.

At the end of a Worship Service one of the parishioners grabbed my arm. It was obvious that he was upset. We had recited the Apostles Creed in the service. He was offended by the statement, *He descended into Hell*.

"I believe the Bible, Chaplain," he exclaimed. "I don't like the Apostles Creed. I know my Bible. The bible doesn't say that."

He agreed to wait until the worshippers left and meet me in my office. I handed him a New Testament and asked him to turn to 1 Peter 3.

In his recounting of Jesus' passion Peter makes a strange statement. After recounting that Christ died for the sins of all, he went on to say "...Being put to death in the flesh but made alive by the Spirit...He went and preached to the spirits in prison." (1 Peter 3: 18,19)

Here I must pause to tell you that what I am about to say is conjecture on my part. You can be on firm Biblical grounds and disagree.

I believe that rather than lying in a suspended state of some kind, while His body was in the tomb, Jesus was at work:

Listen up everybody!
I have finished your redemption, to which the old sacrifices pointed!
Your waiting is over!
Your salvation is complete!
Gather around me!
We are leaving this place!
It will soon be sunrise!

"He shall see the travail of His soul and be satisfied...."
Isaiah 53:11

What is true, and wonderfully true, is that God loved you through Jesus. And that Jesus died for your salvation. That, dear readers is Biblical fact. Amen

April 23

The very same sycamore tree! We were in the ancient city of Jericho.

The guide pointed to the tree and claimed that it was the one that Zacchaeus had climbed to see Jesus pass by. Yeah. Right. And ocean front property in Arizona. And a bridge for sale between Manhattan and Brooklyn. I knew something about how long sycamore trees live.

But the Garden of Gethsemane was different. Olive trees do live hundreds of years. It is believable that some of the trees in Gethsemane are over 2,000 years old. And when I noticed how gnarled and weathered they were my spirit knew that my Lord Jesus had been there.

There were two other chaplains on the tour and the three of us conducted an early morning service in Gethsemane for the tour members.

My emotions overwhelmed me.

I had the profound sense that I had come to the very place where Jesus went on the night that He was betrayed. That I was walking where He walked. That he probably had knelt right there by that old tree and prayed in great agony of spirit, until drops of blood fell from his pores. I felt like taking off my shoes.

What I realized that morning, and need to realize over and over again, is that Jesus *really* was there.

He really did come into the world. He really did bear our sins on the cross. He really did arise from the dead.

He really does love you. Amen

"...They came to a place which was named Gethsemane and...He said to them, My soul is exceedingly sorrowful, even unto death...watch."
Mark 14:32,34

April 24

Some folks give up too soon.

The first major league home run by Willie Mays came off a pitch by Warren Spahn.

Spahn, like Mays, was on his way to the Hall of Fame. It was a clear day, perfect for baseball. From the mound, 60 feet, 6 inches away, Spahn threw a sizzling fast ball. Mays blasted it 400 feet. When asked later about the pitch, Spahn remarked, "It looked good for the first 60 feet."

The trouble with many of us, in our spiritual life and discipline, is that we don't persevere. We get off to a great start serving Christ, but our fervor wanes over the years.

Remember the great joy you had at your conversion, your baptism, your confirmation? When you first became a member of the church? What happened to it? Is it still there, radiating brightly? Or has it cooled to mere embers?

Being a Christian is a lot like being married. We must work at the relationship. Success isn't automatic or guaranteed. But the rewards for both efforts are great.

Dear Lord, I have loved You all of my life. I loved You even before I met and loved my wife. Then why am I so lethargic in my Christian witness? And why am I not more excited about You and me? Lord, I need a second honeymoon. With You! Let's go off somewhere together and rekindle this romance. When all else has gone it will be just You and me. I know that I must work harder at this relationship, Lord. Bless me indeed. Amen

"He who goes out weeping, carrying seed to sow, will return with songs of joy, carrying sheaves with him."
Psalm 126:6

Sow your seed, brother, sister. Joy comes in the morning.

April 25

What are you living for? Before you answer let me give you some Biblical illustrations of wrong answers.

Zacchaeus. Prior to meeting Jesus, Zacchaeus lived for *profit*. Why else would a man become a publican, a tax collector? No profession was more hated. Zacchaeus had practically sold his citizenship and birthright to enrich the hated Roman occupiers. Read it yourself in Luke 19.

Salome. She lived for *posterity*. As a sister of Jesus' mother she tried to take advantage of her relationship to Jesus and secure prominent positions for her two sons. She wanted James on one side and John on the other side of Jesus in the kingdom. Check it out in Matthew 20.

Simon the Sorcerer. He craved *power*. He already enjoyed considerable influence in the community. However, when he saw Paul casting out devils, Simon saw power the likes of which he had never witnessed. He had to have that power. So he faked his conversion. Claimed to be a Christian. Paul really smoked the guy. It's in the book. Acts 8.

Diotrephes sought the *preeminence*. After he had gained a leadership position in the church, Diotrephes refused to allow the Apostolic party of John to visit. He prated against them with malicious words. When others would receive John, Diotrephes cast them out of the church.

Unlike Zacchaeus, we must seek first the Kingdom of God.

Unlike Salome, we must be willing to take the lowly seat in the kingdom.

Unlike Simon the Sorcerer, we must acknowledge that all power, glory, and honor belong to God.

Unlike Diotrephes, we must eschew the preeminence and seek to do humble service for Christ.

Lord, let me always do as I have preached above. Amen

"For to me, to live is Christ...."
Philippians 1:21

April 26

If God died this morning, how long would it take for you to find out? And how would you get the message?

Of course God can't die. He is *eternal* (without beginning or end), *omnipotent* (having all power), *omnipresent* (everywhere present), and *omniscient* (all knowing). That's what we learned in our religious education classes. And I am pleased to tell you that I believe it.

But just for discussion please allow the premise in the first paragraph. How would you find out? Would your minister tell you? Would you hear it on the Today Show? On CNN? Read it in your newspaper? Or hear it on Radio?

What I'm asking is how are your lines of communication (LOC) with God. LOCs are a big thing in the military. There are both sea and air LOCs. A good commander gathers information from every possible source in order to best protect his soldiers and to accomplish the mission.

How are you hearing from God? I hope you are getting the news from the Bible, from good religious literature, from worship experiences, and from daily prayer. It is a humbling privilege for me to assist you through these devotions. I hope that you are making them, and the Scriptures, your first experience each day.

God is alive and well. He is near you. I pray that you have a great day.

The Psalmist tells us how:

"...Early (*i.e., first thing in the' morning?*) will I seek You. My soul thirsts for You...."
Psalm 63:1

Lord God, I could never thank You enough for reaching across Eternity to find me. Nor could my words ever suffice to thank You for the rich salvation that You provided through Christ Jesus. But I am going to keep trying anyway. Help me Lord, through your indwelling Spirit, to keep my lines of communication open with You. Amen

April 27

A clinical report of the medical treatment of Charles II of England goes:

"A pint of blood was extracted from the royal right arm and a half pint from the royal left shoulder. Followed by an emetic. The royal head was then shaved and a blister raised, then a sneezing powder and a plaster of pitch on his feet. Finally, 40 drops of extract of human skull was given. After which his majesty gave up the ghost."

We've come a long way in medicine since the days of Charles II.

We now have miracle drugs and laser (bloodless) surgery. We can exchange body parts from one person to another. And artificial parts are now implanted successfully in humans. My daughter recently had laser surgery on her eyes to cure near-sightedness. She now has perfect vision. No glasses. No hassle.

There is a growing movement in the churches that fosters wellness in its totality: body, mind, and spirit.

Staid old traditional congregations are having "healing" services where prayer and anointing are administered for the sick. Fundamentalist congregations are filling the week with programs that promote physical, and emotional health, as well as spiritual. The emphasis is always on wholeness.

What are you doing about it? The three are connected. Don't forget spiritual health. Nor emotional. Nor physical. God gave you all three. Keep them fit.

Let's substitute the word wholeness in a verse of Scripture and see how it works. It's a bit of a stretch, but the idea is sound. God expects us to be *holy* and wants us to be *whole*.

"(God)...disciplines us for our own good, that we may share in His *wholeness.*"
Hebrews 12:10

Ever hear of the nervous angel?

If angels are like all of God's other creations, they must have their differences, just as humans, frogs, birds, and kangaroos do. None of the living creatures are monolithically the same. Check out DNA, and fingerprints. So if angels come in various types, there must be at least one nervous angel.

If there is at least one, he probably was with Jesus at Bethany. Think of the scene, a day or two before the first Holy Week. Lazarus, Jesus' very good friend, had died and had lain in the grave four days.

The nervous angel must have figured that something was moving. He observed the deep emotional response in Jesus to the distraught sisters Mary and Martha when they met Him at their front door, in tears.

Surely the nervous angel moved in close when he heard Jesus ask to be taken to the tomb where Lazarus was buried. Even closer when Jesus prayed to the Father that the onlookers could believe that He sent Him.

"If he does what I think He is going to do," thought the nervous angel, "I had better caution Him."

The nervous angel must have whispered into Jesus' ear, "Sir, You must be specific." So Jesus did not say, "Dead be raised up." Or, "Let the dead come alive." He said, "Lazarus, come forth." Not you Joseph, Elizabeth, Jacob, Isaac, or Malachi. Not yet! Just you, Lazarus.

What a wonderful lesson for us, too. Jesus will call us, the believers, from the dead in the resurrection, by name!

But He wants to lift you to new spiritual heights and life now. He wants you to experience the power of His resurrection in your life today. And He wants you, *specifically*, to share that power.

"...Whoever lives and believes in Me shall never die. Do You believe this? She said to Him, 'Yes, Lord, I believe that You are the Christ, the Son of God....' "
John 11:26

April 29

Want to step back in time?

If you travel to Lancaster, Pennsylvania, you can come about as close as anywhere to seeing what America was like 100 years ago. Wooden planked barns and silos dot the rolling hills. Windmills still power farms and horse-drawn plows till the fertile soil.

The people are Amish, Mennonite, and Brethren, good people, The *Plain People*. Their lifestyle and culture make their region of Pennsylvania a true gem and offer an insight into the simpler life of a bygone era.

A brochure for Lancaster County reminds visitors that the residents are "not actors or spectacles but ordinary people who choose a different way of life."

Don't you suppose that God loves ordinary people best? He surely made a lot of us.

And what makes a person extraordinary? Is it wealth that he earns? Or inherits? Is it the rare, high IQ? Is it a result of something she does? Political office? The family he happens to be born into? Or the power she manifests?

The answer is none of the above.

What makes a person truly extraordinary is if that person is really at peace with himself or herself. We hear too many horror stories of the rich and powerful to believe otherwise. And we meet too many *ordinary* folks who have little of the world's goods but radiate a persistent happiness.

Thank You, Lord, for things you didn't give me. Amen

"Peace I leave with you, my peace I give to you: not as the world gives do I give to you. Let not your heart be troubled, neither let it be afraid."
John 14:27

April 30

There was a play a few years ago entitled, *Stop The World, I Want To Get Off.* I understand the sentiment. Sometimes things move too fast; I find myself wanting to slow everything down.

Consider the poor cosmonaut, Sergei Krikalev, who spent 313 days in space. He left the Union of Soviet Socialist Republics and returned home to the Commonwealth of Independent States. While he was in space, his nation dissolved and a new one formed. As my kids used to say, "far out!"

I was about to write about the ultimate space travel but maybe it would be best described as travel between dimensions. I am referring to the ascension of Jesus Christ to the right hand of God in Heaven.

I don't know whether Heaven is *up* in a geographical sense, or *out* in a dimensional reality beyond human understanding. But I do know that Heaven and the Second Coming of Christ are important and recurring themes in the Scriptures.

A lot happened during Sergei's 313 days. But nothing compared to the different world Jesus will see when He returns. My mind boggles at the differences between now and then.

But the people he will see will be basically the same. They will still need a Savior. And didn't He promise to come back? Get a dozen Christians together and I bet that most of them will know many of the words to *I'll Fly Away.*

Talking about newness, what is newer, every morning, than the fresh realization of God's grace? *New Grace!*

"Then He who sat on the throne said, 'Behold, I make all things new.' "
Rev. 21:5

Lord, technology has moved so fast in the last few years that I have started to wonder what's left to discover. Then You tell me that I will be caught up, in *space*? And taken somewhere *out of this world.* Wow! Help me to be ready. Amen

Ascension Sunday

He was crucified, buried, and raised from the dead. Then He *ascended into Heaven.*

How?

Did He disappear into the sky like a huge jet does when it gets smaller and smaller as it climbs into space? And finally it is so far away that it is invisible to the human eye?

Or did he dematerialize into invisibility like the image on a television screen does when the cameraman makes it fade into blankness? Was it like something out of Star Trek?

The Scriptures tell us that "A cloud took Him out of their sight" (Acts 1:9).

And what does it matter anyway? How is it related to the Gospel? What is the good news from the story?

Jesus' ascension proclaims a colossal victory over human limitations.

Remember His visit to the disciples on Easter Sunday night? He didn't knock on the door. He entered *through* the wall. The resurrected Jesus was not subject to the same material and spatial limitations as humans are now.

The ascension of Jesus provides us a peephole through which we can see into Heaven. From the Scriptures we can learn where Jesus is. He "Has sat down at the right hand of the throne of God (Hebrews 12:2). And we can see what Jesus is doing there, "He ever lives to make intercession for them" (i.e. those who come to God through Him, Hebrews 7:25.)

The great news in this marvelous story is that Jesus will return to the earth. He will come again.

"This Jesus, who was taken up from you into heaven, will come in the same way as you saw Him go into heaven."
Acts 1:11.

Dear Lord, I want to be ready when You return to the earth. But there are so many distractions, so many claims on my time. Help me to BE ready and STAY ready for your reappearance, Lord. Amen

Pentecost Sunday

Happy Pentecost Sunday.

Pentecost in the Old Testament was the second of the three great annual festivals. The others were Passover and Tabernacles.

The festival of Pentecost was also referred to by other names: the *Feast of Weeks*, because it was celebrated seven complete weeks after the Passover; the *Feast of Harvest*, because it concluded the harvest of the later grains; and the *Day of the First Fruits*, because the first loaves made from the new grain were then offered on the altar.

In the New Testament Pentecost is associated with wind, fire, and other tongues.

That is because it was on the first Pentecost after Christ's ascension that God poured out the Holy Spirit on the disciples of Jesus. They were waiting, prayerfully, in an upper room, anticipating the fulfillment of Jesus' promise that He would send them another comforter who would bring them power. (Refer to chapters 1 and 2 of the Acts of the Apostles.)

The effect on those receiving the Holy Spirit was so pronounced that the Apostle Peter had to assure the crowd that the Christians weren't drunk.

What about Pentecost and us? You? Have you ever been so full of the Spirit that someone thought you were drunk? Or have you ever been so full of the Spirit that anyone even noticed?

Do you fail to pray for the Spirit because you are afraid that something embarrassing might happen to you? Or because your church tells you that you have all of the Spirit you need?

Let us pray, not for as much of the Spirit as others think we need, but for as much as Christ wants us to have. Amen.

"...Do not be drunk with wine...but be filled with the Spirit."

Ephesians 5:18

May 1

A bluebird sang the day that Anwar Sadat died.

Anwar Sadat was a hero of mine. As the President of Egypt he exhibited monumental courage by accepting the invitation of Prime Minister Menachem Begin to travel to Israel on a mission of peace.

In March of 1979 the two nations signed a peace treaty and the world breathed a little easier. In 1978 the two men shared the Nobel Peace Prize. For the first time in my lifetime I actually felt that there was hope for Israel, an end to the bloodshed and bitter feelings that had plagued the region for centuries.

Then they killed him.

Muslim fundamentalists in President Sadat's own military shot him dead on October 6, 1981. I friend of mine was on the very platform with Sadat when he was shot.

The news of the assassination came over the radio in my office at Fort Polk, Louisana and I was devastated. A dark sadness seeped into my spirit. I knew that all of the good that had been done would now be undone.

I was still despondent when I went to the Post Office to get stamps. As I left by the side door of the old wooden building I was awakened from my deep funk by the singing of a Bluebird. He was right there, about a yard above my head, in the crape myrtle tree. Singing for all of his might. I stood there and listened, and had a spiritual experience as light shined in my soul.

"Lord," I prayed, "Bluebirds are still singing. The future of the world isn't lost. You are still the Lord of history. The hope of the world does not end with its Sadats, its Begins, or its Carters. Thank you for the sermon from this Bluebird. Do help me to remember its message. Amen"

"Therefore know this day, and consider it in your heart, that the Lord Himself is God in heaven above and on the earth beneath; there is no other."
Deuteronomy 4:39
Remember, Jesus told us to watch the birds.

May 2

Daddy was relaxing, reading the paper, after a hard day's work. But nine years old Johnny was ready to play. So he kept pestering his daddy to put the paper down and pay attention to him.

There was a map of the world in the paper he was reading so Daddy tore it into puzzle-size pieces and threw it on the floor. "OK, Johnny, when you put the world back together, I will play with you," said Daddy.

Johnny did it in about a minute. Daddy was surprised. "How did you do it so fast?" Daddy asked.

"There was a picture of the Simpson family on the other side of the map," Johnny answered. "I didn't know how to put the world together, but I knew how to put the family together."

Get the message? The way to put the world together is to put the family together. Children are God's most precious gift. They deserve the very best that life can offer: parents that love and nourish.

Lost from the American family is the parent as teacher. Children learn from television. And what they are learning is tragic. Violence is normal behavior. Drugs are fun. Personal satisfaction in sex, work, and play is a civil right.

Who is teaching your children? What are they being taught?

Dear Lord, bless families everywhere. And bless children especially. All children, Lord, and particularly those that live and learn where there is only one parent available to help them grow. Help them to grow up to be good, honest, and strong adults. Bless parents, Lord. Help them to teach by word and deed.   Amen

"...You shall lay up these words of mine in your heart...You shall teach them to your children...."
Deuteronomy 11:18,19

Jesus was not a wimp.

I get so sick and tired of those who characterize Jesus as a sissy, a weakling, and a doormat. During the approximately three and one half years of His ministry He probably spent most of his nights sleeping on the ground. His days were spent walking miles at a time over rough trails.

Yet, Jesus was a man of deep emotion. Picture this. The furniture had been reversed in the little house in Bethany, a suburb of Jerusalem. There had been four days of mourning, weeping, and wailing. Neighbors had come.

During that time the family had done no work, had not bathed, and had eaten only austere food. They were observing a religious ritual of mourning the dead. A sort of "keeping up with the Jones" mentality had developed over the years. So it was that Mary and Martha were marking the death of their brother, Lazarus. Their loud weepings were for their own sake and for the neighbors' sake too.

This was the family that Jesus probably loved most. His friend Lazarus was dead. Jesus was *deeply troubled.* The Greek word underneath that phrase is *Embrimasthai,* which is often translated angry.

Jesus was angry! At death. At Satan. At the evil that had produced so much pain to so many good people. Some folks don't like to think of a Jesus that could get angry, weep, and plat a whip and physically drive people from a temple. I refer to them in the first paragraph of today's devotion.

In the eleventh chapter of his Gospel John showed how Jesus reveals how God is. Great power. Great passion. Deep emotion. Great love.

"...When Jesus saw her weeping...He groaned in the spirit and was troubled."
John 11:33

Lord, You showed real and deep emotion when You were here on earth. And You still care deeply for me. Everyone else, too. I really thank You. Amen

May 4

A boy who wanted to learn jade went to study with an old teacher.

This teacher put a piece of jade into the youth's hand. While the youth held the jade in his hand the old man talked for about an hour of philosophy, men, women, the sun, and almost everything under it, before sending the boy home.

The procedure was repeated for weeks. The boy became frustrated--when would he be told about jade?--but he was too polite to interrupt his venerable teacher. Then one day the old man put a piece of regular stone into his hand. The boy cried out instantly, "That's not jade!"

A great example of hands-on training. The military does it well. They *train* constantly by *doing* their military tasks. When they stop doing their training, they lose their sharp edge.

A few years ago, the fad in counseling was behavior modification. The theory was that *by doing we become*. Or to put it differently, feeling follows actions. Most folks go at it backwards: one first has a feeling (like being in love); then one takes an action (like getting married).

I see a lot of merit in the approach. Put in laymen's terms, if you want to love your spouse more practice doing loving things.

It is true in your spiritual life. Christ commands you to love your enemies. Now a person can command her behavior but not her feelings. So love can't be just feeling. It must be an action. Jesus knew that when a Christian acts out love toward his enemies, his feelings change.

As Christians we train to be Christians by being Christian. That is when others will look at us and say, "That's Jade."

"...Let us not love in word or in tongue, but in deed and in truth."
I John 3:18

Help me Lord to be content in Your hands. Amen

"Did you ever see such a thing?"

"My, I never...."

It was bad enough that Simon was a leper. (Cured of the disease of course, or he would have had to live outside the city.) And bad enough that Jesus would even enter the house of such a person, a known sinner.

In those days people ate while reclining on one elbow at a low table. Now it was a violation of hospitality codes not to offer to wash a guest's feet. It was routine. Dusty roads and streets. A refreshing experience for tired feet. It was a servant's duty, if there was one.

The other part of the hospitality rite was for the host to sprinkle perfume on the guest's head. Now perfume was very expensive. Only a few drops. Once in a blue moon, if you had a very important person in your home, you might break a bottle and pour it all out on his head. Much like retiring the number of a sports hero. But that was indeed rare.

Simon had neither of these two things.

A woman came in off the street and shocked them. As Jesus was reclining it was easy for her to get to His feet. She washed His feet with her tears, and dried them with her hair. They were scandalized. A real lady would never even let her hair down in public.

In the Scriptures hospitality is a spiritual value. Are you a hospitable person? If Jesus rang your doorbell would you invite him in? The feet-washing woman touched a nerve.

They berated her but Jesus thanked her. More tomorrow.

"If I then, your Lord and Teacher, have washed your feet, you also ought to wash one another's feet."
John 13:14

Hey folks, have you washed anyone's feet lately?

May 6

Does worship have to make human sense?

When a woman washed Jesus' feet with her tears and dried them with her hair the onlookers were shocked, scandalized, outraged.

Then when she broke an alabaster jar of pure nard, a very expensive perfume, and poured it over his head they went bonkers. "That was worth 300 denari, a whole day's work. Why wasn't it sold and given to the poor?" they screamed.

Don't get sidetracked here on whether we need to give to the poor. We all agree that we do.

But if you stop there you will miss the point: *true love is always extravagant*!

Watch any grandparent.

Or any young guy in love and looking at rings.

Or a mother protecting her baby.

When my Grandfather Jordan lay a corpse in the funeral home, my Mother wanted to sit up all night with him. My Sister and I chided her until she finally consented to let us take her home.

We were so smart. *And so wrong!*

It didn't make sense to us for her to sit up all night. But it made sense to her.

She could have said, "Dad, we haven't been as close to each other as we could have. But I am here with you now. We can have this night together, just the two of us, like old times. I love you, Dad."

Farfetched? To human sense, yes, but not to love.

"She has done a beautiful thing to Me."
Mark 14:6 (NIV)

Lord, if true love is always extravagant, help me stop being such a miser. Amen

May 7

Ray and Dot Caulder were coming for a few days' visit. Shirley had already baked a cake, and there was a ham cooking in the oven.

The Caulders are among our closest friends. Ray is a retired Army Chaplain like me. We share a common background and know the same songs. We once sang all of the way from Fort Lee, Virginia, to New York City, with only a fifteen minute break to hear the news on the car radio.

We have been friends since October, 1968. I had just come home from an unaccompanied tour in Korea and was being assigned to Fort Gordon, Georgia, near Augusta. Shirley and I went to look for housing.

Our sponsor was supposed to arrange for our stay in Augusta, but hadn't. Ray heard about our plight and took us home with him, where we stayed several days. Dot treated us like family. Since then we have visited numerous times in each other's home.

So, today I thank God for the gift of friends, and urge you to do the same.

Friends are the true riches. Children grow up and find their own space, but friendships (not just acquaintances) endure. If you measure riches by the good friends you have, as I do, how rich are you?

Jesus enjoyed a similar relationship. There was a family at Bethany where He often stopped over to rest and recuperate. Martha would cook His favorite meals and Mary would engage Him in great discussions. Their brother, Lazarus, may have been Jesus' best friend. When Lazarus died, the sisters were angry at Jesus for not rushing to their side. Then, at Lazarus' tomb Jesus wept.

Today, nourish your friendships. They are gifts from God. Be thankful. And always remember, "What A Friend We Have In Jesus."

"...Peace to you. Our friends greet you. Greet the friends by name."
3 John 14

May 8

A Martyr and not yet dead?

Everyone should be so blessed as to be able to hear Buckner Fanning preach. He is the pastor of the huge Trinity Baptist Church in San Antonio, Texas.

The sermon was brief on the Sunday I attended, and the preaching was extemporaneous. There were deacons to ordain.

The text was from Acts seven, where Stephen gave his marvelous witness to the person, nature, and work of Jesus. He was one of the original deacons. Stephen concluded his sermon by accusing his hearers of killing the Christ. They where cut to the heart and stoned Stephen. Thus Stephen became the church's first martyr. Martyr, that is, according to the popular understanding that a martyr is someone who has died for his or her testimony.

It was the idea of a living martyr that stuck in my mind.

We have all heard of someone's being called a living saint. Popular personalities are sometimes referred to as legends in their own time. But a martyr in his own time! Her own time!

The words martyr and witness are the same in the Greek language. So, *martur* in Greek becomes *martyr* in English. The practice is called transliteration. It means to write words in the corresponding characters of another language. A good example is Revelation 17:6, where the text in English is *martyr*. However, in at least three instances (Acts 2:8; 22:20 and Revelation 2:13) *martur* in the Greek is translated into *witness* in English.

Get the point?

While we, as faithful Christians, are living our lives in obedience to the claims of Christ, and are bringing glory to His name, we are martyrs. Because we are martyring (witnessing). Living martyrs! In the text below the word in italics is my translation from the Greek.

"...You shall be *martyrs* in Jerusalem, and ... to the ends of the earth."

Acts 1:8

May 9

"Through persistence the snail made it into the ark."
(John Hagee)

Glenn Cunningham, who once held the world record for the mile run was severely burned when he was a child. As a result of the accident, which killed his brother, some said that Glenn would never walk again.

But his mother would not allow talk of giving up.

Every day Glenn's mother would massage his scarred, lifeless legs, sometimes until her hands and arms were numb. Then when she had to turn to other chores she would make him continue. "Keep working at it son," she would say. He did.

After six months he was walking.

Then a few months later he could trot a little, with only a slight limp. At age twelve he ran and won a schoolboy race. His mother didn't see that as the end of anything. "Just keep working at it son." she would say. Glenn said that not even running in the Olympics was more important than that schoolboy race.

Back to the snail. He went at top speed. Kept oozing along. Perseverance is the word today.

What about you? You got off to a good start. Are you still running? Has the Christian race lost its excitement for you? Become too tiring? Have you forgotten the importance of enduring until the end?

Today I pray that you can catch your second wind spiritually. Get a fresh new picture of the prize that awaits. "Keep working at it...."

"...*Continue* in the things which you have learned and been assured of...which are able to make you wise for salvation through faith which is in Christ Jesus."
2 Timothy 3:14,15

May 10

My knowledge of science is limited.

Since I never liked the subject, I wasn't a good science student. In fact, I learned more science teaching it in the sixth grade than I did in eight years of post high school education. I remember one lesson well.

A professor rapped his knuckles on the wooden podium and exclaimed that it wasn't solid. He went on to explain that even though it appeared to be solid the podium really was composed of millions of molecules in motion. He said that if we were able to magnify the substance sufficiently we would be able to actually see space between the molecules.

It boggles my mind. Space between the whirling components of a solid piece of oak.

Remember the first Easter night? The disciples were gathered (hiding?) in a room behind locked doors. They were afraid that the same authorities that had killed their Lord would also be coming for them.

If Jesus had tramped on the wooden sidewalk, then knocked loudly on the door, they might all have nearly died of heart attacks.

So He *appeared* in their midst.

Hello God!

There is no indication that anyone opened a door to let Him in. Did it have anything to do with the molecules in the wooden walls and the space between the molecules? Or did it even matter to the resurrected Jesus? Probably not.

Keep molecules in mind when your pastor conducts the Ascension Sunday worship service.

The wonderful mystery grows when you remember that He promised that we would be like Him in our resurrection. Moving through molecules? Space.

Boggle along with me.

"... What if you were to see the Son of Man ascending where he was before?"
John 6:62 (RSV)

A lot of folks criticize the government, but there is at least one good thing that it has done: it set aside a day to honor mothers. And a Sunday near this date will be designated Mothers' Day.

The government acted at the insistence of Miss Anna Jarvis of Philadelphia, and her supporters.

Aside from the gift of His own Son to be our Savior the dearest gift God has given to mankind is mothers. They bore us, enduring great pain. In their arms we found shelter and protection. They kissed away our hurts and assured us that we could get up when we fell down.

Next to the love of God the greatest thing in the world is the love of a mother.

God's love is eternal but a mother's love is enduring. It lasts through failure as well as success, through adversity as well as prosperity, through sickness as well as health, through degradation as well as exaltation.

A true mother, like the mother of Jesus, is someone who will always love you. As you grow older she will love you no less.

A Rabbi once said, "God could not be everywhere so He gave us mothers." One could quarrel with his theology of the deity, but hardly with his sentiment about mothers.

I thank God for my own mother, Nettie Marie Jordan Hunt.

She worked her whole life to enable my sister and me to get an education. Compared with the austerities of her childhood we lived in luxury.

Her sense of humor was infectious. Her faith was profound and real. Her daughter served alongside her preacher husband, and I accepted the call to preach the gospel. It must have been easier for God to call us. Mother had already set the context of ministry.

"My son...do not forsake the law of your mother."
Proverbs 1:8

May 12

"Oh, well, I can always do it tomorrow."

Not really. You may not have a tomorrow. You should never boast of something until you have it.

Once long ago, a wise child prince asked his tutor to prepare him for the life beyond. The tutor replied that there was plenty of time for that when the lad was old. The boy disagreed, "I have been to the cemetery and measured the graves and there are many shorter than I."

A number of years ago a cartoon appeared in the paper in three parts. In the first scene, a busy young man was at his desk. At his shoulder was Christ inviting him to be saved. His answer, "Tomorrow."

The second scene showed a middle-aged man, busy, heavier, and better dressed, at a larger desk stacked with papers and reports. Christ again was at his elbow. Again the answer was, "Tomorrow."

The last scene showed the man old, thin, stooped, and sick. Christ was not at his shoulder now, Instead there was the gaunt, bony specter of death. Again he answered, "Tomorrow," but it fell on deaf ears.

Someone greeted me with, "Isn't it a wonderful day." I answered, "At my age, any day that I can get out of bed, put on my shoes, and leave the house is a good day."

Don't waste today.

If there is a heart that you broke, mend it. If there is a promise that you made, keep it. If a child is reaching up to you, take her hand. You don't have to be morbid to understand the value of time. If Christ is tapping on your shoulder, let Him in. It is a wonderful day!

"Do not boast about tomorrow, for you do not know what a day may bring forth."
Proverbs 27:1

May 13

"Hey, Sergeant, how long have you been here?"
"Four years, Sir."
"Then tell me, is this rain or fog?"
"It's fog, Sir."
The famous San Francisco fog!

It was an early June morning, and I was processing into the Sixth U.S. Army at the Presidio of San Francisco. Something was sticking to my glasses.

The fog dampened the air and settled on the growing things. It reminded me of God's providence.

I don't know much about ecosystems but everywhere I have been things had their own particular way of fitting together. Even the desert is alive with living things, each one dependent on the other.

What a marvelous, beautiful, and complicated world God has created. And what love He has shown the world in giving His Son to be our Savior.

I hope that you will bow to thank God for the gifts He has given you. The pleasures of earth. The blessings of Heaven. And don't forget to thank Him for the Holy Scriptures, the church, and the gift of saving faith.

Dear Lord, I thank you for Jesus my Savior and for this beautiful world to live in. I am indeed rich in spirit and material things. Help me to be a good steward of all of Your blessings. Amen

"Therefore God give thee of the dew of heaven, and the fatness of the earth, and plenty of corn and wine."
Genesis 27:28 KJV

May 14

At a seminar preceding a National Prayer Breakfast in the nation's capital, Congressman Tony Hall told about his family's initial move to Washington, D. C. after his election.

The night before they left, his then three year old daughter was saying her prayers with the usual, "God bless Mummy, Daddy, the Cat, etc." She got through about twenty God blesses when she concluded, "Well, God, I guess this is good by, we're moving to Washington, D. C."

The little girl was learning about the pain of Permanent Changes of Station, PCS to those who have served on Active Duty.

Soldiers and their families could teach a class on the subject. I never became tired of wearing the uniform, but, I really got tired of moving. I don't even know how many times Shirley and I did move.

The Bible is full of PCS. I suppose that the first one is when God kicked Adam and Eve out of Eden. He just kicked them out. No pinpoint assignment, no sponsor to assist in the move.

My favorite PCS story is that of Abraham. "He went out, not knowing where he was going." (Hebrews 11:8) At least I always knew where I was being assigned. I guess soldiers (i.e. all military) have it pretty good, after all. Thank God for moving companies. And supportive families.

Dear Lord, bless our military members and their families. They will be doing a lot of moving this year, some leaving the Service and some getting new assignments. Go with them all, even with those going to Washington, D. C. And Lord, richly bless each person who is reading this now. In Jesus' name. Amen.

"...The Lord your God is with you wherever you go."
Joshua 1:9

Of course the greatest challenge we all face, and it is coming whether we are ready for it or not, is to be ready for that final PCS.

May 15

Is your pump primed?

When I was a kid our pump was at the edge of our back porch. It sat atop a pipe that reached down to the cool water below the ground. We operated the pump manually. I was convinced that having to "pump water" amounted to cruel and unusual punishment.

There was one cardinal rule: never let the pump go dry.

When for some reason the pump went dry, lost its prime, we could work the handle all we wanted to but no water would flow. One of us would have to walk to a neighbor's house to borrow prime water. When we poured the prime water into the top of the pump and worked the handle the pump regained its prime.

What about your spiritual prime? Are you available, ready, when opportunity presents itself for Christian service? Are you a reliable witness for our Lord? Are you "prayed up?" Can you be counted on to respond immediately to the Spirit's leadings?

To be a "primed" Christian you need to be faithful in prayer and Bible study. The Bible, the Word of God is the bread that nourishes us. It is in prayer that we keep in touch with our source, Jesus.

Do you have a daily schedule? Weekly?

Christian fellowship is another factor in staying "primed." Spiritually minded friends, who also love Jesus, give us valuable feedback, and encourage us.

If you feel that you have lost your prime listen to our Lord.

"...If anyone thirsts, let him come to Me and drink...As the Scripture has said, out of his heart will flow rivers of living water."
John 7:37,38

Lord, help me to keep my prime. Keep my gaskets moist from Your Spirit's presence in my life. Amen

May 16

Posted in a Paris hotel elevator: "Please leave your values at the front desk."

Now everyone reading that would understand that the writer meant to use the word valuables, but missed on the translation into English

Do you sometimes leave your values at the front desk? That is a nasty question. So let me talk about myself, which only seems fair, since you can't talk back.

I have a tendency to try to keep two separate patterns of behavior: one as a Christian, and another as just another human being.

Do you get it? Behaving one way when I am in my *Christian* mode and behaving differently when I have switched into my *just another person* mode. Or, behaving one way in a group, and another way when I am alone. Again, behaving one way when I am with one crowd, and another way when I am with a different crowd.

It really is about the lordship of Jesus. For as long as I reserve a part of me for my own personal pursuits I am denying Him full control over my life. And, until Christ is Lord of all of my life He is not yet Lord. And that scares me.

Dear Lord, keep after me. Don't let me get away with half-heartedness. It sounds too much like hypocrisy, Lord. Work with me until I am completely surrendered to Your will and Lordship. Until you have filled every hidden place with Your divine presence and control. Amen.

"...Whoever wants to save his life will lose it, but whoever loses his life for me and for the gospel will save it."
Mark 8:35 NIV

May 17

Sometime this month our nation will observe Armed Forces Day.

On that day, military members and their families around the world receive numerous accolades, justly deserved.

In searching the Scriptures for this devotion I learned that soldiers didn't always look good.

It was soldiers who made a crown out of thorns and smashed it on His head. Soldiers took Jesus' garments and split them into four parts. They divided the garments, one for each soldier. They also broke His legs. Of course they were carrying out routine procedures. Soldiers also pierced His side with a spear.

But there are also positive examples.

It was a Centurion (a commander over 100 Roman soldiers) whose profound spiritual understanding drew from Jesus the remark that "I have not found such great faith, not even in Israel." (Luke 7:9) Also read about Cornelius in Acts 10. So, the Scriptures show the good and the bad about soldiers.

Soldiers are America. They are you, us, our sons and daughters, the people. Hard training, long deployments, low pay, and constant moves take a heavy toll on young soldier families. I hope that you will become well informed about the needs of these American heroes and become their advocate.

Reflecting on the meaning of Armed Forces Day I am truly thankful for the privilege of being a soldier and a chaplain. It is the best ministry in the church. I wouldn't have missed it for the world.

You can be a soldier, too. You don't have to be in the Army to be a soldier for God. Let's have a sharp salute.

"...Endure hardship as a good soldier of Jesus Christ."
2 Timothy 2:3

Lord, I have been privileged to be a soldier in Your army and in the army of my Country. It's been an honor serving, Lord. Thank you. Amen

In his book, *Hanging By A Thread*, pastor Mark Rutland maintains that only a rediscovery of biblical values such as courage, honesty, and reverence, can prevent our post Christian society from unraveling at the seams.

He identifies three descending levels for the disintegration of society.

The first is the seminal stage when we formulate our noblest ideals and make some attempt to live by them. The founding fathers pledged their "sacred honor" as well as their material possessions to the success of the American experience.

The second stage is when we remember what it means to be noble, but we can't live that way. That causes an inner conflict. Humanity cannot live for long in contradiction to what it believes. It will either change how it lives or change how it believes.

We may now be in his third stage. We, as a society, don't seem to be willing to change the way that we live. We have gained a high tolerance for violence, promiscuity, theft, and lying, to name but a few things. Little wonder that we are changing the way that we believe.

We change our values to fit our lifestyle. Then we give the new values noble definition. Violence is aggressive behavior. Promiscuity becomes self-expression. Lying is done to protect the sensitivities of another. Theft is okay if the victim is rich. The whole society spirals downward.

These are days in which those who really love America can exercise a most patriotic service: Pray for her.

"If My people who are called by My name humble themselves, and pray and seek My face, and turn from their wicked ways, then I will hear from heaven, and will forgive their sin and heal their land."
2 Chronicles 7:14

Dear Lord, let Your heart go out to us, and bless America. Help us to be a good and honest people, filled with compassion, and determined to seek justice. Amen

May 19

Friendly fire! Now isn't that phrase an oxymoron?

The high-tech battlefield of Desert Storm brought that most regretful result. The loss of life in any battle is tragic, but it is compounded terribly when our own weapons cause the deaths.

My only injury in Vietnam came from a "friendly" 105 round. The injury was light; I didn't report it, and the highly accurate fire bought time for the airmobile company I was in to regroup, surely saving lives.

I am often saddened by the casualties to "friendly fire" in our churches.

I once invited friends to attend services at the chapel we attended. Immediately upon their taking their seats, one of the "leaders" of the congregation leaned forward and informed them that they were in the "general's seat." There was no general's seat, and my commander would have been as mad as a wet setting hen if he had known about that thoughtless remark. My friends never came back.

Young people, criticized for their music, appearance, boisterous youthfulness, or worldliness, never return. Good people, blasted by unfeeling members or pastors, leave the church. Preachers, targeted by caustic critics, drop out. (I had a deacon threaten me with a pistol when I wouldn't agree to let him have his way. He didn't shoot, thank God. He was a stinking coward.)

It would take pages to discuss adequately the casualties from friendly fire in the home and in the workplace.

If you are shooting at a loved one or co-worker it is not *friendly* fire.

Unload! Stack your arms. You are not on a firing range. Find a better way to communicate. Christ will be pleased with you.

"...Be kind to one another, tenderhearted, forgiving one another, as God in Christ forgave you"
Ephesians 4:32

At their breakfast table the little boy prayed: "We thank you, God, for this beautiful day." Everyone at the table glared at him. Driving wind and sleet were making the bitterly cold morning even more intolerable.

His father admonished, "You must never pray insincerely like that again." His older siblings allowed that he was always trying to be a smarty.

"What do you mean, son, a beautiful day?" his mother asked.

Reaching for the jam the youngster answered, "You can't judge a day by its weather."

Nor can you judge a day by your schedule, the number of trips, meetings, the in box, or the busyness of your telephone. Nor must old failures and broken relationships ruin today.

Each new day gives us a fresh start, another chance at doing it right.

So close your door, put your feet up, lean back, close your eyes, and thank God for the great gift of today. Thank Him for life! Thank Him for health! Thank Him for your family! If you are fortunate enough to be employed thank God for your job. Your vocation. For everything.

And don't waste your time and energy worrying. Trust in God. He loves you. A lot. Amen

"So do not worry, saying, 'What shall we eat?' or 'What shall we drink?' or 'What shall we wear?' for the pagans run after all these things, and your heavenly Father knows that you need them. But seek first His kingdom and His righteousness, and *all these things will be given to you as well*...Each day has enough trouble of its own."
Matthew 6:31-34

Lord, I am a worrier. You know that I always have been. After all these years I am still praying, "Lord, increase my faith, help me to cast my cares on You." Amen

May 21

Doug Murren, senior pastor of a large church in Kirkland, Washington, wrote about his reaction to his son's coming home from work wearing an earring.

Pastor Murren had already noticed a number of earrings appearing on the lobes of the youth in the congregation. He had admired them jokingly, not making much of them. Actually, his son's earring was small in comparison to the others, but in the pastor's eyes, it looked like a tire dangling from his son's ear.

I remember the hassle I had trying to get my oldest son to keep his hair short in the 70s. I lost. Years later, my youngest son, perhaps remembering how I had allowed myself to be hooked by my oldest son's long hair, tried to hook me too. I had noticed that he was wearing his hair long but had said nothing.

"How do you like my hair, Dad?"

"It's fine with me."

"But you don't like long hair."

"But I like you."

"Look, son, I learned my lesson with your brother. I tried to force him to wear his hair to please me and we had nothing but hassle. I won't make that mistake again. It's your hair and your responsibility."

He was soon wearing his hair neatly trimmed, and has ever since.

Raising teenagers can be the most awesome, difficult, and exasperating experience in life. It can also be the most blessed and rewarding experience in life. Often it is both of those in the same day.

Dear Lord, bless every parent today, and every son and daughter. Help them to get along, to love each other, and to have peace in the home. Amen

"Behold, children are a heritage from the Lord...."
Psalms 127:3

Are you a member of the "ASAP Tribe?"

Most of us are ASAP-ers, whether we work with deadlines or not. It seems that people everywhere, in all walks of life, live under the mandate or issue mandates, to do everything "as soon as possible."

Where would we be without microwaves, personal computers, fax machines, cellular telephones, speed dialing, and instant potatoes? Yet It seems that the more time we save, the more we find to do.

In a devotional address to The Evangelical Press Association, Evangelist Leighton Ford spoke of the *tyranny of the urgent*. He pointed out that wisdom is in knowing the difference between what is *urgent* and what is *important*.

When our daughter and her family were visiting us I looked in on my grandson one night and saw his dad stretched out with him on the bed, reading a children's story. A tough soldier! But with good priorities.

Then the next day I accompanied one of our generals to inform a wife that her husband had died the previous night while on Temporary Duty (TDY) in Atlanta. After she had a few minutes to regain her composure she said, "I guess we should say goodbye every time they leave for TDY."

Amen Alice, Reverend Ford, and Zachary.

There is a world of difference in what is urgent and what is important.

Heavenly Father, help each reader today to be able to make the distinction. It is important to earn a living, vote, and care for others. But it is urgent that we keep our connection with You, and that we encourage our families to do the same. Make it work for me, Lord. Amen

"...He who is impulsive exalts folly."
Proverbs 14:29

May 23

The pastor offered the couple the choice of having a traditional or a contemporary wedding ceremony. They chose the contemporary.

On the day of the wedding, it rained snails and bullfrogs.

The groom had to drive a circuitous route to even reach the church. When he got there, he had to roll up his pant legs so his trousers wouldn't get muddy.

He had barely made it inside the door, when they hurried him into the service.

He had forgotten to roll his pant legs down. So there he stood with his bride and with his pant legs still rolled up.

The pastor whispered, "Pull down your pants." The groom stared at the pastor but did nothing.

"Pull down your pants."

The groom finally whispered to the pastor, "Reverend, I've changed my mind. I want the traditional service."

I love to perform weddings.

On one of my first, I was reading the vows in little pieces for the groom to repeat. He stumbled over "I plight thee my troth" a couple times before blurting out, "Aw shoot, I can't say that."

The bride hit him with her fist.

Marriage is society's fundamental institution.

It is God's gift to the human race. People, like me, who have been blessed with an enduring marriage should give humble and sincere thanks to God. I do.

"Therefore a man shall leave his father and his mother, and be joined to his wife, and they shall become one flesh." Genesis 2:24

Lord, there are so many marriages on the rocks today. There has been so much grief and pain, and it continues. They need Your help, Lord. Step between those that are fighting and help them to see how senseless it is. Bring healing, and reconciliation Lord. Amen

A church bulletin told of Mrs. Craig, an eighty-one- year-old lady, who had not missed Sunday School in 1,040 Sundays, a perfect record for twenty years. What was wrong with that lady?

Didn't she ever have company on Sunday? Didn't she ever have headaches, colds, flu, feel run down, or get an upset stomach? Didn't she like golf or ever sleep late? Didn't it ever rain or snow or get too hot or too cold where she lived? Didn't she ever get mad at the preacher or get her feelings hurt? Did she not like television?

Was the attendance thing really just her way of getting attention? Or is it possible that she genuinely loved the Lord and cared about people. And felt strongly about accepting and carrying out her responsibilities.

May God bless the Mrs. Craigs of the world. And God bless you and give you encouragement and strength to do your spiritual duties. You may not be serving the Lord to *break* a record, but you are *making* a record, in Heaven.

The first place that my wife, Shirley, was ever taken was to church. That is probably true for me too.

Counting Sunday School, youth activities, mid-week and Sunday evening services, I have been to church over 6,500 times. Seems like more.

I ask you now, what is your record of attendance at worship services and other church events? I hope that you are not just an Easter and Christmas Christian. What counts for spiritual growth and family cohesion is to adopt a regular schedule of spiritual worship and training and sticking with it.

"Let us not give up meeting together, as some are in the habit of doing, but let us encourage one another--and all the more as you see the Day approaching."
Hebrews 10:25 (NIV)

Thank you, Lord, for all of the churches where Jesus is clearly portrayed as Savior. Amen

May 25

An old legend tells of a merchant in Baghdad who one day sent his servant to the market. Before very long the servant came back, pale and trembling, and in great agitation, said to his master: "Down in the market place I was jostled by a woman in the crowd, and when I turned around I saw that it was Death that had jostled me. Master, I am frightened. Please lend me your horse, and I will ride to Samarra where I will hide, so that Death will not find me."

The merchant lent him his horse and the servant galloped away in great haste.

Later the merchant went down to the market place and saw Death standing in the crowd. He went over to her and asked, "Why did you frighten my servant this morning? Why did you make a threatening gesture?"

"That was not a threatening gesture," Death said. "It was only a start of surprise. I was astonished to see him in Baghdad, for I have an appointment with him tonight in Samarra."

Each of us has an appointment in Samarra. But Christians know that Jesus holds the keys to the city.

Brigadier General Dick Sharp was my supervisor and hunting buddy when we both were stationed at Fort Polk, Louisiana. He was an active, vivacious person. We kept in touch after we both were reassigned. Early one duty day he went jogging and fell dead.

The little chapel where he worshipped in Hunter Army Air Field near Savannah, Georgia, had a tradition of saying goodbye to those leaving before the next Sunday. The chaplain would ask them to raise their hand so that they could be sent away with the congregation's blessings.

Mrs. Pat Sharp sent me a copy of the chapel bulletin for General Sharp's last Sunday there. "Lamar," she wrote, "I guess we ought to raise our hand each Sunday."

"...It is appointed unto men once to die, but after this the judgment.

Hebrews 9:27 (KJV)

A missionary and a new convert were discussing stewardship. "If you had a hundred sheep, would you give ten of them for the Lord's work?"

"That I would."

"If you had fifty cows, would you give five to the Lord's work?"

"That I would."

"But if you had twenty hogs, you wouldn't give two of them to the Lords work, would you?"

"Oh yes I would."

"But if you had ten chickens, would you be willing to give one of them to the Lord's work?"

"No, I wouldn't. And you have no right to ask me when you know I have only ten chickens."

I love that story. Another great story is the one about The Widow's Mite.

Have you ever wondered what motivated her to shake the last two coins out of her handkerchief into the offering plate at the synagogue? It must have been the presence of Jesus, sitting there, watching. "...Jesus sat opposite the treasury and saw how the people put money into the treasury...." (Mark 12:41).

Did you know that Jesus watches the collection plate when you go to church?

If you are still dropping a dollar in the plate after twenty years of pay increases aren't you stealing from God? And think of the blessings you have missed. One of the rich ways God has of blessing you is through your stewardship. These blessings flow from a gracious God who rewards a generous spirit.

Jesus watches the collection! Is it time for you to examine your record of stewardship? And increase your giving?

Bless you. Amen

"...Assuredly, I say to you that this poor widow has put in more than all those...."
Mark 12:43

May 27

Are we making progress or what?

The guardians of the nation's morals were worried. "There is no doubt," a 19th century clergyman solemnly warned his New York congregation, "that we are dealing here with a contraption of the devil himself."

A noted policeman bewailed the injuries the contraptions caused and wished that they could be outlawed.

The bicycle!

Brought to America in 1866, that "contraption of the devil put women into pants and speed cops on the highway. And things haven't slowed down since.

America's churches have provided a good, positive influence on American society. Our emphases on volunteering, charity, and education (many of the country's greatest universities were founded by churches) have enriched America.

But America's clergy have often missed the mark.

Even after the Berlin wall has fallen and the Soviet Union has been disbanded, some seminary professors and pastors still praise communist goals and lambaste the United States.

There are some compromises I wish folks could make.

I wish my Catholic brothers and sisters would re-look their position on contraception. It would be easier to join with them in their abortion position if they would take this one little step which seems so reasonable.

I wish that folks in my church would balance their social agenda with a greater emphasis on spiritual experience.

I pray that my fundamentalist brothers and sisters will accept those of us who love the Lord, too, but disagree with their positions on some things.

"Some indeed preach Christ even from envy and strife, and some also from good will."
Philippians 1:15

Lord help us to find better things to preach about than bicycles. Amen.

May 28

Do you ever have enough?

The story is told of a widow of meager means who, nevertheless, was quite liberal in her giving. Unexpectedly, a large legacy was left her, and she was wealthy. However, where she had been giving twenty dollars each Sunday, she now gave only one.

When asked why there was such a change in her giving, she replied candidly, AAh, when day-by-day I looked to God for my bread, I had enough and to spare. Now I am rich and have to look after myself. I must save every little bit I can"

A famous actress, when interviewed, spoke with surprising candor. AThere was a time when tangible things were important to make me happy,≅ she admitted. AI enjoyed my big home and my furniture, my jewels, my paintings, and my Tiffany silver. But, my possessions finally possessed me. I got to the point where I wouldn't leave if the servants were out. I had to have a baby sitter for the house."

Shirley and I had a terrible time choosing the house we now live in. It is the first house we ever bought thinking that we may have to live in it the rest of our lives. Also, buying this home has caused me much thought along other lines.

We already own several houses, as investments. How much of my anxiety is about growing up poor? Why have I been so fixated on owning land and houses? And how do I reconcile that need with following the One who walked on sandaled feet down dusty trails, and had "no place to lay His head?"

Don't become so concerned with earthly things that you forget your heavenly destiny. Life is short, but eternity is forever. Maybe we need to have a *garage sale for the soul,* clearing out all of the things that clutter and corrupt our spirits.

"...One's life does not consist in the abundance of the things he possesses." Luke 12:15

Dear Lord, thank you for blessing me with an earthly home, but don't let it in any way obstruct my view of the home I have in heaven with you. Amen

May 29

How old are you?

The Chapel Choir was enjoying its fall retreat in the glorious mountains of western North Carolina. We were having a wonderful time, working on Christmas music.

Of course, it was particularly interesting to me since I had written the cantata that the director had chosen to use.

We were staying in the mountain home of a retired Army Chaplain, the father of our chaplain at that time.

On Saturday afternoon the sun was shining bright so we cooked out. The fresh air and brilliant color were wonderful.

Our host gathered us together for the blessing, spread his arms out to us, hugged as many of us as he could at one time, and prayed: "Lord, I thank you for all these *young people*."

Young! I was 56 at the time and felt it. Our average age was over 50.

What does it mean to be young? Is age chronological or attitudinal? (The chronology is nipping at my heels!)

And what about people who feel old but think young? I go days at a time thinking of myself as young and then something happens to remind me of my age.

A senior citizen freebie. Aching back. What a bummer.

After Israel had occupied the Promised Land there were still pockets of resistance in the highlands. Caleb, then 85 years old, petitioned Joshua for his share of the land.

To Joshua he said, "Give me this mountain. I am as strong as I was 40 years ago when you and I first reconnoitered it."

Dear Lord, I will not tell the readers how old I am. You already know. Please bless me with many more good years. But don't let me ever get old. Amen

"They shall still bear fruit in old age...."
Psalms 92:14

May 30

Happy Memorial Day!

Today's devotion deals with two piles of stones.

The first is the twelve stones that Joshua and the elders of the people placed by the river Jordan to commemorate their miraculous crossing into the Promised Land. The stones have long since been washed away, but the meaning remains.

The second is at Stonehenge, on the Salisbury Plain, Southeast of London. The stones remain but no one knows for sure how they got there or what they mean. I have read dozens of explanations but they all leave me wondering. Was Mary Stewart right? Did Merlin the magician really did do it.

The meaning of Joshua's stones is known because subsequent generations were taught the meaning.

The meaning of Stonehenge is lost because subsequent generations were not taught the meaning. Our task as parents, teachers, leaders, and ordinary citizens is to teach the meaning.

On this Memorial Day there will be thousands of speeches and observances, all intended to teach the meaning of: FREEDOM, HONOR, EQUALITY, COURAGE, DISCIPLINE, PATRIOTISM, and FAITH.

Wave the flag and remember. Many of us who wore the uniform will remember buddies lost.

Within our Nation's capital there is a long black wall
Where heroes' names are etched into the stone
Among the many thousands who heard the Nation's call
I found the name of James Montgomery Jones.
  I bowed my head in sorrow with memories in my mind
  Of youthful dreams that we had shared back then
  And knew that I would never be fortunate to find
  Another time so wonderful a friend.
(From *The Ballad Of Monkey Jones*, by this author)

"Pray for the peace of Jerusalem (and America). May they prosper who love you."
Psalms 122:6

May 31

Have you ever been accused of having a disrespectful face?

Due to a misunderstanding between me and a member of his staff, Brigadier General (then colonel) Joe Ecopi was giving me a royal chewing. And me a lieutenant colonel already! He was a great soldier and we are still friends. (I even let him buy my lunch recently to prove it.) But I wasn't enjoying the chewing. So I popped to rigid attention to register my displeasure.

"Why are you standing at attention, Lamar?"

"Sir, if I am getting chewed out like a private I think I should stand at attention like a private would."

"You are being disrespectful to me."

"Sir, I am being very careful not to say anything disrespectful to a senior officer."

"You are disrespecting me with your face."

And he was right.

We sometimes say more with our bodies than we could ever say in words. And counselors have made body language a virtual science.

Consider the significance that Pentecostal believers give to hands upraised in worship. An act of spiritual surrender? An expression of openness to God? A request to be taken up in the Lord's arms?

Catholics use their bodies in worship, too: genuflecting; crossing themselves; and kneeling, to name a few.

Have our denominational strictures kept us from seeing the value in worship styles that enrich the souls of others?

Dear Jesus, I will eat at anyone's spiritual table where you are Lord.

"...You shall love the Lord your God with all your heart, with all your soul, with all your mind, and with all your strength...."

Mark 12:29

June 1

Do you feel boxed in? If so you can have sympathy for the Children of Israel, and learn from their experience.

As slaves in Egypt they had been forced to do heavy manual labor. Each time the Jews complained Pharaoh increased their workload. Then Moses appeared to lead them to freedom.

When they were finally freed Moses led them on a round about way to the Promised Land to avoid the warlike Philistines. And that is how they found themselves boxed in.

While encamped by the Red Sea they learned that Pharaoh's army was chasing them with a force that included 600 war chariots. What to do? The way behind was denied. Their left and right flanks were blocked by impassable terrain.

They complained that if they were to die it would have been simpler to die as slaves in Egypt. When Moses prayed for guidance God instructed him to lead the people forward, *through the waters*. God divided the sea and Israel crossed over on dry land.

Now back to you.

Do you feel boxed in? Is a great sadness blocking you on the right? A painful family situation obstructing from your left? Hostility dogging your trail, blocking you from the rear? And a vast and fearful unknown ahead of you?

If so, the answer for you is the same as the one for the Children of Israel: *through the waters*.

The prize is ahead, not back, or off to the sides. God is calling you forward, and He will be there to make the way.

"...Tell the Children of Israel to go forward."
Exodus 14:15

Dear Lord, I can identify with the Israelites. I have known my own bondage. Like them I have set out to follow Your lead, even when it has taken me into new directions. Like them I can see no option but straight ahead. So I am going Lord. And I am counting on Your being with me.

Open up the sea. Divide the waters. Make a path. Amen

June 2

A man was traveling on foot and came to a mountain pass. It was in winter and snow began to fall. He quickly became very cold.

After a great struggle he reached the top.

But alas, he found a stranger lying there unconscious and near death from the bitter cold. Forgetting his discomfort the man hurried to the suffering stranger and began to massage his body and limbs vigorously.

Before long the stranger showed signs of life. After much brisk exercising the stranger was restored to full consciousness. The amazing thing the man discovered was that by working hard to save the stranger's life he himself had become warm.

He eagerly lifted up the stranger, and together they descended the mountain to safety. Which of the two received the greater blessing? He who gave the help, or he who received it?

Are you a giver or a taker? Do you clutch every asset to yourself lest someone else might see it and need it more than you? Would you be willing to risk your own safety to help someone in worse condition than you?

Will you tell someone today about God's love and redemption in your life through Jesus Christ?

Dear Lord, I will be climbing a mountain today. I may meet some person in great distress from the cold, or some lost soul who doesn't know the warmth of Christ. Help me to keep warm by warming someone else. You have warmed me, sweet Jesus, with Your love, and by Your death on the cross, carrying my sins. Thank You. Amen

"...Freely you have received, freely give."
Matthew 10:8

See you at the top.

June 3

Don't you love to walk along the water's edge?

When we were stationed at the Presidio of San Francisco, Shirley and I often did a power walk near the Golden Gate Bridge. I remember that on one particular day the wind was fierce. Gusts must have reached thirty to thirty-five miles per hour.

Walking westward, toward the Pacific, the wind was blowing against us. I found myself leaning forward, pushing against its force.

At the turn around, the wind became a friendly force, assisting us, increasing our speed, actually nudging Shirley into a brief jog at one point to recover her balance.

When you write a daily devotion, you always have your antenna up for ideas. And I thought of the word for spirit, "ruach" (wind) in Hebrew. "In the beginning God created the heavens and the earth... and the Spirit (wind) of God was hovering over the face of the waters" (Genesis 1:1,2).

The New Testament word is *pneuma*. Think of pneumatic. The word pertains to air. Automobile tires are pneumatic.

"...When the Day of Pentecost had fully come... suddenly there came a sound from heaven, as of a rushing mighty wind (pneuma)...." (Acts 2:1, 2).

Hello God!

I wonder how many times, when I have struggled against my own "winds of adversity," that I was really walking against the direction God was blowing for my life. I do know, for sure, that when you walk with the wind it is easier.

If you find yourself walking against the wind you should ask yourself if you are moving in the direction that God intends for you to walk.

Lord, help me to walk the way Your wind blows. Amen

"...It shall come to pass...that the Spirit (wind) of The Lord will carry you...."
1 Kings 18:12

June 4

Did you hear Garth Brooks' hit song that thanked God for unanswered prayers? The song hooked my homiletical mind and a sermon is cooking that will probably be called, "Fruitful Detours."

Someone that I thought I loved dropped me for another guy, breaking our engagement, and leaving me with a broken heart. Then Shirley came into my life. Boy, did I ever luck out.

Whistler, the artist, earlier flunked out of West Point.

Victor Hugo, at forty-eight, was banished to the island of Guernsey by the French emperor. There he wrote several books, including *Les Miserables*. Later, he said that he should have been banished earlier.

A boy in Decatur, Illinois, was interested in photography and spent twenty-five cents for a book. He was mistakenly sent a book on ventriloquism. He became fascinated with the subject and created a wooden dummy that he named Charlie McCarthy. You know who he was, don't you?

The Apostle Paul was heading to Spain, to the rim of the known world, to plant the Christian message. Instead, he landed in a Roman prison, the worst place for an activist like Paul. A place where one could only think and write. He did. Many of the New Testament writings came from a jail cell.

In the Christian faith it is not "how I can bear this," but "how will God use it?"

The great example of this truth comes from Joseph. His brothers had sold him into slavery. However, he became a powerful person in the Egyptian government and literally saved them from starvation in the draught that followed. They met Joseph in fear but Joseph reassured them that he would protect them.

Joseph: **"You intended to harm me, but God intended it for good...to accomplish...the saving of many lives."**
Genesis 50:20 (NIV)

Lord, when I am so sure of what is best for me I am sometimes off by a mile. Help me to trust in You. Amen

Use your imagination!

How many times have you said that or had someone say it to you?

A great imagination is the preacher's most valuable gift. Remember the boring sermons you have heard? How unimaginative they were: point after point, doctrine after doctrine, subheading after subheading and a few stale jokes.

And do you remember how you wished the speaker would add something spicy, exciting? Like a story?

In his book, *All I Ever Needed To Know I Learned In Kindergarten*, Robert Fulghum wrote that imagination is stronger than knowledge, and myth is more potent than history.

Jesus is history's greatest storyteller.

He used birds and lilies to preach grand truths. He used mankind's most fundamental experience, birth, to illustrate heaven's grandest reality, the Kingdom of God.

I have known great commanders and great preachers, but none that weren't also great storytellers. Each was endowed with a great imagination and knew how to use it.

When is the last time you used your imagination?

How will Jesus look when you see him? What is heaven like?

In what form or shape will your departed loved ones be when you see them again in heaven?

What is the value of a soul? What is the shape of a spiritual treasure?

Do angels smile? Can God laugh?

Lord, you have given me a great imagination. Help me to use it to find ways to serve others and better please you. Amen.

"Eye has not seen, nor ear heard, nor have entered into the heart of man the things which God has prepared for those who love Him."

1 Corinthians 2:9

June 6

It happened on this date in 1944. Military planners referred to it as *Operation Overlord.* The book by Cornelius Ryan, and the movie that followed, was called, *The Longest Day.*

History's largest armada was putting American and Allied soldiers ashore at Normandy, on the Northeast coast of France. There were 1,200 fighting ships, 4,126 landing craft, 10,000 airplanes, 804 transport ships, hundreds of tanks, and 156,000 troops. Ten percent of the troops would become casualties

The Normandy coast was divided into five beaches: Utah, Omaha, Gold, Juno, and Sword. The first landings were by the United States 82nd and 101st Airborne divisions. General Dwight D. Eisenhower was the overall commander.

I stood on the windswept beaches of Normandy many years later and let my imagination run: to the thunderous noise from bombs, artillery, and assorted other arms; the roar of landing craft, tank, and aircraft engines; and the screams of the wounded. History has seldom, if ever, witnessed such fierce fighting. The beaches were red from blood.

We owe much to the patriots at Normandy. They truly were *The Great Generation.*

We can never repay them, but there is much that we can do.

We can honor their service and teach our children to do the same. We can learn the meaning of their sacrifice; that they ended the Nazi pogrom against the Jews, and other ethnic groups; and that they cleared the way for a new Europe.

And we can pray: for the WWII veterans and their families; for our men and women in the military today; for our national leaders, that they be good and honest people, and for America, that she will always remain strong and resolute against oppression.

"Show us Your mercy, O Lord, and grant us Your salvation." Psalm 85:7

Let us pray.

June 7

An open-air preacher was telling the story of redemption when a mouthy youth called out, "You tell us about the burden of sin. I feel none." Then he added, "How much does sin weigh? Eighty pounds? Ten pounds?"

The preacher answered, "Tell me, if I laid a four hundred pound weight on the chest of a dead man, would he feel it?"

"No, because he is dead," answered the youth.

The preacher responded, "And the man who feels no load of sin is dead spiritually."

We don't hear much of that kind of preaching anymore. But the Bible still speaks of those who are "*Dead* in trespasses and sins." (Ephesians 2:1)

When I was young and worked on the farm, my hands became very callused. Once, as an experiment, I stuck a knife blade into a callus far enough that it swung free but didn't fall to the ground. And it did not draw blood.

Hearts can become hardened, too

Our spirits can be like the sponge that my wife, Shirley, keeps at the sink. With disuse, the sponge dries and hardens. Likewise, when our spirits become insensitive or resistant to the tug of God's will for our lives, they need the watering of His Spirit.

Is your spirit tender? Is your will pliable? Are you able to change an opinion or a direction when you hear God's word?

Lord, keep us warm, moist, responsive, and tenderhearted. Alive! Don't let the scratches, tears, abrasions, and blows of daily living harden us to Your voice. Amen

"...Reckon yourselves to be dead indeed to sin, but *alive to God* in Christ Jesus our Lord."
Romans 6:11

June 8

Was he ever good!

When he was just a kid he learned the value of a buck. When other kids rushed to the candy store to spend every penny they had he always kept some back.

When he was in the first grade his dad started him on an allowance and paid him ten percent a month for all that he saved. He caught on so fast that his dad discontinued that deal quickly.

In high school he got a job at the shoe store earning six percent on all sales. He quickly learned to push polish and matching handbags to up his sales. All of the time he was saving a good portion of his earnings.

In college he didn't go out for many of the campus activities. He now had a job as a night watchman on weekends and was janitor of his church. His combined earnings now equaled those of many men who had families to support.

Soon after graduation he landed a well paying job as a regional sales representative, making a good salary and a percentage of the sales of those he supervised.

He began to invest in the stock market at what proved to be the beginning of a long bull market. He bought real estate in the right places and tripled his investment. In a few years he was rich beyond all reason.

But he was troubled in spirit. It was not easy finding places to put all that money. And he was afraid he would loose it somehow.

He worried about what he would do with all of his money. Maybe cash in a few millions stocks and buy his own bank. Then he could tell his soul to take it easy, to eat, drink, and have fun.

"Surely he will have no respite from his craving; he cannot save himself by his treasure."
Job 20:20 NIV

June 9

You can now purchase every word of poetry published in England from Anglo-Saxon times (roughly the sixth century) until the present, on computer disks. The complete works of nearly 1400 poets and almost 5000 volumes is stored on disks that a person can hold in one hand.

The Lord's Prayer has 56 words; Lincoln's Gettysburg Address has 266 words; the Ten Commandments use 297 words; and the Declaration of Independence has 3,000 words. A U.S. Government document setting the price of cabbage had 26,911 words.

In Old Testament times folks believed that words had movement, and power. Think of movement. They thought of words as entities set in motion. Once set in motion they could never be recalled. Imagine an arrow flung from its bow. Thus the writers caution against every idle word.

Words are reality. If you don't believe it explain how, upon hearing words (perhaps a message of great loss), a person suffers an immediate heart attack.

Jesus comes to us as the *Word* of God. He is not idle chatter. He is the movement, the message, and the power of God.

Be careful with words. We seem to think that they don't matter. But they do. Spoken in anger or haste, words can injure a loving spouse, trusting child, or faithful friend. Conversely, a kind word can heal, nourish, and inspire.

Sticks and stones can hurt your bones, and your words can kill.

"A word fitly spoken is like apples of gold in settings of silver."
Proverbs 25:11

Lord, I can toss words around as though they were no more than fluffs of cotton. I can be very flippant. Teach me to be more careful when I speak. Amen

June 10

A chicken and a pig were walking down the road discussing church support. When they passed a restaurant advertising Ham and Eggs the chicken suggested that they step inside and provide some worthy person a meal.

"No thanks," said the pig. "For you it would be just a contribution; for me, it would mean total commitment."

I know Christians, good people, who live well, earn good money, wear fine clothes, live in a grand home, send their kids to the best schools, and drive two expensive automobiles. They go to church regularly and contribute their time and money.

I also know Christians, good people, who left the United States and live in primitive societies as missionaries. They burn out, get strange diseases, watch their children struggle with a foreign culture, and come home old and sick. Their average income is pitifully low. They will retire on Social Security, and little more monetarily.

Isn't the disparity between those two examples too much?

If God doesn't call me to a mission field, but permits me to live in the comfort that America affords, don't I owe a greater debt? Now understand, I am not talking about good works to earn salvation. To be fair to Ron, David, Bobby, and Roland, and their families, missionary friends, shouldn't I be doing more than just perfunctory giving in support of the church's mission? If we are permitted to make a *contribution* instead of a *commitment*, to stay with the illustration above, shouldn't it require a more painful stewardship on our part?

Dear Lord, I am humbled by how others have given so much more than I have. I don't mean just money. Make me truly grateful, and cause me to be more generous in my stewardship. More than generous, Lord. Let it hurt a little. Amen

"Give, and it will be given to you...for with the same measure that you use, it will be measured back to you."
Luke 6:38

June 11

The preacher said, "There's a difference in making a living and making a life."

He was referring to the fifth chapter of Ecclesiastes.

Upon revisiting the chapter I found it rich in commentary about possessions and poverty.

Having experienced being poor in my early life and now possessing cars, cash, houses, and equity I am troubled by my need for things. Listen carefully to the wise man in Ecclesiastes 5:10-13:

He who loves silver will not be satisfied with silver; Nor he who loves abundance, with increase..." Verse 10

"When goods increase they increase who eat them..." Verse 11

"The sleep of a laboring man is sweet, whether he eats little or much; but the abundance of the rich will not permit him to sleep." Verse 12

There is a severe evil which I have seen under the sun: riches kept for their owner to his hurt." Verse 13

I am certainly not rich enough to stay awake nights worrying about possessions. Yet, in my life I have striven to obtain things, as though my future safety depended on how much I could amass.

Such values embarrass me as a follower of Jesus. Birds had nests and foxes had holes but He had no place to lay His head. And He calls me to follow Him. Help!

Heavenly Father, even though I am retired now, I am still fretting over the future, worrying about making more money. Help me, dear Lord, to learn to trust more in You, and not in my own abilities. Amen

"...What profit has he who has labored for the wind?"
Ecclesiastes 5:16

June 12

I am a landlubber, and had no business acting like a ship's captain.

I had taken a group from the chapel out into the Pacific aboard the sixty five-foot sailing ship, the Chief Aptakisic. She was a worthy vessel, having sailed all of the way to New York City in 1976 for the gathering of tall ships.

When we reentered the Panama Canal I learned too late that I had not anticipated a very key element of nature. I had overlooked the tide!

On your starboard side as you enter the canal, high up on Ancon Hill, is a beacon. Sailors sight on the blinking light as they approach the harbor and use it as a navigational aid. I noticed that I was not moving. Our small diesel engine was still running, going wide open, in fact. But the flushing effect of the Miraflores Locks and the push of the outgoing tide had stopped our progress.

As long as the engine didn't fail we could sit there, dead still, in the canal.

But what if the engine failed? I would lose all power to navigate. We could crash into another ship. Or be washed out to sea.

The tide changes about every six hours. I determined that the next change was about an hour away. So when my mate asked what we were going to do, I said, "Steady as she goes, Mate. The tide will change in about an hour and we will begin to move." It did. And we did.

You may feel that you have gone as far as you can. That you are sitting dead in the water even though your engine is going wide open. Strong currents buffet you. A spouse, child, parent, or friend continues a destructive path. Things take time. Kids and adults can grow.

When you are doing right and things are going wrong don't give up. The tide always changes.

So don't give up. Ever. *The tide always changes.*

"Those who sow in tears will reap with songs of joy."
Psalm 126:5

June 13

Symbols. We all make use of them. And not just those of us who are in the military. Symbols communicate.

One can look at a soldier's dress uniform and know if she is an officer, her rank, if she were in combat, her current unit of assignment, her branch, if she jumps out of airplanes, or flies them, and her military service. Military ribbons give a general account of where one has been and how he has performed.

One's clothing and grooming also give out messages. In this morning's service Shirley and I sat behind newlyweds, 7 days married. Both of them had ponytails. Some pastors wear the off white alb when conducting services. Some wear the black robe. Some wear the robe with stripes on the sleeves to indicate graduate degrees.

We are surrounded by symbols: earrings, gold chains, yellow ribbons, Christmas lights, automobiles, hair, and clothing, to name just a few.

Tomorrow is Flag Day, the day that we honor our Nation's most visible symbol. The flag draped casket speaks of the nation's embrace of the fallen warrior. On television I saw a father hug the folded flag from his son's casket, and pat it, like he was caressing the boy himself.

It's okay to love America, and to honor her flag. That flag is recognized the world over as a symbol of freedom, justice, and opportunity. I will fly mine proudly.

But today's devotion is not just about flags. It is about symbols.

There is one symbol that is most important to me. I wore it on my uniform and I wear it in the lapel of my suit. It graces my ecclesiastical vestments. It hangs on the walls of my home. The *cross!* The cross reminds me that God loved me to a degree that I cannot yet comprehend.

"...God forbid that I should glory except in the cross of our Lord Jesus Christ...."
Galatians 6:14

Thank you, Lord, for enduring the cross for me. Amen

June 14

Happy Flag Day.

Did you know that the basic flag of the United States is one of the world's oldest national flags? Only the flags of Austria, Denmark, Great Britain, the Netherlands, Sweden, and Switzerland are older.

The first official flag of the United States was created by an act of congress on June 14, 1777. It consisted of 13 alternate red and white stripes in a field of blue, representing the 13 colonies that declared their independence in 1776. It has grown and changed over the years to reflect the addition of new states.

As a soldier of over 30 years I have seen "Old Glory" waving in over 35 countries. I have seen it in jungle command posts, on soldiers' uniforms, draped over coffins, and in our Nation's capital. I love our Country and respect the flag, and cannot understand why some would desecrate it.

In fairness we must note that there are many good people who would never desecrate the flag but are never the less uncomfortable with undue reverence being given it. As though it were a form of idolatry.

God has richly blessed America.

Our wealth has allowed us to send hundreds of thousands of missionaries to every corner of the globe. And to get the Scriptures translated into all major languages and dialects. That spiritual ministry has brought freedom to millions. So how can we honor the flag, our national symbol, in a way acceptable to all Christians?

When I fly the flag today I will fly it as a prayer. A prayer of thanksgiving for God's rich blessings on our nation. And a prayer of entreaty that God will help our people to be as good as His blessings have been generous. Amen

"...His banner (flag) over me was love."
Song of Solomon 2:4

God, bless America. Amen

June 15

A soldier came to me in an overseas assignment and said, "Okay chaplain, I have been downtown and gotten my dose of VD. So maybe the guys will leave me alone now and stop harassing me about coming to chapel. Can you help me somehow?"

In the twisted logic of the men in his unit he wasn't a man until he had gotten his "case." And he was immature enough to let himself be pressured. Although I suspect that his own lust may have been a major part of his decision to go down to the "Village."

Peer pressure! Can it ever have been worse than now? And can it get even worse? Alcohol? Drugs? Sex? Vulgarity? Disrespect? Lawlessness? Violence?

My daughter is now a mature adult, good mother, and careful manager of resources. Yet she complained, while in high school, when my wife bought clothes for her that were on sale. It didn't matter that the clothes may have been from a fashionable company. Kids were boasting about how much their clothes cost. She was afraid that her friends might think her cheap, even though her clothing was the same brand as theirs.

Someone asked the Queen of Sweden why she was so strict on her daughter. "She is being trained for the throne," The Queen answered.

Picture a fly looking for a place to alight. He sees a bunch of other flies dancing around on a "landing strip" and thinks that it must be okay since everyone is doing it. He makes a perfect four-point (How many legs does a fly have?) landing. On flypaper.

"...Has not God made foolish the wisdom of the world?"
1 Corinthians 1:20

Lord, help me to be different when peer pressure would force me to go in a wrong direction or participate in evil. Amen

June 16

A God for all occasions!

God revealed Himself by seven different names in the Old Testament. Each name reveals a different aspect of Him as it pertains to His relationship with His people. It is a rich study, too full for a brief devotion, but with great potential for reading in depth. The names of God that follow are transliterated from Hebrew into the English text listed.

Do you need food, clothing, or other provisions? Call on Jehovah-Jireh, the God who provides, Genesis 22:13,14.

Sick? Jehovah-Rapha is the God who heals. Exodus 15:26.

Feel defeated? Call on Jehovah-Nissi, the God who is victorious, Exodus 17:8ff.

Prone to stray? Jehovah-Raah is the God who shepherds, Psalms 23:1.

Troubled? Call on Jehovah-Shalom, the God of Peace, Judges 6:23,24.

Torn by guilt? Sinfulness? Pray to Jehovah-Tsidkenu, the God of righteousness, Jeremiah 23:6.

Lonely? Jehovah-Shammah is the God who is there, Ezekiel 48:35.

Oh great Jehovah, You have revealed Yourself to us as the truly all sufficient God. We worship You, we praise Your holy name.

Lord, our needs are as numerous as the ways You have revealed Your power and grace. Bless us, Oh Lord. Bless us and make us a blessing. Amen

"...When...they say to me, what is His name? What shall I say to them? And God said to Moses say...I AM has sent me to you."
Exodus 3:13,14

June 17

While driving around San Francisco I noticed a bumper sticker on the car ahead of me that read, "Question Authority." The driver didn't sport an orange Mohawk or drive an expensive sports car. Rather he was a non-descript 30-35 year old driving a beat-up Japanese import.

Saint Paul urged that "prayers... be offered to God... for kings and all others who are in authority, that we may live a quiet and peaceful life with all reverence toward God and with proper conduct (1 Timothy 2:1,2).

In Romans 13 he also urged the church to "obey state authorities, because no authority exists without God's permission, and the existing authorities have been put there by God" (Verse 1).

Saint Paul's guidance troubles me almost as much as the bumper sticker. Progress in civil rights has always come when people question a corrupt status quo and the authority that allowed the evil to become entrenched.

So what does it mean? The meaning of Paul's guidance to me is that I should pray for and be obedient to, *proper* authority. I don't believe that Paul, himself, would have prayed for the success of Hitler. So let us pray for those in authority that they will govern justly and with compassion. And that the citizenry will be respectful of government when it is just.

Oh Lord, I pray today for all people who have authority over me. May they exercise that authority justly and with compassion. And help me to be a good citizen. Amen.

The wise man said,

"When the righteous are in authority the people rejoice; but when a wicked man rules, the people groan."
Proverbs 29:2

A Sunday near this date will be designated Fathers' Day. I hope that it will be a blessed day for you.

As a chaplain I always thought of myself as the bringer of good news. But that didn't keep commanders from asking me to deliver death messages.

So, early in my career as a Chaplain, when a commander called and asked me to come to his company and tell a young soldier that his father had died I went right over. The soldier was in the commander's office when I arrived.

"Son," I said, "I have bad news for you. I regret to tell you that your father died."

"That's not bad news," he replied.

I was taken back by his answer, and he obviously saw the surprise on my face.

"I'm not trying to be a wise guy, Chaplain," he continued, "But that man was so mean to me, my mother, and my brothers and sisters that I doubt that any in my family considers his death bad news."

You can see how easy it is for us to get into trouble when we talk about the fatherhood of God. That soldier gave me a valuable lesson early in my chaplaincy.

Now when I refer to God as father I never say that God loves you like a father. I always say that He loves you like a father ought to love his children. That He is the kind of father that a good father ought to be.

Imagine the confusion in a young child's mind when she is told that she should love the heavenly Father while she is being sexually abused nightly by her earthly father. God is not just father, He is the Good Father.

"...God...our Father...has loved us...."
2 Thessalonians 2:16

Dear Lord, I thank you for my father, Henry Edward Hunt, who is now in Heaven. He was a good father who loved his children. Help me to be like him. Amen

June 19

Our brigade was in a field training exercise in Korea, near the tiny village of Il San. The Harry Holt Orphanage was located there.

Harry, a successful Oregon businessman, had been moved by the plight of the orphans of Korean and American parents and had created a very successful adoption service. By the time I arrived in Korea, Harry had died and his daughter Molly was carrying on his work.

I decided to visit the orphanage.

As our jeep approached the facility the children were quick to notice our arrival. They crowded, hundreds of them, along the road, against the balcony, and around the jeep.

As I toured the facility I became aware that all of the kids were yelling the same thing to me. Now I had received forty hours of conversational Korean, but I didn't understand what they were shouting. So I asked Molly. "Oh, Chaplain Hunt, they are just saying 'pick me up'," Molly answered. "Well," I responded, "I can handle that. My youngest son was only six months old when I left the States. I have been wanting to pick up a kid."

I threw off my field gear and began to pick up kids. I tossed them into the air, caught them, and then put them down. They squealed with delight. Everyone had to have a turn.

After 40 or 50 kids, I realized that I wasn't going to be physically able to pick up all 500 of the orphans, many of whom were 5-6 years old. Nor would I have had the time. Molly saw the fix I was in and eased me out a side door.

The children at Il San were a sermon to me of what the Lord does. He lifts us up! He lifted ME up.

I ask you, what have you done this week to lift someone up? What do you plan to do today to lift someone up? That is the Christian's task. Start lifting. Amen

"I will extol You, O Lord, for You have lifted me up...."

Psalms 30:2

June 20

I already knew that it wasn't music. Then it was revealed
that a certain musical group had not sung a word of their
award-winning album. Others had dubbed the songs for them.
The industry was embarrassed. The group was shunned. I
gloated!

That sorry trick fueled my distrust, and distaste, for much
of what is going on in the music industry. The public buys
and listens to millions of records that are filled with vulgarity,
advocate violence, and denigrate women.

Such trash mirrors society then significantly contributes
to establishing society's norms. It is a sad, tragic cycle.

Seventy five percent of high school students admit to
cheating. Fifty percent of college students admit to cheating.
Thirty percent of resumes contain deliberate misrepresentations
of background and credentials.

How is a Christian to act in a society where lying and
cheating is condoned? How is one to withstand the pressure to
conform?

Jesus requires a severe honesty of His followers, "'...Let
your 'Yes' be 'Yes,' and your 'No,' ' No.'..." (Matthew 5:37).

That is indeed a tough standard for living in a world of
situational ethics.

As Christians, we must challenge as dangerous, both
practically and spiritually; attitudes that seek to justify
dishonesty on any grounds, whether it is artistic, academic,
occupational, or professional.

And we must guard our own hearts and minds, to insure
that we don't adapt our own values to society's standards.

**"As obedient children, do not conform to the evil
desires you had when you lived in ignorance."**
1 Peter 1:14

Lord, keep me from the values of a decadent society.
Amen

June 21

For years I have kept a print of the painting of Christ Knocking at the Door hanging over my desk. It helps to keep my attention centered.

It also gives me an opening to discuss my personal faith when counseling. People bring a variety of problems to military chaplains, some of which aren't strictly spiritual. Honesty requires me to deal with the problems that they bring. Afterward I usually try to turn the conversation toward Christ.

A young couple came asking me to pressure the housing section into moving them up the list ahead of others. I wasn't convinced that they deserved special treatment and told them so. They were angry, and disappointed in me.

I told the couple that sometimes our lives get out of sort, relationships suffer, and resentment and bitterness fills our hearts, because we are not in right relationship with God.

I pointed out that when we are in right relationship with Him other things tend to fall into place.

I pointed to the portrait and commented on Christ's being outside the house, and the doorknob being on the inside, meaning that Christ only enters our lives when we open the door and invite Him in. I told them that I was sorry that I couldn't give them what they asked of me but that I hoped that they would remember Christ knocking at the door of their hearts.

About six months later I got a call at midnight from the young man asking if his wife and he could see me.

I said sure, tomorrow. He said tonight. "We couldn't get the picture out of our minds," he said. "We realize that we need to ask Christ into our hearts and home." "Come on over," I said.

"Behold, I stand at the door, and knock. If anyone hears My voice, and opens the door, I will come in to him, and will dine with him, and he with Me"
Revelation 3:20

June 22

At the little country church my family attended when I was a kid we practiced "foot washing" as a part of the Communion Service. The idea derives from John 13 and remains part of the liturgy of some denominations.

Our pastor gave great emphasis to searching our hearts and confessing our sins as we prepared for the foot washing and as a prerequisite for receiving the Lord's Supper.

He was big on getting us to seek out people that we had wronged and confessing to them personally. As he continued on the subject I began to think back for something I had done or said and sure enough I found something.

I had said some mean things about one of the elders of the church. It was nothing really bad, like hate or murder. I had gossiped that, for a church leader, he wasn't very "Christian" to his son, my buddy.

Well, guess who I was paired with for the foot washing! My heart sank. I was trapped, and knew that I would have to confess before proceeding. The brother was very generous. "It's all right, brother Hunt," he said. "I know that you meant no harm." I felt clean inside and was nourished by the Sacrament that followed.

Jesus washed His disciple's feet at Passover that night in the Upper Room.

In the New Testament, foot washing was a hospitality rite that servants did automatically for visitors in the home. Since the Passover was conducted in an upper room, it was no one's home.

No one volunteered to do the servant's chore so Jesus did it Himself. "If I, your lord and teacher, have washed your feet, you also ought to wash one another's feet," Jesus said.

The most impressive Christians that I have known have been foot washers. They saw their role as serving others, not being lord and master over them.

"If anyone desires to be first, he shall be last of all and servant of all."
Mark 9:35

Have you ever been lost? Do you ever feel like the guide who was hired to take some hunters into the backwoods of Northern Maine?

After several days they were hopelessly lost, and began to question the competence of the guide. "You said you were the best guide in Maine," they chided. "I am," he said, "but I think we are in Canada now."

In our prayers most of us are quick and to the point. "Lord, do this and this; Lord, give me that and that; Lord, don't let that those bad things happen."

Divinity students call that laundry list praying: shallow, and self-centered. It's not that we ought not to pray for specific things. But if that is all our praying consists of we are falling way short in the praying department.

Great praying sometimes transcends human language and effort. "...The Spirit also helps in our weaknesses. For we do not know what we should pray for as we ought, but the Spirit Himself makes intercession for us with groanings which cannot be uttered." (Romans 8:26, 27).

Will you join me now in a different style of praying? Let us pause, lean back for a few minutes, kick our task oriented minds into neutral, take a deep breath, exhale slowly, and then pray this prayer (after a minute or two of quietness):

Dear Lord, I am not asking for anything specific this morning. I don't know what to even pray for, except that your will be done in my life. Help me to be and do what You want. I praise your name, Lord. Amen.

"Praying always...in the Spirit...with all perseverance...for all the saints."
Ephesians 6:18

June 24

You have to clear an adding machine for it to work right.

And for God's Spirit to work freely in you your spirit needs to be clear and clean. It's like the adding machine.

If you leave something in it from an earlier transaction you will get a wrong answer every time. You see why the Scriptures give such emphasis to the daily Christian walk.

During World War II pilots in the huge bombers, having so far to fly over enemy territory, and with every gallon of fuel so precious, removed the paint from their planes' exteriors. Some of the large planes had as much as sixty-four pounds of paint on them. By removing the paint they extended their range.

Which leads me to tote sack Christians?

A tote sack Christian is one who carries a sack of grievances every where she goes. Every wrong that has ever been done to her is carried in the sack. And don't even try to get her to empty the bag.

The hurts are part of his spiritual persona. He seems to treasure them. Tragically they cloud his mind so that he can't see clearly and honestly the other person's motives. Thus he can assign motives to a perceived adversary and react in kind.

The hurts clutter his soul and hinder the movement of the Holy Spirit in his life. They weigh him down. Be sure that you understand: what he or she is carrying in that bag is not cute. It is SIN.

"...Let us cast off the works of darkness...."
Romans 13:12

Lord, help me to empty my tote sack. Thank you.
Amen

June 25

A Montana herdsman, in a very remote area, needed to tune his violin.

But he didn't have a tuning fork. So he wrote to the radio station whose signal reached him and asked for help. At an agreed upon time the station broadcast the E note for a full minute from their studio piano.

Out there in the hills the herdsman tuned the 1st or E string as the radio broadcast the signal. Then all he had to do was tune the A string down a fourth, the D string down a fourth, and the G string down a fourth.

As a former disc jockey at station WHPB in Belton, South Carolina, I can identify with that story. We really worked hard to accommodate the needs of the community.

It is the Holy Scriptures that tell you if you are out of tune. Prayer is how you tune your spiritual life. In prayer you dial the heavenly frequency and hear the divine tone.

Violin strings tend to stretch and go flat over time. They need constant tuning. So does your spirit. No musician performs until he has tuned his instrument. Nor can you give an effective witness if you are out of tune.

Jesus taught us to pray for daily bread. Daily blessings accompany daily prayer. It doesn't work to pray annually for daily blessings. Nor monthly. Nor even weekly.

It is through daily prayer that you stay in constant tune. Amen.

"Then He spoke a parable to them, that men always ought to pray and not lose heart."

Luke 18:1

Let us pray.

June 26

He was a popular guy.

His friends were many. He was invited to every party. All of the girls were pretty. Everybody thought him clever. He was on a roll. Until his money ran out.

You can get along over there, in an alien lifestyle, if you have lots of money. You can buy your way, even some love. But you are in deep trouble if you appear and sound strange and are broke. And if you belong to a religious group that requires strict adherence to religious taboos and requirements you are always under surveillance.

He had persuaded his father to divide the estate and give him his inheritance. So the prodigal son, with pockets full of money, left home. Fun, travel, and adventure. Big time.

When he ran out of money he sought work. But who in that gentile world was going to hire a Jew! Finally he found a job, feeding pigs. Swine were unclean in Jewish law. The ultimate humiliation.

With hunger gnawing a hole in his belly, eating the husks from the hog food, he came to himself. He decided to return to his father, to throw himself on his father's mercy. He was received joyously.

There is a great lesson here. You are never completely right until you are right with God. You may have lots of money, fame, friends, and things. But if you are away from the Heavenly Father you need to come to yourself.

Do you recognize a bit of the prodigal in yourself this morning? If so, do what the Prodigal Son did:

"...When *he came to himself* he said...'I will arise and go to my father.' "
Luke 15:17,18

Folks, until you are *right* with God you are never really *at* yourself.

June 27

The whole world knew and revered Mother Teresa. And properly so. But have you ever heard of Mark and Huldah Buntain? Their work is also in Calcutta.

When they arrived there in 1954 they saw a city where poverty, hunger, and disease had laid cruel claim to millions of people. They dreamed of touching those lives with the love of Christ. Within a few years their congregation grew into a great ministry that reached thousands.

When Mark's heart stopped beating on June 4, 1989 he left a junior school for over 2,000 students, a high school for 2,500 seniors, a school of nursing, a 120 bed hospital, a Bible school to train pastors, a boys' home, a correspondence institute, radio ministries, and a printing plant.

After Mark's death Huldah continued and even extended the ministry. She opened feeding stations in garbage dumps, and added a daily noon meal for several thousand homeless.

I never met the Buntains, although I feel that I have known them for years. They were good friends of missionaries that are good friends of our family.

Someone once said that there is no limit to the good a person can do if he or she doesn't care who gets the credit.

It seems that God lifted Mother Teresa up before the world as an inspiring symbol of the power for good that one life can have. He has also greatly blessed the Buntains' ministry, but their work never captured the attention of the world.

That God selects some for highly visible ministry does not mean that others, who are just as selfless and hard working, are demeaned. Remember that it is God who will ultimately reward humble service, not the media.

"There will be...glory, honor, and peace, for everyone who does good...for God does not show favoritism."
Romans 2:9-11

June 28

When I boarded a plane for a flight from Atlanta to Seattle I discovered that someone was in my seat.

"Ma'am, are you in the right seat? According to my boarding pass you are sitting in mine," I said, tentatively.

"I'm not getting out of this seat. This is my seat. I called the airline before I left my home, and this is my seat," she established. "Very well, ma'am," I conceded.

The flight attendant got the same response from the lady then put me in first class. What a treat for a flight of several hours. If I had persisted I might have won a right but lost a blessing.

Serendipity: an unexpected or unintended benefit; something good that comes to you while you are working something that may be completely different.

To me, the blessings of Christianity are serendipitous. Whatever my motives were as a young person for accepting Christ I serve Him now because I have learned to love Him. The blessings of believing are inner peace, an assurance of forgiveness, confidence in prayer. Heaven. The blessings are too many to list.

In poor areas of the world Christian converts are sometimes ridiculed as rice Christians by their detractors. It is really a back handed compliment, for the converts are always better. They may be poor in physical comforts but they are rich in spiritual blessings.

As a Christian I am not better than others, but I am better off than anyone who is without Christ. And it is all because of God's grace.

"...My God shall supply all your need according to His riches in glory by Christ Jesus."
Philippians 4:19

Lord, how many times have I fought for what I thought was best for me when all along You knew that something else was better for me. Don't let me have my way, Lord. Help me to know Your will and let You have Your way. Amen

He lived beside the railroad. The railroad crossing was not properly guarded and illuminated. His job was to stand at the crossing and wave a lantern to warn approaching vehicles.

He had fallen asleep.

When he heard the train's whistle he raced to the crossing and frantically waved the lantern.

A car, filled with young people, did not stop. The train crushed it and all of the young people were killed.

There was a hearing. He was questioned closely by the judge. "Are you sure you were there in time? And that you waved the lantern?" the Judge asked.

"Yes your honor," the man replied, "I am sure."

Later, at home, when he recounted the experience to his wife, he was still shaking. "What's wrong honey? You were at the crossing. The judge believed your statement that you were there, and that you waved the lantern to warn the young people. Why are you still so upset?"

"I was afraid that the judge would ask me if the lantern was lit," he answered.

Jesus, who said that He was the light of the world, later said, "Now you are the light of the world."

I ask you to begin this day by checking to see if your wicks are trimmed, if your fuel is adequate, and if your lantern is lit.

Dear Lord, it's such a dark world. Help me to shine. Don't let me fall asleep by the tracks. Amen

"...If...the light that is in you is darkness, how great is that darkness."
Matthew 6:23

June 30

Thomas Edison defined genius as "1% inspiration and 99% perspiration." His secret for discovery was to seek.

Edison was an intensely curious child, always asking questions. How does a hen hatch chickens? How does a bird fly? Why does water put out fire? When answers were not forthcoming he tried experimentation. Once he sat on some eggs.

Another time he persuaded a kid to take a triple dose of seidlitz powders in an effort to see if the kid could generate enough gas to fly.

By his death in 1931, Edison had over 1,300 patents that covered just about every possible field.

Persistence, not brilliance, is also the key to spiritual growth. If you want a loftier view of the scene you can climb a tree. Sitting on an acorn won't work.

Spiritual growth comes about through effort. The prophet Isaiah lists several key ingredients (Isaiah 55:6,7)):

(1) Seek the Lord while He may be found,
(2) Call upon Him while He is near,
(3) Let the wicked forsake his way, and the unrighteous man his thoughts,
(4) Let him return to the Lord.

Oh Lord, don't let me be satisfied with a shallow, peripheral relationship with You. Inspire me to perspire, until I know You better and please You More. Amen

"Ask, and it will be given you; seek, and you will find; knock, and it will be opened to you."
Matthew 7:7

July 1

A former prostitute, and cocaine addict, became infected with AIDS. As her illness grew worse she recalled a childhood experience of seeing people singing joyously in church. She asked for a pastor to visit, and was converted. She died two weeks later.

On the counselor's last visit to her bedside she was unable to speak. She handed him a note and gently dismissed him with her eyes.

"Please tell everyone that Jesus loves people like me," the note read. "Tell them that I became a Christian and went to heaven to be with Jesus."

Christians have to decide how they will respond to people with AIDS.

Many Christians strongly deplore, and believe that the Scriptures condemn, the behavior that most often results in infection. If people persist in behavior that results in AIDS how far must Christians go to love (minister to) them?

Then there are the "innocents." Such as people who are infected through blood transfusions, and children who get the disease from a parent.

The leprosy in Jesus' time is an imperfect parallel to AIDS today.

Lepers did not get the disease through sexual improprieties and drug abuse. However, it is just about the best example one can find. Lepers were outcasts. It was a capital offense for a Jew to touch a leper. Yet Jesus did.

As this calamitous plague spreads, it will be impossible for us to remain uninvolved as individuals. And the church will have to face the issue honestly and provide ministry to AIDS patients.

"...Jesus answered and said to them, 'Go tell John the things you have seen and heard...the lepers are cleansed...the poor have the gospel preached to them.' "
Luke 7:22

July 2

While his dad was stationed in the Sinai, my first grandson and my daughter spent a few weeks with Shirley and me in the Presidio of San Francisco.

He taught me a lot. Take trust, for instance.

He was still a little top heavy, and reached out for a strong finger from Poppa when stepping up on a curb. When Nanna had one hand and Poppa the other he climbed stairs fearlessly, and with abandon. Sometimes his feet would get so far ahead that his body would be almost horizontal.

He was eager to learn. For instance, he learned the difference in a rock and a clod of dirt. Poppa could crush the clod, but not the rock.

Being closer to the ground He saw beauty that I missed. He was always bending down to pick those little yellow blossoms that grew in our yard. I had viewed them as weeds, pests.

Imagination too.

He got a kick out of straddling a tree fork across the street, and riding horsy. While whee-ing in the swing he was really driving his car, and his lips provided the motor noise.

I really missed him when he left. But every time I remember him I will do it with a prayer and a smile. How long since you have been instructed by a child?

Oh Lord, help me to be more like Zachary Ian was, and less like a grumpy old adult. Make me quicker to see the beauty in Your creation, slower to think ill of any of Your children, and more eager to learn. Amen

"...Unless you are converted and become as little children, you will by no means enter the kingdom of heaven."
Matthew 18:3

July 3

Just after the end of Desert Storm I was awaiting my flight at the Butte, Montana Airport. There also, was a group of Desert Storm mothers. They were awaiting a returning Marine, the son of one of them.

I identified myself as an Army chaplain, was given an American flag, and joined the demonstration. No gender discrimination there.

The mother, whose son was really on the bus, didn't know that it was her son that was coming home. To keep it a surprise they had told her that another mother's son was returning.

The passengers arrived, two hours late, on a bus from Bozeman, Montana. We had become snowed in. So as to not miss any of the excitement of that homecoming, I positioned myself to observe the Marine's mother.

It was predictable: screams, hugs, and tears. All of the mothers hugged the young man. I wanted to hug him too, but was afraid that it would be misunderstood. He reminded me of my own son.

I wasn't able to meet my son's ship in Charleston when it returned from service in Desert Storm. The episode in Butte made up for it.

Christians know that there will be a great homecoming in the sky. The Scriptures teach that we will be gathered from the east, west, north, and south. We will be gathered together by Jesus and ushered into Heaven.

Families will be reunited. The crippled will walk. The deaf will hear. The blind will see. All things will be made new. The joy so abundant at the Butte, Montana, airport will pale in comparison.

"We...shall be caught up together with them in the clouds to meet the Lord in the air. And thus we shall always be with the Lord."
1 Thessalonians 4:17

Tomorrow is Independence Day. What are your plans?

July 4

Happy Independence Day!

We hold these truths to be self-evident: that all men are created equal, that they are endowed by their creator with certain unalienable rights, that among these are life, liberty, and the pursuit of happiness.

Those incendiary words from the Declaration of Independence were indeed radical in their time. The document concluded with a declaration of war against England.

Fifty-six men from the 13 Colonies signed the document. They pledged their lives, honor, and fortunes to the new country. And some of the signatories did lose their lives and fortunes for the independence that they so nobly declared had to be won on the battlefields. Names like Lexington, Concord, Bunker Hill, and Valley Forge come to mind.

The Declaration includes lofty concepts indeed:
Equality.
Unalienable rights granted by the Creator.
Life, liberty, and the pursuit of happiness.

On this Independence Day I hope that you will reflect on the meaning of freedom and equality. And I hope that you will recognize just how central the Founding Fathers understood God's role to be as the author of these rights.

"Blessed is the nation whose God is the Lord...."
Psalm 33:12

Lord God, You have richly blessed America. I pray that You will bless Americans. Help us to be charitable to our fellow citizens and generous to those less fortunate. Bless us with good and honest leaders. Make us a Nation that others will see and emulate, not for our riches, but for our goodness. Amen

July 5

When I was young I didn't know any people who did bad things.

I had an uncle who was alleged to have killed someone but I don't remember ever meeting him. My dad boasted of having hauled "shine" to the lumberjacks in the backwaters of Lake County, Florida, when he was a kid. But that ended when he was ten.

During my high school days I occasionally ran around a bit with the guys, but when they decided to steal watermelons I opted out. I had this fear that one day I would have to confess to the farmer and pay for the melons. It would have happened as sure as the world. Our pastor was big on making recompense. One of his favorite words.

By the time my kids were at the getting-into-trouble age the world was different. There was profanity on the airwaves, sex selling household products, and pornography at the newsstands. And drugs!

My friends and I would have boasted of smoking a cigarette out behind the barn, or sharing sips of a warm beer someone had hidden in his coat pocket. But now kids were being shown that drugs are cool and that sex is the expected recreation for teens and pre-teens.

Dear Lord, I pray for parents of teens and pre-teens. It is much harder today, Lord, to teach young people to do right. There is so much to compete with honesty, family, goodness, faith, and work. Thank for you for them, Lord. I wouldn't take anything for them, but You have to help. Amen

"Do not be deceived: bad company ruins good morals."   1 Corinthians 15:33. (RSV)

The future is counting on you, parents. You have a tough job. But think how nice it will be to be a grandparent. Then you can spoil the little ones and let your kids take the hassle. It all evens out. Hang in there.

I knew her, but not well. Her husband and I were of equal rank, and occasionally met when working in the same areas. They lived down the street from us, but we weren't friends. We knew each other just well enough to cause me to be a little more attentive than I might have been.

During a typical week I had been seeing about fifty soldiers and/or family members a week. And was burning out. No one can keep a counseling load like that and be worth a flip. As a result I had drifted into a get-it-down-quick approach to counseling: hear the problem, suggest a solution, have a prayer, and send them on their way.

She began to pour out her heart about her relationship with her daughter, blaming herself.

"Chaplain, I feel like a failure as a mother. Every time my daughter does or says anything I jump down her throat. I can't keep her at home. I know that she is slipping off to be with a wild bunch. But she is still my daughter. I am so afraid for her, and don't know how to deal with it. I just wish I were a better mother."

I just let her talk, pour it all out. She went into considerable detail about her failings as a mother. After several minutes she calmed down, dried her tears, and waited for me to speak.

"I forgive you," I said, shocking myself at my response. Her face brightened, "Oh thank you. I was afraid that you would just try to reassure me. I needed to have someone hear me out. Thank you for forgiving me."

When Jesus spoke to Peter about the awesome power He was giving His church did he also include the power to convey God's forgiveness?

"Assuredly, I say to you, whatever you bind on earth will be bound in heaven, and whatever you loose on earth will be loosed in heaven."
Matthew 18:18

July 7

It was fun seeing the Desert Storm soldiers on television with their greetings to the folks back home. Moms and dads, brothers and sisters, spouses. A male soldier greeting his wife would invariably call her name.

However, one soldier's greeting was generic, global, "I want to say hello to my girlfriend." No name at all. He could have had several and each girlfriend would have thought that he was sending greetings to her.

It reminded me of how God thinks of us. It is always by name, never by group or category. God does not just love a formless mass of humanity. He loves people, individuals.

Sometimes when I am speaking or writing about loving people I feel hypocritical. Like I don't really love people, but I love the idea of loving people. Or that I can love the world, but I will do it generically, sweetly. But how about loving that homeless man sitting at the traffic light. Or that bellicose neighbor.

Look at the great text, John 3:16 (KJV): "...God so loved the *world*" sounds as though it could be love in the generic sense. However, the next phrase, "That *whosoever* believeth in Him," is personal.

God doesn't have group plans like insurance companies. His will is individual, for each of us. He not only knows us, He knows *about* us. Jesus said, "...The very hairs of your head are all numbered." (Matthew 10:30)

In the early church the Christians at Antioch were praying about whom they should send as missionaries. God knew the members' names.

"As they ministered to the Lord, and fasted, The Holy Spirit said, 'now separate to me Barnabas and Saul for the work to which I have called Them' "
Acts 13:2

God's love for you is personal!

July 8

Two brothers were convicted of stealing sheep and were branded on their foreheads with the letters ST (sheep thief).

One brother fled to a foreign country, and wandered from place to place, hoping to escape his guilt. But he found no peace at any place that he stopped.

Finally, he died in a distant land, alone. No one there knew him. No family member or friend knew to grieve for him. His funeral was low budget, the cost born by the state. His grave was unmarked.

The other brother repented of his crime. He was determined to prove himself as a human being worthy of respect. So he stayed, bore his shame, acknowledged his guilt, and set out to make things right. After many years the people learned to trust him, and the folly of his youth was forgotten.

He had also gained a reputation for great honesty and kindness.

One day a stranger traveling through the area saw the old man with ST branded on his forehead. He asked a villager what it meant. The villager responded, "It happened a long time ago and I have forgotten the details. But I think it's an abbreviation for saint."

The great power of the Gospel and the magnanimity of the love of God assures us that we can outlive our past, get a second chance. Start over.

When one repents of his sins and embraces Christ as his Savior he gets a clean slate. The state will still prosecute any crimes he may have committed, but in God's eyes and heart the sins never happened.

"...If anyone is in Christ, he is a new creation; old things have passed away; behold, all things have become new."

2 Corinthians 5:17

July 9

Was it ever a bum rap, or what?

He was with God. In the form or image of God. He didn't consider it presumptuous to think of Himself as equal with God.

Then He took on the likeness of man. He came as a person of no reputation. He mingled freely with sinners. Prostitutes were drawn to Him. Lepers handled Him. He washed the dirty feet of itinerant fishermen. He became the servant of people less than Himself.

For His good deeds and message of hope and salvation He was scorned, ridiculed, criticized, ignored, put down, beaten, and spat upon.

He was obedient to their sentence of death. To being nailed naked to a cross. To die a mortal's death. To be buried in someone else's tomb.

What a picture. From the very highest to the very lowest. From God to man. From supreme to servant. What a price to pay. And for what? There was nothing in it for Him, but everything for us. Salvation from our sins. Eternity with Christ in Heaven.

As Christians what are we supposed to learn and do as a result of Christ's sacrifice?

Lord, I pray to be like Jesus. But who am I fooling? Here's what I want, Lord: to *really* want to be like Jesus. Then I will work at it, and see results. Keep me honest, Lord. Don't let me get away with being a fringe Christian, one talking one way and walking another. Amen

"Let this mind be in you which was also in Christ Jesus, who...made Himself of no reputation, taking the form of a servant, and coming obedient to the point of death...."

Philippians 2:5

July 10

He stood at the podium, looked strait at the congregation and said, "I have cerebral palsy, what is your problem." He was born with the disease.

The speaker was David Ring. He was speaking at the Cornerstone Church, in San Antonio, Texas. He was celebrating the twenty-ifth anniversary of his ministry as an evangelist.

The theme of his message was *turning lemons into lemonade*. He walks with difficulty. Because of the disease his speech is slurred. It is not easy to understand him. Yet he is a most powerful speaker.

With the congregation in rapt attention he told of his struggles at home with the early death of his father who was a preacher. And then the death of a mother that loved him as a "Mama's boy" is loved. He recounted the difficulties in school, and in doing those things most young people do easily, such as riding a bicycle.

His sermon was loaded with zingers that encouraged us to stop whining so much about real or perceived maladies. He reminded us that God never says oops. He was saying in summary, "Look at me. If God can do this much with me just imagine what He can do with you." And, of course, he was right.

He told how good folks tried to discourage him from entering the ministry. Family members, ministers that he trusted, and who loved him. *He only had 800 invitations to speak last year.*

If life has dealt you a hurtful blow, a lemon, remember that God can turn lemons into lemonade. David Ring's life is living proof of it. So is mine, probably yours, and millions of others. The power is God's. Amen

"Although I am less than the least of all God's people, this grace was given me: to preach...the unsearchable riches of Christ."

Ephesians 3:8

July 11

Flunking that test was a blessing.

I scored so low on the English placement exam when entering college that I had to take remedial English, for half credit. So now I really do understand the agreement of subjects and verbs. And I can diagram sentences. Can you?

Also, I liked my teacher. I asked her to evaluate a paper of mine for creative ability. The paper came back covered with red ink. What I intended as creative style were only errors in grammar and punctuation to her.

She answered the wrong question. I bet you do the same thing.

When your husband asks how you like his new haircut you had better know that he isn't asking if you think that he is getting bald, or if you still think him handsome. A real hunk.

When your wife spins around, and swirls a new dress in front of you, and asks if you like it you had better be sure you know the question. It may be simply if you like the dress. My wife does that to me. But the real question may be if the dress makes her look fat, or makes her ankles look thick, or if you still think she is gorgeous.

What a wonderful truth. God never misunderstands the question. He knows our hearts, our innermost thoughts. He hears what we say and knows what we leave unsaid, the part too painful to speak.

"It shall come to pass that before they call, I will answer; and while they are still speaking, I will hear."
Isaiah 65:24

Dear Lord, thank You for knowing me. That scares me. But I am reassured in that You answer before I even call. That lets me know that You are committed to me in love. Again, thank You.

July 12

A call after midnight summoned a highly acclaimed surgeon to the hospital. A little boy had been severely injured in an accident and only the good doctor had the skill to save him.

The quickest way to the hospital would take the doctor through a very rough neighborhood. So he had no choice. Time was critically important.

While stopped at a traffic light his car door was opened by an agitated man demanding the car. He was literally pulled from his car, and then the man sped away in it.

It took the doctor nearly an hour to get a taxi.

Then they raced to the hospital. When he entered the hospital the nurse shook her head sadly. "It's too late," she said, "The boy died half an hour ago. His dad is in the chapel. Maybe you ought to go see him. He couldn't understand why you didn't come." The Doctor hurried down the hall.

Kneeling there in the chapel was the man who had taken the doctor's car. He had thrown aside the only one who could have saved his son.

If you were asked to name history's saddest record how would you answer? Would it be the slaughter of innocents by despots, the killing plagues of less advanced societies? Or, maybe evil done in the name of religion?

The saddest record in history is related by Saint John: "He came to His own, and His own did not receive Him,"

However, history's best news follows in the next verse:

"But as many as received Him, to them He gave the right to become children of God, even to those who believe in His name.'

John 1:11,12

July 13

Did you ever notice how *things lost take on new value*?

Take the morning newspaper for example. Everyone knows that you can stop off at the service station and buy one for 50 cents. But let the paperboy fail to leave one and the hassle of not getting it greatly exceeds its monetary value.

But the monetary loss is not the main point. You are denied an experience that part of your life: enjoying a second cup of coffee while leisurely reading the sport section; scanning the editorial page to get the political spin on your favorite issue; glancing over the crossword puzzle before you leave for work. A piece of your life has been lost.

In the parable of the lost coin (Luke 15) Jesus tells the story of a lady sweeping diligently to recover the coin. She couldn't rest until it was found. Never mind that she could earn other coins. Or a family member might replace it. It wasn't just a coin. It was a lost coin.

Every grandparent knows the importance of spending time with his own children. The giggly walks with a toddling granddaughter, and the fishing trips with an all hands and feet grandson recall painfully the times you didn't have with your own kids. Opportunities lost forever.

Woe unto the parent who rushes so fast and works so hard to provide for her children that she loses them.

More sad, even, is the man who hears the message, time after time, and puts off accepting Jesus until it is too late. It's hard to concentrate when you are lying on a gurney in an emergency room.

"...What is a man profited if he gains the whole world, and loses his own soul? Or what will a man give in exchange for his soul?"
Matthew 16:26

July 14

A modern day Philip Nolan? You say who was he? He was *The Man Without A Country*, popularized in a novel by that name many years ago.

For some evil and traitorous deed he was put out to sea and never allowed to go ashore again, *in any country*. Not only homeless. Country-less! I had great compassion for the fictional Nolan as an early-teen reader.

Then there was the traveler living under the departures board at the Charles de Gaulle International Airport. The Iranian born traveler, born to a Scottish mother and Iranian father, was unable to leave the airport because he had no passport, for anywhere. He had lived there over two years when I lost track of him. Is he still there?

Home is the universal anchor of the human spirit, the hub around which we move in living out our lives. Changing one's home can be a stressful thing. Not even having a home must be terrible indeed.

Where is your home? Is it where you came from? Where you live? Or where you are going?

Abraham "...Looked for a city which hath foundations, whose builder and maker is God" (Hebrews 11:10 KJV). His search was not just for the correct geographical location, but for the proper spiritual connection as well.

The Christian is dual-based. We have our earthly home. But we also have a heavenly home which is our spiritual destination. Our earthly addresses change. But our eternal location will be permanent. Which home gets more of your attention?

"...Our citizenship is in Heaven, from which we also eagerly wait for the Savior, the Lord Jesus Christ."

Philippians 3:20

When you are homesick what are you saying?

They were a striking couple.

She was always on his arm when they came into the club, straight, thin, and regal in her bearing. He was so protective of her, guiding her, with his hand on her arm, through the buffet line and later to the dance floor. And they danced every dance. Slow, fast, and in between. He wrapped his arms around her as they danced. She glided, gracefully. He was more wobble and bounce than style.

One night I saw him sitting alone, with crutches leaning against his table. He told me of his early morning stroke, of his fall and injury, and of lying on the floor until a neighbor happened to come by. Where was his wife, I asked. He answered that she had Alzheimers, and usually just wandered around, not knowing where she was. Her one great pleasure, that she could still enjoy, was dancing.

He looked so sad, so forlorn, when he asked, "Who's going to dance with her now?"

As I walked back to my table I noticed her wandering around the room, trying to find him. A friend, with both of her hands full from the buffet table, had not been able to physically guide her and she had become disoriented.

When back at their table, I saw him place his hand on her arm, then it all made sense: his protectiveness, his holding her so closely, and his dancing until he nearly dropped.

It was love, a pure, profound, and unselfish love. There was so much she could no longer do but she still loved to dance.

At first I was sad, as I remembered Lamentations 5:15, "Our dance has turned into mourning." But then I remembered what Jesus had said,

A man shall

"...Leave his father and mother, and *cleave* to his wife"

Mark 10:7

Oh Lord, help them to keep dancing. And bless marriages and families everywhere. Amen.

July 16

A businessman, who manufactured various soap products, was also quite critical of Christianity. He prided himself in never attending church services.

One day he was riding through a rough area of town with one of the town's pastors. "Your Gospel hasn't done much good in the world," the businessman observed. "Just look at all of the mean and wicked things that people do."

The pastor didn't comment immediately.

Soon they passed kids playing in the mud.

"Soap hasn't done much good in the world either," the pastor remarked. "I still see a lot of dirty people." To which the businessman responded, huffily,

"Soap is useful only when it is applied." And with a smile the pastor replied, "So it is with the Gospel."

Applied Christianity. Someone wrote a book with that catchy title several years ago. The real challenge is to apply Christianity to your daily life; to let your faith modify your behavior, and not the other way around.

Take love, for instance. It is easier to love people than persons, especially persons with dirty, loud, mouths; weird attitudes; and destructive behavior.

Sometimes I wonder if I'm not copping out by handling much of my stewardship through the mail. It's a lot easier than working the neighborhoods. And a lot safer than the streets.

Christianity is a hands-on religion. The Scriptures teach it. The example of our Lord affirms it.

How long since you got your hands dirty for Jesus?

"...Be doers of the word, and not hearers only, deceiving yourselves."
James 1:22

Lord, I talk Christian love and service a lot better than I do it. I want to HEAR the Word, but I also want to DO it. Don't give up on me, Lord. I'm working on it. Amen

July 17

On a cold, dreary Sunday in Jacksonville, Florida, she pedaled past my life.

I had left successful evangelistic work at age twenty to attend Bible School. It was Christmas break of my first year. I had gone from being somebody as an evangelist to being just another student. I was broke and depressed. The sermon that I had preached that morning had bored me, too.

Doubts about my gifts and calling for Christian ministry plagued my mind and spirit. I was strolling around the block behind the pastor's house, lost inside my own head, thinking that maybe I had chosen the wrong direction for my life. A failed romance had added to my depression.

Then I saw her.

She was about 4 years old, all legs and knees pumping up and down, pedaling a shiny new red tricycle. As she approached, I opened my mouth to say, "My, what a pretty tricycle. Did Santa Claus bring it to you?"

But I didn't have a chance to utter a word. She must have read my mind.

As she flashed by she shook her head, long braids flapping, smiled, and said, "Hit ain't mine, dough." It wasn't her bicycle. I watched as she entered a run-down tenement house.

With her words like arrows piercing my soul I realized that she was a message from God. My life wasn't mine, either. And right there I rededicated my life to preaching the Gospel.

Hello God!

Remember this, "God works in mysterious ways, His wonders to perform?"

Well, God spoke to me through a kid on a tricycle. How have you heard the voice of God lately? He is talking. Are you listening? And are you willing to let Him have all of your life?

"You do not belong to yourselves but to God, He bought you for a price. So use your bodies for God's glory." 2 Corinthians 6:19,20

July 18

Illusion: *a false mental image produced by misinterpretation of things that actually exist.*

Mirage: *an illusion produced by reflection of light against the sky.*

We were aboard the Chief Aptakisik, sailing from Contadora Island back to the Bay of Panama during the rainy season. I had set our course on the exact azimuth that would lead us to anchorage. She was a worthy ship. It was a strait shot. Nothing in between. Piece of cake.

Then why was there an island off to our port side. I could see it perfectly as it rose out of the sea, its rocks and ridges. It was real.

The Sea Scouts owned the ship and I had picked their best sailor to be my mate. "Mate, what do you see on our port side?" I asked. "An island, Captain," he responded. "It isn't supposed to be there."

There were twenty eight persons from our chapel aboard and I was responsible for them. I was afraid. Our radio was broken. Were we sailing in the wrong direction? Out to sea? I kicked the compass to see if it was stuck. It's arrow shuddered, then settled back on the same azimuth.

I had two choices: go by what I saw, or trust my compass.

"We'll hold her steady as she goes, mate," I said, with all of the composure I could muster.

So I stood there, at the helm, and waited. And watched the "island" dissolve into clouds.

We have a compass, you know, that is trustworthy. Our compass is Holy Scripture, and it points directly into the outstretched arms of Jesus.

"...When He had risen...they believed the Scripture and the word which Jesus had said."
John 2:22

Lord, It is so easy for me to *see* things that aren't real. I perceive slights when there are none, feel hurt when it wasn't intended, and often respond inappropriately. Let me SEE what is real and not an illusion, Lord, and follow faithfully. Amen

You never get a second chance to make a first impression.

Isn't that a sweet slogan? How many times have you heard it? The phrase is silly on its face. Of course you can't get another chance to make a first impression. It's a matter of math. There is only one first anything.

However, first impressions are important.

Humans tend to view subsequent behavior through the prism of the first impression.

A man dressed as a country bumpkin becomes one in the viewer's eyes.

A woman made up like a floozy likewise becomes a floozy.

A person acting a fool in public is marked as a fool in the minds of others.

That's how humans regard others. Quick to judge. Reluctant to change original opinions. But, thank God, that isn't how God views humans.

God's view is loftier than our ours. He knows that people can change for the better.

God forgives sinners, even when their sins have brought pain and injury to others.

God loves even the worst among us. He is long-suffering, full of compassion and of tender mercy.

So, don't be too quick to judge others. You might be positioning yourself on the opposite side of the issue from God.

For you see, God doesn't see YOU as others see you. They see your worst faults and judge you by them. God sees you as a person capable of changing. One He loves, and for whom His Son died.

"...As Christ was raised from the dead through the glory of the Father, *we to may live a new life.*"
Romans 6:4 (NIV)

Lord, help me to not be so quick to judge others. I know that You love me. Help me to love You with all of my heart. Amen

July 20

There was an old key lying on the parking lot this morning. Part of it was broken off, and the remainder was scratched and corroded. It once could open things, but now it is discarded. Like a broken dream.

I got to thinking about the things that are key in my life. The list has changed over the years.

As a teenager the key to my happiness was getting to drive the car, then getting a car of my own, dating girls, and being a big man on campus.

Next was choosing a vocation, getting an education, a family, and amassing creature comforts.

In the middle years I was concerned with giving my kids a good start in life.

Later I am more concerned with my personal security, health, and comfort in retirement.

Yesterday's keys may not open tomorrow's doors. So which keys still work, and are basic and foundational, for the long haul?

Good values can last a lifetime. Honesty, charity, loyalty, duty, and industry are some of the main ones.

However, faith has been the indispensable key to my life.

Faith enabled me to hear and accept a calling above the din of commerce. It helped me choose a direction when I couldn't see to the end of the road. It caused me to hope when despair crowded my soul.

Faith lifted me up when I was down.

My faith in Christ the Savior is the master key to my life! Jesus said:

"Fear not, I am the first and the last, and the living one; I died, and behold I am alive for evermore, and I have the *keys* of death and Hades."
Revelation 1:17,18

The Western movie, *Broken Arrow*, has an exchange between James Stewart and Jeff Chandler that ought to be required viewing.

Chandler, the Indian youth, told Stewart, the government representative, that he had to get home because his mother would be worrying about him. Stewart appeared surprised and remarked that he didn't know Indian mothers worried about their children.

Before Hitler could succeed in the murder of millions, he first had to portray the victims as inferior as a class, less human than others.

When I have treated other human beings badly it has always been after I first viewed them stereotypically. Yet I continually amaze myself at how often I grow to like persons after I get to know them. All sorts of persons.

The old proverb comes to mind: before we criticize someone we ought to first walk a mile in their shoes. Are you too judgmental?

Effective communicators have the ability to convey their genuine concern for the other person. Even when they are speaking to a group. Conversely, poor communicators usually speak to stereotypes or categories. You hear phrases like "you people," "those people," and "them."

When Jesus healed a blind man (Mark 8:24) his vision wasn't clear at first. Men appeared as trees, walking. After Jesus laid his hands on the man again he saw everything clearly. Do you need the second touch?

Dear Lord, I am more like the blind man than I want to be. Help me to not stereotype people. Touch my eyes a second time. A third. A fourth. Until I cease to see people as trees, as groups, as a mass, but as persons that you love. Amen

"...Anoint your eyes with eye salve, that you may see."
Revelation 3:18

July 22

You asked, "What does the image of God mean?"

My honest answer is that I don't know for sure. I don't think it means God's physical form, because God is a spirit. Some questions will help shape the discussions.

Does it mean having spiritual capabilities? Does it mean having the attributes of personality, self-consciousness? Does it mean that mankind was created pure, holy, like God? Does it mean the capacity to love? And exercise dominion? Does it mean having the ability to communicate intelligently?

Yes to all of the above, and more.

Adam was incomplete without Eve, in the sense that the pair, together, like God Himself, had the power to create human life.

So, is the divine image the power to create? Perhaps? Or is the answer even more tantalizing?

The Scriptures describe God as pure light (1 John 1:5). What you read next is only a hunch. My honest hunch, but only that.

Adam and Eve were creatures of light that sinned, lost their light, and needed covering.

When our redemption is complete we "shall be like Him" (1 John 3:2) and will be restored as creatures of light.

Here are some scriptures that I believe support my hunch: Exodus 3:2; 13:21b; Daniel 7:9; Matthew 17:2; Daniel 12:3; Matthew 13:43; John 1:4, 8:12; and Matthew 5:14.

I know it's a stretch. Not the usual devotion. But why not spend some time today and check your light meter.

"And God said, let us make man in our image, after our likeness..."
Genesis 1:26

Lord, I have heard the preachers say that in the good old days the saints would get so close to You in prayer and worship that their faces would glow. I always thought of such statements as mere rhetoric. But can it be true? If so I'm ready to shine. Amen

July 23

"Saint Who?" you ask.

Saint Polycarp! In the second century he was the Bishop of Smyrna in what is now Turkey. He was martyred in 156 A.D under Emperor Antoninus Pius.

It had been a capital offense to be a Christian, however under Roman Emperor Trajan, Christians were not pursued as diligently and could save themselves by recanting their faith.

Severe persecution usually resulted only when mobs were incited to attacks upon Christians, which was the case of Polycarp. He escaped the mob at first, but when he was discovered and pointed out by a child he accepted his martyrdom as God's will.

Polycarp requested one hour to pray and prayed with such power that his guards expressed regret at having taken him prisoner.

When the flames grew intense and the crowd fell back from the heat Bishop Polycarp continued in prayer and sang praises to God. The fire didn't kill him. It took the executioners' spears to finish the 86 year old Bishop. Then the mob finished burning his body.

The Greek word *Martus* is used for both *witness* and *martyr* in the English New Testament.

The Scriptures make no distinction in degree for our witness, whether it is simply a word for Christ fitly spoken, as in a free society, or paying the ultimate price for one's faith, as has happened throughout church history. And which happens today in too many places of the world.

Are you a faithful martyr? Am I? If not Polycarp shames us.

"And they stoned Stephen as he was calling on God and saying, 'Lord Jesus, receive my spirit.' "
Acts 7:59

Lord, I pray today for Christians who are being tortured and killed for their faith. Bless them. Sustain them, Lord. Amen.

July 24

I miss Louis L'Amour.

L'Amour's western novels, cranked out at a regular pace, were a true delight and something to look forward to every six or eight months. His capacity for homespun philosophizing enriched a great capacity for story telling.

In *The Lonesome Gods*, L'Amour argued that while people seek peace and comfort it is their enemies that give them strength. He believed that strength only grows from struggle.

Glittering successes are fun but you probably don't learn anything from them. In fact, success can blind you to needed improvement. After all, if you are so successful maybe you aren't so dumb.

We learn from our failures.

The hardship that you are presently enduring, or the suffering that you are now experiencing, can result in great blessings. Not that they themselves are blessings. It's what you can learn from them. They can cause you to look inside yourself, to examine your attitude, your behavior, and grow.

It is when we walk through the "valley of the shadow of death" that we are most aware of God's presence with us.

It is in the fiery furnaces of life that our true mettle develops and we gain strength for future trials. History, the Scriptures, and, I imagine, your life experiences, are full of examples.

So let us not pray for easier trials, but for greater struggle.

"...We rejoice in our sufferings, knowing that suffering produces endurance, and endurance produces character...."
Romans 5:3,4 (RSV)

Lord, I am afraid to pray for greater struggle lest I should fail in the struggle. But Your grace is sufficient for me. Bless me oh Lord. Help me to grow in spirit. Amen

July 25

Did you ever have anyone keeping book on you?

I have. For thirty years. During my entire career in the Army I was rated at least annually by two supervisors. They kept book on me. Maybe not a daily log, and not just bad stuff. Their files on me provided them data to use in writing my efficiency report.

And during that entire period I kept book on others. You see, I also supervised those who were subordinate to me in rank. It wouldn't have been fair to them for me to not have kept a record of their service. How else would I have been able to rate them on their accomplishments.

It is all right to keep a record of good.

Then there are those whose motives are less pure.

They note every failure. They nag about each faux pas. You just can't please them. They remember every offense. And look for every opportunity to bring up past misdeeds.

How refreshing to learn that God isn't like that.

"Out of the depths I cry to you, O Lord...let Your ears be attentive to my cry for mercy. *If you, O Lord, kept a record of sins, O Lord, who could stand?* But with you there is forgiveness..."
Psalms 130:1-4

Dear Lord, I know that each day adds to the record of my life. It is written in the hearts of my wife, my children, my family, my friends, my neighbors, and my associates. I want them to have good memories of me.

Help me, Lord. Give me wisdom and courage, and strength, to live an exemplary life. Not just for them, O Lord, but for You, too. So that my life can be a light that shines brightly and beckons others to You. Amen

July 26

Jesus will be with you today. What ever your needs are you can turn to Him and find Him near.

If a sense of sin troubles you, look to the *Lamb of God* that takes away the sins of the world.

If you are wandering, feeling like a lost sheep, Jesus is the *Good Shepherd* who seeks until the lost is found.

If the ground on which you are standing seems unstable you can feel secure because you are anchored on the *Rock of Ages.*

If you are spiritually famished He is the *Bread of Life.*

If your soul is dry and thirsty He is the *Living Water.*

If sadness darkens your spirit He is the *Bright and Morning Star.*

If you are doubtful about the future, fearful about life's uncertainties, Jesus is the *Way,* the *Truth,* and the *Life.*

If the ugliness of a culture speeding out of control threatens you, look to Jesus, the *Rose of Sharon,* and the *Lily of the valley.*

If you are plagued by sickness, weak to the bone with a persistent disease, Jesus is the *Great Physician.*

If you are lonely He is a *Friend* that sticks closer than a brother.

When you are wronged you can rely on Jesus, because He is the *Righteous Judge.*

Get the point? Then look up.

"Looking unto Jesus, the author and finisher of our faith...."
Hebrews 12:2

Lord, I thank You for the rich resources You have provided for my spiritual growth. Help me to take advantage of every one of them.

I know that You are with me today, and I turn to You with all of my heart. Amen

A friend will soon retire after over 30 years of active duty in the Army. I asked him where he plans to retire and what he plans to do. He didn't know.

I tried to make a joke of it, saying that at least he was Scriptural, that "Abraham (also) went out, not knowing whither he went" (Hebrews 11:8 KJV). It wasn't funny to him, and I felt like a jerk. But it got me to thinking.

Abraham marched off his map. He left friends and familiar surroundings and found a new, a promised, land. He fathered a child in his old age and became the father of a nation, and an ancestor of the Savior.

Mary Pickford, America's sweetheart from an earlier generation, wrote that failure was not falling down, but staying down.

Many years ago a little girl was bedridden from a severe auto accident, maybe never to walk again. Determined not to give up she took up singing lessons. Her name is Doris Day, the heartthrob of a whole generation of American males.

The Gospel of Christ is "Good News" in that it promises a second chance. You can start afresh. It's never really over for the person of faith.

Moses lived 120 years. He spent the first 40 getting an education. The next 40, after a premature effort to lead Israel, were spent on the "backside" of the desert, hiding out. The last third of his life was actually spent doing what God called him to do.

Don't get in too big of a hurry. Nor give up too soon.

"By faith he (Moses) forsook Egypt, not fearing the wrath of the king; for *he endured as seeing Him who is invisible.*"
Hebrews 11:27

That's what I need, Lord, better spiritual sight. Give it to me, Lord. Amen

July 28

There is an old song I used to sing entitled, *You're Nobody 'Till Somebody Loves You.*

It's a pretty song, but I can't even imagine that there could be a person that has no one to love him or her. Even the worst among us has someone.

But how terrible it would be to feel so alone as to believe that no one in the whole world loves you. How empty, how useless, life would be. I suppose you would really feel like a nobody. Well, forget it because there aren't any nobodies.

Everybody is a somebody because God loves everybody. No one is so down that His love can't reach them. If you feel unloved today it is a false feeling. Resist it.

So nobody, but nobody, is a nobody anymore. God's love makes that would-be nobody a somebody.

Please pray this prayer with me:
Dear Lord, I thank you for the people that love me. I don't know how I would make it alone. May I never have to find out. I especially thank You for loving me. I promise to pass that love on to others every way I can. Help me to love You with all of my heart, and my neighbor as myself. Amen

The song ended by the writer's urging the hearer to find somebody to love.

"You shall love your neighbor as yourself."
Matthew 19:19

Lord, You know that I am better at talking about loving people than I am at actually loving them. I guess I love the idea of loving people. I know that doesn't cut it.

With Your help, dear Lord, I will do my very best to really love, as You taught and require me to love. Amen

July 29

Happy anniversary of the Army Chaplaincy.

With collegial respect for the other services I want to highlight the Army Chaplaincy in today's devotion. It was on this date in 1775 that the Army Chaplaincy was organized.

The Chaplaincy has been good for soldiers and their families. It have been good for the Army and the Nation. No other country's military approaches ours in providing quality pastoral care for its troops.

Chaplains have a record of starting good things and then handing them off to others. For example, chaplains began the Drug and Alcohol Rehabilitation Program, and the Army Community Service.

Chaplains are always seeking new ways and areas of ministry, but they always remain true to their primary mission of providing pastoral care to soldiers and their families.

I have served under eight Chiefs of Chaplains: two United Methodists, three Roman Catholics, two Lutherans, one Presbyterian, and one Baptist. They all contributed to my professional growth. What I have appreciated most is their encouraging me to do spiritual ministry in a collegial setting. Nowhere does that work as well as in the Army Chaplaincy.

Please give your support and prayer for the Chaplain ministry.

Dear Lord, please pour out a special blessing today on Chaplains and their assistants. In each of the services. Prosper their ministries, whether at home or abroad. Keep them safe, and make them a rich blessing to our military members and their families. Amen

"He...makes His angels spirits, His ministers (Chaplains) a flame of fire."
Psalm 104:4

July 30

When I was a pre-schooler my family lived between a twenty acre orange grove and a huge open field. Old Wolf, our German Shepherd, and I hunted rabbits to add excitement to our days. And meat for our table.

Wolf didn't have a great nose, so she chased the rabbits by sight. When she would lose the rabbit in the tall grass she would leap into the air, quickly scan the area, locate the rabbit, adjust her direction as required, and resume the chase.

The rabbits often ran into holes. We called them gopher holes, although they weren't really dug by rodents, but by land turtles. Tortoises.

Old Wolf would begin to dig them out but the dirt would pile up behind her. I would then crawl in behind her and push the dirt past me with my feet. We were a real team, and a great terror to the rabbit population.

One day we chased a rabbit down a hole that a skunk had already claimed.

Imagine our predicament: old Wolf whining, scratching my face while trying to back out of the hole; and me in total panic. Picture a dirt-caked, stinking, kid, and a very sick dog, running home to Mother.

Needless to say, Mom wasn't pleased with what she saw. She made me pump two tubs of water, one for me, and one for old wolf. Then she scrubbed us. Good.

Today, you might fall into a hole. Or dig yourself into one. You can crawl out. You may run head-on into a skunk. He can stink you up, but he can't kill you.

Open the window, breathe the fresh air, say a prayer of thanksgiving to God for the gift of life. His hand is reaching down for you. Grab hold. Amen.

"He brought me up out of a horrible pit...and heard my cry...."

Psalm 40:2

Mark who?

On their first missionary journey, Paul and Barnabas took along a young man named Mark. His mother apparently was a mainstay in the infant church. She had provided hospitality to the Apostle Peter. She had also allowed the early Christians to meet in her house.

So Mark apparently went along as an apprentice minister, of sorts, or as a personal assistant to the missionaries Paul and Barnabas.

As the missionary party traveled they encountered hostility in some places. In fact, Paul was actually stoned at Lystra.

This may have frightened Mark. Or maybe he was still too much of a mother's boy. For when they reached a coastal town in Pamphyllia, Mark left the group and returned home.

On the next journey Paul refused to take Mark along.

What a blow to a young preacher with such a bright future.

Paul had become the obvious leader in the young Church's expansion into the world. With himself now alienated from Paul what was Mark going to do? How would his ministry be received?

How was he ever going to write a Gospel for the New Testament?

Mark didn't give up.

In Christ there is always forgiveness and hope. Mark learned from his failures and grew. And his subsequent Christian service must have been remarkable, for many years later, from prison, the aged Paul urged,

"...Get Mark and bring him with you, for he is useful to me for ministry."
2 Timothy 4:11

Guess who wrote the second Gospel.

August 1

During the last few years there has been a lot of media coverage of misbehavior by high governmental officials.

Was it really lying or was it just falsifying, and what was the intent?

I have real difficulty with the attempted distinctions.

This lie is okay, but that lie is not okay. A political lie is permissible. Adultery (i.e. breaking the vow that you made in the marriage ceremony) is okay, but lying about it is not okay.

Do whatever you want to as long as there is plausible deniability. Then if there is no denying it, and the truth hurts, claim that you can't remember.

There seems to be a consensus that it is okay to lie as long as you don't lie under oath.

The Christian is always under oath.

Understand though, honesty doesn't require you to be brutal with the truth. Truth isn't a club with which you can beat someone over the head for your own personal reasons.

You aren't obligated to tell an ugly person that he is ugly. Even if he asks you if you think he is. You can spare him the hurt without telling a lie. And you ought to do so.

Honesty doesn't require you to say that her dress looks like something out of the funny papers. You don't always have to give a yes or no answer to be honest. You might simply say, "I like you. Our friendship doesn't hinge on liking each other's dresses."

We as Christians have to be truthful. Always.

Our Lord IS the Truth. If we are not truthful how are we different from everyone else? But the truth doesn't have to be brutal. The Scriptures instruct us to speak the truth in love.

"Speak each man the truth to his neighbor."
Zechariah 8:16

August 2

Dreaming is the language of the Spirit.

While pastoring a church in a South American country the speaker had dreamed of reaching multitudes. As increasingly large crowds flocked to hear him, drug lords were threatened by his preaching.

He was ambushed and took several bullets. Undeterred, after months of recuperation, he resumed his ministry and his congregation grew to include thousands.

His dreaming was not the nocturnal happenings that sometimes result from too much food or drink, or the wrong kind. Rather it was the insistent longing for a yet unrealized success, the persistent hope of reaching a cherished goal, the pull of a powerful promise.

The patriarch Abraham lived comfortably in Ur of the Chaldees, a city rich in commerce and art. Yet he left there and journeyed to a distant, unknown land.

God had promised to make of Abraham a great nation, to bless him and make his name great, that through him all of the families of the earth would be blessed (Genesis 12:1-3).

Abraham was not driven out of Ur. The promise pulled him. The dream compelled him.

What great faith!

What about you? What is your dream? Does it still tug at you, pulling you out of your comfort and into your potential? Don't give up on the future.

"So Abram departed as the Lord had spoken to him...and Abram was 75 years old...(he) took Sarai his wife...and all their possessions...so they departed to the land of Canaan...."
Genesis *12:4,5* (KJV)

Lord, don't ever let me stop dreaming. And I pray that you will bless everyone that reads this devotion today. Enlarge their dreams. Increase their faith. Pull them, compel them, ever onward and upward. Amen

August 3

To many, WWII is symbolized by marines raising the flag on Iwo Jima. When some think of Vietnam they will remember a little girl fleeing a napalm attack, her clothes burned from her body.

How do you remember the Persian Gulf war? Viewing a scud attack through a newsman's eyes from a rooftop? A reporter dangling a microphone out of the hotel window to pick up the sounds of exploding bombs and air raid sirens? The thousands of burned out vehicles that didn't quite make their escape? "Stormin' Norman" briefing the press?

My favorite image is of the non-commissioned officer who flushed a handful of enemy soldiers from a bunker. They tried to kiss his hand. He pushed them back gently, rejecting their subservience, while reassuring them.

For them to live they had to surrender the "safety" of their bunker. Their hope had to overpower their fear. They had to trust the NCO. He enabled them to do so and thus portrayed what is best in Americans.

Images are only as powerful as the reality they portray. I hope that you portray strength and compassion that pleases the Lord and points others to Him.

Each of us, as a Christian, is a message of Christ to the world. They read us like a letter. What is the message that you convey?

"You are our epistle…known and read by all men."
2 Corinthians 3:2

Dear Lord, help me to be readable. And let the message that others read in me be the Gospel of Your love and forgiveness. Let me be a living symbol that points others to You as Lord and Savior. I don't want to be a bystander. Nor do I want my appearance and behavior as a Christian to give an unfaithful representation of Your grace to others. I am counting on Your blessing Lord. Amen

August 4

Are you walking wet?

The pastor talked about walking wet in a sermon on baptism.

I had trouble following him. He was trying to say that one's baptism should show. But the imagery was confusing because nothing stays wet. Everything dries out sooner or later. Nevertheless he made a good point.

Our baptism should show.

Let me make it clearer for you.

Christians must be distinguishable. I don't mean by looking or acting stupid, but by living honestly, showing mercy, and pointing the way to Christ the Savior.

When you tell the truth while those around you lie, you are walking wet.

When you keep your vows while others don't, you are walking wet.

When you refuse to cheat and steal while others do so routinely, you are walking wet.

When your behavior and demeanor causes others to focus on the words and work of Christ, you are walking wet.

You will be visible whether you are trying to be or not.

"I have been crucified with Christ; it is no longer I who live, but Christ lives in me; and the life which I now love in the flesh I live by faith in the Son of God."
Galatians 2:20

Dear Lord, don't let me dry out. I want to walk wet. I want to be an example of the true believer. Help me to be a light that shines and points others to you, the Light of the World. Hose me down when I need it, Lord. Amen

August 5

A most often told lie is that everybody does it. And kids didn't invent the lie. They learned it from their adults.

When Cynthia was ten she was with her mother when they were caught speeding. Her mother handed the officer her driving license, wrapped in a $50 bill. "It's okay honey," her mother said as they drove off. "Everybody does it."

When she was fifteen she broke her glasses, but her mother persuaded the insurance company that they had been stolen. They collected $175. "It's okay honey," she said. "Everybody does it."

When she was nineteen she was approached by an upperclassman who offered the test answers for $100. "It's O.K., honey," he said. "Everybody does it."

Cynthia was caught and sent home from school. She was devastated. Her family was scandalized.

"How could you do this to your father and me?" her mother screamed. "You never learned anything like that at home."

Her aunts and uncles were also abashed. For if there's one thing adults can't stand, it's a kid who cheats.

"Train up a child in the way he should go, and when he is old he will not depart from it."
Proverbs 22:6

Heavenly Father, help me to be the kind of parent I ought to be. Help me, always, to *model* the behavior that I hope to *see* in my children, and in others. You have loved me and saved me Lord. Fill me so full of Your Holy Spirit that there will be no space left for evil. By Your power and grace I will set a better example. Amen

August 6

"Who do folks say that I, the Son of Man, am?" asked Jesus.

"Some think that You are John the Baptist, some are convinced that You are Elijah, and others believe that you probably are Jeremiah, or another of the prophets." The disciples muttered.

"But who do YOU say that I am?" Jesus persisted.

They were dumbfounded.

They knew that His name was Jesus, of course. They already had high hopes that He would become the political leader of the Jews. They sensed in Him someone who could deliver them from the Roman occupation of their homeland. They had experienced His power, His wisdom, and His compassion.

But who *was* He? They weren't sure. And they were embarrassed. They waited.

Then Peter cried out,

"You are the Christ, the Son of the living God." (Matthew 16:16)

He had answered correctly, but where did he get the answer?

"Blessed are you, Simon Bar-Jonah, for flesh and blood has not revealed this to you, but my Father who is in heaven. (Matthew 16:17)

A popular teacher once observed that God has no grandchildren. By that he meant that the Christian faith demands a personal response to Christ's offer of salvation.

It is never enough to rely on what others say or believe. Your mother's faith in Christ will get her to heaven. But her faith won't get you there. However, your faith in Jesus can get you there. So what do you say?

Who is Jesus to YOU?

August 7

Peter's confession of faith was "You are the Christ, the Son of the Living God."

Biblical scholars call this the Great Confession of Faith. Peter's confession is indeed great. But it is not the greatest.

To me the greatest confession of faith came from one remembered by many as the doubter. It happened the next Sunday night after Easter. And it was strikingly personal. In the first person singular. And that is the point I hope that you will understand.

Thomas had been absent Easter night when Jesus appeared in the midst of the disciples. Perhaps his grief had driven him away from the group.

When they told him later that Jesus was alive Thomas would have none of it. His hopes were shattered. The Romans had killed Jesus. Everyone knew it. It was over.

With a sob in his throat Thomas cried that for him to believe that Jesus was alive he would have to push his hand into Jesus' riven side and run his finger into the nail holes in Jesus' hands.

Bully for Thomas. It is to his credit that he didn't quickly swallow such a fanciful story. Remember, he had missed Jesus' first visit. How would you respond if someone told you that a popular leader, someone that you knew had died and had been buried, had risen from the dead?

At their next gathering Thomas was with the disciples. Jesus *appeared* in their midst. "Come here, Thomas, and see the hole in my side. Look at these hands. Go ahead, stick your finger in the holes. Do whatever you have to do, Thomas. Just believe."

Hello God!

"...Thomas answered and said to Him '*My* Lord, and *My* God.'"

John 20:28

August 8

Do you have a favorite novelist?

For years I kept hoping that another last novel would emerge from the great novelist, John D. MacDonald. He died a few years ago having written sixty-six books, most of them best sellers. I read every one of them.

MacDonald's great strength as a writer was his ability to understand and comment on human nature. He would often insert, in the midst of a great yarn, a lofty discourse on some pet philosophical point.

MacDonald's most famous character was the detective Travis McGee, a burly, physical type, whose sidekick was Myer, an accountant. Myer was the means that MacDonald often used to get his own personal philosophies into the narrative.

In *Free Fall In Crimson* Myer mused over the many different people that we are. He explained that we become different people in response to different challenges, responsibilities, duties, and opportunities. Different settings.

So I am many people. You too.

To some I am Shirley's husband. I am also Betty's brother and Ann's brother in law. To others I am Alan's Dad. Children on a certain street know me only as Priss' grandfather. I am Dania's father-in-law.

So who am I really? I am a many faceted human that no other person can truly know as I know myself and as God knows me.

My most essential relationship, however, my most predictable perspective, my most consistent value, is that I am, more than anything else is, a child of God. What wonder. What privilege. What grace. What about you?

"...One is your (my !) Father, He who is in heaven."
Matthew 23:9

Do you have a favorite chapter of the Bible? Mine is the twentieth chapter of John. It is the great VICTORY chapter.

There is victory over *death*. Jesus is raised from the dead. The tomb is empty. Victory over *despair*. Mary, weeping outside the tomb, is comforted by the risen Lord. *Doubt*. Thomas, who had missed Jesus' earlier visit to the disciples, was helped to believe.

From this chapter we also learn much about Jesus?

He is the one who breaks through our locked places to get into our lives. The disciples were locked in, hiding from the authorities. Jesus *appeared* in their midst. You can't keep Jesus from finding you.

Jesus is the one who identifies Himself by His wounds.

He could have strolled down Main Street bouncing the stone that had sealed His tomb. Or twirling the cross like a baton. But Jesus *showed them His hands*. Status in the kingdom is determined by humble service.

He is the one who forgives and commissions us to forgive.

He further promises us that when we forgive someone on earth they are forgiven in heaven. Give the *gift of forgiveness* today. Look around you. Someone needs your forgiveness. It is the greatest gift you can give.

He is the one who deals carefully and effectively with doubt. Jesus wasn't picking on Thomas. Rather, He was gently helping a struggling disciple to believe.

Finally, He is the one who blesses us for *believing when we cannot see*. Someday we will see. Today we can believe. Hallelujah.

"...Blessed are those who have not seen and yet have believed."

John 20:29

Are you a fisherperson?

When Jesus called Simon and Andrew, two fishermen, to be His disciples, He promised that they could still be fishermen. But they would now be catching people.

They immediately left their nets and followed Jesus. Does that mean that we, too, must leave what we are doing to really follow Jesus? Be sort of an empty handed, wandering, nomad?

No! Obedience to Christ's call doesn't mandate that. The real lesson is that our lives take on a new dimension. A wonderful, heavenly, other worldly, dimension.

We are no longer just painters, farmers, secretaries, clerks, and builders. We still do what we have to do to make a living. But at the same time we are doing something else. We are at work temporally and eternally. At the same time.

A pastor told of visiting an old lady in his church and finding her crying. When he inquired about what was wrong she said, "Oh pastor, when I was young I wanted to do something for Christ. But all I have ever done is wash dishes, cook meals, scrub floors, take care of children, and mend clothes."

The pastor thought for a few minutes then asked, "Where are your children?" She answered that Suzy was a nurse, Mark a missionary, John a builder and deacon, and that Jim was a Peace Corps volunteer. In her sadness she had completely discounted her vital role as mother. She *raised* fishers of people.

Are you a fisherperson? Have you made any catches lately? What are your plans for catching someone for Christ today? Be a witness. Amen

"...Come after me, and I will make you become fishers of men."

Mark 1:17

August 11

How many times have you said or heard someone say, "Why doesn't God do something?"

The question, accompanied by a sad shaking of the head, is usually asked about the suffering of innocent people, tragedies, and the like.

Well, I recently heard a preacher say, "God doesn't get into the struggle until we do." Not that He can't, of course, just that He doesn't. To illustrate the point the preacher referred back to the crossing of the Jordan River.

It was only when the priests waded into the water that the parting occurred. Now that's not the way I want it.

"Lord, you just go ahead and part the water while I look on. Hold it back awhile until the ground is good and dry. I don't want to take any chances, or get my feet wet. Then, when I am sure it is safe I will commit. When I can see the end I will begin."

But God tells us to believe.

You may show me a boat or ship and tell me it is strong and safe. You may even show me its blueprint. After much persuasion I may believe IN it. But that's not the same as believing ON it. At some point I must climb aboard.

Faith that makes us people of God is the sort that acts. It is not just an intellectual assent, but a commitment, a climbing aboard. So, the question is not, "Why doesn't God do something?" but, "Why don't we?"

"Blessed is the man who trusts in the Lord, and whose hope is in the Lord."
Jeremiah 17:7

So, dear reader, have you placed all that you are and have on the belief that Jesus is who the Scriptures say that He is? We are not talking here about intellectual assent. It is time to start across the Jordan, to wade in. Amen

August 12

In 1970-1973 I was stationed in Kaiserslautern, Germany. Those were sad days for the Army in Europe. Priority of assignments was to Vietnam. Units in Germany were often understrength. Morale was low.

Those were also days of intense racial strife. I remember watching a group of thirty or so soldiers of a certain race, armed with baseball bats and sticks, running across the chapel grounds, heading toward a confrontation with soldiers of a certain other race.

Much of my counseling was dealing with anti-establishment attitudes and behaviors, and perceived racial prejudices by the leadership.

One soldier was wonderfully different. He was a minority soldier from an American inner city. His struggles were not with the competing versions of how to respond to authority, but with his sense of sin. And how to find salvation.

John asked about forgiveness. About heaven and hell. He recounted his tragic life on the streets and expressed his yearning for something better. John wanted to know what Jesus could do for him then and forever.

The Gospel was good news to John. He eagerly accepted the message of redemption, of forgiveness, of salvation, and of a new beginning. He was born anew.

John was a prolific writer. Often sharing his writings with me.

When he was processing out of the company to return to the States John came by my office and dropped a paper on my desk. It was poetry, entitled "I Have Risen." The last line captured the truth: "I have risen, *from there to here.*"

"...Put on the new man...created... in righteousness and true holiness."
Ephesians 4:24

Jesus lifts us from the *there* of doubt, despair, and defeat to the *here* of victory over self, sin, and Satan.

August 13

When I was in Bible College, *way back then*, a famous Christian song was entitled *I Know Who Holds Tomorrow*. Reverend Ira Stanphill, a great songwriter and preacher wrote the song.

I had the privilege of meeting Reverend Stanphill at camp meeting and later preaching in his church. He was a great person.

The message of the song is that we don't need to know about tomorrow because we know who holds tomorrow. I still occasionally find myself singing that song. Still remember most of the words.

Isn't it funny how folks spend so much time and money trying to know the future? Fortunetellers and horoscopes. Clairvoyants. Tealeaves and the intestines of chickens. Ugh.

Maybe not knowing is better. What if you suddenly had dumped on you all of the bad things that might happen in the rest of your life. And you had to carry all of those burdens each day, as long as you live.

I would rather not know. I would rather take one day at a time. Our assurance comes not from knowing the future, but from knowing God.

Believers know that Jesus will never forsake us. That He will walk with us through sorrows and rejoicings. That He will be with us as a loving, guiding, strengthening, comforting, healing, and sustaining friend no matter what happens in our future.

Dear Lord, I thank You that You know me and the future. And I thank You for allowing me to know You through faith. I trust myself to You, for my future is in Your hands. Amen

"We walk by faith, not by sight."
2 Corinthians 5:7

A country preacher, tired of making do on meager income, got a call to a larger parish in a swank community. He told his wife about the call, then said, "Hon, you go ahead and pack while I pray about it."

An architect complained that people pay good money to have him design a home for them only to discover that they have already designed it in their minds. They really were seeking his approval of their plans.

Prayer should be to determine God's will, not to seek His approval on our plans.

Are you in God's will?

Does it shock you to be asked that question? Did you, at one time, know and follow God's plan for your life only to turn aside later to your own pursuits?

God has a plan for each of us.

It is not like an insurance company group plan. His plan is individual. No one else has the same plan. The God who can give all five billion of us different fingerprints, and numbers the hairs on our heads, surely has a plan for our lives.

It is interesting to listen to some of the exchanges when young people are surveyed:

Question, "What are your plans for the future?"

Answer, "To be happy."

Happiness is not something that you can seek and find. Happiness finds you. When you are in God's will, and doing right, happiness sneaks up on you and grabs you.

"Teach me to do Your will, for You are my God;
Your spirit is good. Lead me in the land of uprightness."
Psalms 143:10

August 15

What does it mean to be honest?

Does it mean telling the *whole* truth all the time, whatever the circumstance?

I know that you swear in court to tell the truth, the *whole* truth, and nothing but the truth. But you really only testify to what you are asked. However, I am not speaking here about testimony. But rather, what is our obligation to tell the truth, as Christians, in everyday communication?

Christian honesty doesn't mean that we have to say everything that enters our mind all of the time.

It may be a fact that you are ugly, but honesty doesn't require me to tell you so. Nor am I being dishonest when I compliment you on your kind attitude and sweet spirit.

Here's a beaming mother who shows me her new baby. I don't have to comment on the flopped ears, crossed eyes, or bad complexion. To do so would be brutal. Nor would it be too dissembling to remark, "My, My, isn't that some baby? Whom does she favor?" (Honesty doesn't require you to ask if the baby is sick, as one person did.)

Say that I am walking out of the sanctuary and the preacher is there expecting me to shake his hand and congratulate him on the sermon. But it was really a pretty boring sermon: too long, and too ethereal. What must I do? I want to say something. Be civil. But I won't lie.

I just say thank you. I learned that from my seminary, the Associate Reformed Presbyterian Seminary. Whether the sermon was great or boring, the students (faculty too) responded with a simple thank you. And a thank you is appropriate, even if it wasn't a great sermon. The speaker probably did his best.

So, I don't feel that I have to tell the *whole* truth on every subject, every time. I am not lying if I leave out the part that hurts when it isn't relevant. And when leaving it out doesn't itself create a lie.

"He who...speaks uprightly...will dwell on high...."
Isaiah 33:15,16

August 16

Have you ever heard the expression, "On fire for God?"

Mr. Thomas Huxley, an English biologist in the nineteenth century, said that in the soil of England lies buried a great variety of tropical seeds. Birds and wind brought them there. He went on to predict that if England could have just twelve months of tropical heat it would bloom out in luxuriance.

Isn't there a lesson here for Christians?

How often do the seeds of spiritual growth lie dormant in us? Seeds that can't germinate because of our lukewarmness of spirit? The coldness of our hearts?

On the first Easter afternoon two men were walking to Emmaus, a village near Jerusalem. They had heard of the crucifixions. They knew that the authorities were looking for disciples of the Nazarene.

A stranger drew near and walked with them. He expounded the Hebrew scriptures to them, explaining that the Christ must suffer, be killed, and raised from the dead. They listened in rapt attention.

When they arrived at their home they urged the man to enter and have supper with them. It was while they were eating that they noticed His hands. They had nail holes in them. *Hello God!*

At their recognition of Him Jesus vanished.

And they said to one another, "Did not our *heart burn within us* while He talked with us on the road, and while He opened the Scriptures to us?"
Luke 24:32

With hearts on fire, and no longer deterred by fear, they raced back to Jerusalem and reported that the Lord was indeed risen. Don't you wish that you could be that on fire for God? You can, you know. The secret is in the text: walking, talking, and studying the Scriptures, with Jesus. Amen

August 17

My wife and I were called home to see my Mother when the family believed that she was dying.

Mom had quite unexpectedly become weak, unable to leave her bed, and wasn't taking food or water. She was virtually non-responsive. She had already instructed us that there were to be no heroics. So we had gathered to be with her as she died. She was eighty-seven years old.

The most important thing to my Mother has always been her love of God and faith in Jesus. So we gathered around her bed and sang the songs that we had heard her sing so often. I played her favorite Christian songs on my mandolin.

Within a day or two Mom started to show signs of reviving, and began to take some nourishment. She even tried to sing with us, but couldn't form the words or keep the rhythm.

One day I heard Mom in the other room but couldn't understand what she was saying. Her words were jumbled, mumbled.

I asked my Sister about it. "Oh, she is praying, Bud," my sister said. Then I understood a verse that has long seemed strange to me:

"...He who searches the hearts...makes intercession for the saints...."
Romans 8:27

Mom had lost the power of speech but not the power to pray. The sweet Holy Spirit which still filled her heart and soul was praying through her, and for her. Within a few days she was eating at the table.

What a wonderful truth! And what a powerful reality! There is no way that you can fail as long as you let the Holy Spirit have full sway in your life. You can be a victor today. And tomorrow. Amen

August 18

The popularity of the nation's leader was at an all time high but rumors about his sexual adventures persisted.

While walking in the cool of the evening he had seen a young woman bathing. He could have saved himself much grief if he had simply looked away. But he didn't. He sent for her. Thus began King David's reckless affair with Bathsheba, the wife of Uriah a popular military commander.

In the parlance of today he slept with her. She became pregnant.

Then began the cover-up.

David summoned the woman's husband, Uriah, and the two of them talked. War stories. Military types love to do this. Then David told the general to go home to his wife. But Uriah was too honorable. He couldn't enjoy a night at home while his troops were deployed. Instead, he slept with the king's servants. When David heard of that he sent for Uriah again, got him drunk, and then instructed him to go home to his wife. Uriah still wouldn't do it.

The cover-up grows.

David sent a letter with Uriah to Joab, the senior commander, instructing him to send Uriah to the hottest battle, then withdraw all support, leaving Uriah exposed to the enemy. Uriah was killed.

And you thought that political cover-ups were a modern invention.

It is true that the truth will make you free. It is also true that the truth, when given quickly, openly and thoroughly, will keep you out of a worse jam.

"...Judge nothing before the time, until the Lord comes, who will...bring to light the hidden things of darkness and reveal the counsels of the hearts...."
I Corinthians 4:5

"O what a tangled web we weave, when first we practise to deceive." (The quote and the spelling are from Sir Walter Scot.)

We dealt earlier with the shameful affair of David and Bathsheba. David let his eyes wander, had an adulterous affair, made the woman pregnant, then had her husband killed to cover up his sin.

The affair started a chain of events that included rebellion against him by his own son, Absalom, civil war in his kingdom, twenty thousand of his soldiers dying in one battle, and much, much more.

David's irresponsible behavior graphically illustrates how one betrayal inevitably leads to larger ones. That is, unless it is dealt with immediately; unless it is admitted and confessed before things get out of control.

Which leads into why I think David was a "Man after God's own heart." It is true that he could goof up badly, sin woefully. But he had a tender heart toward God.

When confronted by the prophet Nathan, David confessed, "I have sinned against the Lord." Nathan responded, "The Lord also has put away your sin; you shall not die" (2 Samuel 12:13). However, Nathan told David that he would still pay a price for his sin. The child conceived in adultery would die.

Folks today seem to think that the wages of sin are canceled by a tearful confession.

It was David, the one who sinned shamefully that prayed:

"Create in me a clean heart, O God, and renew a steadfast spirit within me."
Psalms 51:10

Amen.

The following statement is not true: "Sticks and stones can break my bones but words can never hurt me."

Words can kill.

The battalion firebase in Vietnam was considered safe from enemy penetration. Despite that, sappers made their way through the perimeter defenses and lobbed explosives into several of the bunkers. A fierce firefight resulted with many wounded and several killed.

The medics worked quickly and heroically to save one soldier whose legs had been blown off. In the rush of things he hadn't realized that his legs were gone. But he had been stabilized. He was alive, and aware; all bandaged up, being nourished intravenously, lying on the helipad, waiting for the chopper. By every indicator he was going to make it.

Then his buddy came running up to where he was. "My God, his legs are gone," he shouted. The soldier died immediately.

The Old Testament Scriptures recognized the power of words. Once spoken they moved and carried force. They could never be retrieved.

Remember how Isaac was tricked into giving his blessing to Jacob, instead of to Esau, the son that he had intended to bless?

We moderns would simply have said that we had made a mistake and would have corrected it. The ancients understood words differently. They always had consequence. They were never spoken frivolously.

Be careful what you say and how you say it. Words live on.

"...On the day of judgment men will render account for every careless word they utter."
Matthew 12:36 (RSV)

August 21

Do you like taking tests? I do. I always considered it sort of a game, like trying to outguess the professor. But I never liked unannounced tests. Pop quizzes. And I really got tired of physical fitness tests in the Army.

There are a lot of tests in life.

There are tests of your integrity, as in temptations to lie. There are tests of fidelity, as in temptations for you to break the marriage vows. There are tests of honesty, like paying your debts, and not omitting income on your tax return.

But those are nothing compared to life's real tests.

That beautiful child you prayed for came with a crippling disease. Your spouse was laid off and you are losing your home. Your son has become involved with a group of young people of questionable and frightening behavior. Your daughter wants to go live in the big city because she is bored with the simple (good?) life. Or you discover cancer in your breast. Your husband just had a severe heart attack.

In the Lord's Prayer most of us pray, "Lead us not into temptation." Some translations read, "Do not put us to the test."

I can make you this promise, God will never allow us to be tested beyond what we can bare. And also that our Lord Jesus has promised to never leave us or forsake us. Ever!

The reason I can make you those promises is that they are specifically promised in the Scriptures.

"No testing has overtaken you that is not common to everyone. God is faithful, and He will not let you be tested beyond your strength, but with the testing He will also provide the way out so that you may be able to endure it."
1 Corinthians 10:12-13 (NRSV)

Lord, it is easier to talk this than to live it. Help me to keep my trust in You and know that You are always near.

August 22

It was a 1955 Dodge, and had been my Grandfather Jordan's car.

When Grandpa "Press" Jordan died, the family, my Mother, and her siblings, thought that I ought to have the car since I was studying for the ministry. Knowing how broke I was, they sold it to me at a bargain.

The family had gathered at my Aunt Lessie's house after the funeral. I arrived late and had to park up the hill a ways. I pulled over to the left side of the narrow street, put the car in park, and began to walk down to the house.

My Uncle J. P. raced past me to the car, which was rolling backward down the hill. He jumped into the driver's seat, grabbed the steering wheel, and braked to a stop. There was no park gear in a 1955 Dodge. I had put the car in neutral.

I have thought of that experience many times. It helps me with the question of how faithful Christian people experience bad things.

God doesn't put bad stuff on us. Bad stuff is part of the human condition. Like the rain falling on the just and the unjust, suffering comes to the good as well as the bad. Nor does it mean that we have sinned.

It is like the Dodge and my Uncle J. P. When things spin out of control, when tragedy occurs, and we turn to God for help, He takes the controls, gives direction, and applies the brakes.

I didn't say that the love of God, faith in Jesus, or the indwelling of the Spirit, would keep bad things away.

I do say that when we turn to God amidst the bad things, He works to bring good out of them, and glory to Himself.

"…We know that all things work together for good to those who love God, to those who are the called according to His purposes."
Romans 8:28

August 23

Today is a good day to examine motives.

Why do people do what they do? Is it simply folks following their instincts, as animals do? Is it because of the way they have been trained, brought up, socialized? Whatever. People have the power to choose.

We generally choose what pleases us. What benefits us personally. If it enriches us, or enhances our persona we do it. The subject is "Me, Myself, and I."

But Jesus calls on us to denounce personal self-interest and seek to be a blessing to others. While it is true that one needs good self-esteem to be a healthy person it is nevertheless true that the Christian ethic is service, not self-aggrandizement. So what motivates us?

What motivates you? If you looked into the most secret place of your heart what would you find? Who would be on the throne of your life? The Lord Jesus? You?

"So, whether you eat or drink, or whatever you do, do everything for the glory of God."
1 Corinthians 10:31 (NRSV)

Dear Lord, I am ashamed of my selfishness. I seek money, hoping that it will bring me security. I collect friends to demonstrate my popularity. I give to the needy with satisfaction that I am not like them. My witnessing is not always purely motivated.

Thank You, Lord, that You are longsuffering. Thank You for not spewing me out of Your mouth. It is only Your mercy and grace that gives me hope. Bless me in all the ways that I need it, Oh Lord, and let me truly be an honor to You, and a blessing to others. Amen

August 24

One morning, while I was still in the Army, I was standing around, waiting for my physical fitness test. I began to look for pecans that had fallen from the stately old trees at the parade field at Fort McPherson, Georgia.

I had not eaten breakfast, and the sweet Georgia pecans would provide a tasty treat. But it was in the fall of the year, and leaves covered the ground, making it difficult to find the nuts.

My feet found the pecans. I couldn't see them with my eyes but I could feel them through the soft soles of my running shoes.

I thought of Moses. I had often wondered why God told him to take off his shoes before approaching the burning bush.

Then it hit me.

God is not just a good old buddy, someone that we can pop in on whenever, without serious thought or preparation. He is not a benevolent uncle who smiles, pats us on the head, and tells us it is okay, that sin is no big deal. He is the mighty creator, the righteous judge. The one before whom each of us will stand and give account of ourselves.

We don't rush easily into the presence of such a God. We first take off our shoes. We approach Him uncovered, vulnerable to the stones and thorns; painfully reminded that we are utterly dependent on His mercy.

We search for Him with our eyes, and listen for Him with our ears. But sometimes we find Him with our FEET. Don't let your spirit be insulated from God. Stay tender, uncovered. Take off your shoes.

"...Take your sandals off your feet, for the place where you stand is holy ground."
Exodus 3:5

I'm going barefoot, Lord. Amen

August 25

Daniel was a remarkable young man.

While just a kid he was taken as a slave to Babylon, where he served in the royal court.

Imagine the temptations: he was away from home, in a strange land with many exotic attractions. There were strange foods, and all kinds of wine. He could have taken whatever he wanted. After all, he was a servant in the king's house. He choose to not partake. He was determined to remain true to his faith, to be *guided by a firm purpose.*

This profound sense of purpose helped Daniel to avoid the royal temptations and survive the lion's den. It also made him indispensable to four kings: Nebuchadnezzar, Belchazzar, Darius, and Cyrus.

Purpose is to a person like a secured string is to a kite. It allows us to soar, to use adverse winds as an engine of flight.

Purpose is also like the anchor of a ship, helping us to face the changing tides and ride out the storms of life.

In a training session in Panama I was seated near the window where I could see all of the sailboats anchored along the canal. When I looked out of the window later the boats had done a one eighty, turning completely about. The tide had reversed but the boats had stayed secure. The anchors did it.

Dear Lord, the winds and waves of adversity are buffeting me. The king's meat and wine are attractive. Help me to keep my eyes on you. Fortify me with the same deliberate purpose that the young Daniel had. Amen

"...Daniel purposed in his heart that he would not defile himself with the portion of the king's delicacies...."
Daniel 1:8

I enjoyed the book, *Let The Redeemed of The Lord Say So*, by Eddie Fox and George Morris.

After discussing the sins of *commission* and the sins of *omission* they pointed out that there is another, more insidious, sin, the sin of *permission*.

This is the sin where we look on while evil is committed but do nothing to stop it. A reality that surely has plagued many who lived through the regime of Hitler. People who didn't personally harm the Jews, but had to know what was going on.

As a son of the South I must admit that there were times that I saw evil happening without acting to stop it. Times that I chose not to get involved. And I am humbled by the memories. But one incident comes to mind of which I am very proud.

I attended a rural high school. One day one of the school organizations took a field trip into the next county. As we rode through a small country town an upperclassman noticed a little black girl standing on the sidewalk. The school bus was moving slowly. The upperclassman lowered the window and threw a grapefruit at the little girl, hitting her in the stomach and bending her double.

I was outraged, and flew into him. He beat me up. Badly. Not one member of the group lifted a finger to help me. I searched their faces afterward for any sign that they disapproved of his action. Nothing. It was between the upperclassman and me. And between him and the little black girl. It's has been many years now, and I am still proud of that beating.

Dear Lord, forgive me for the sin of permission. I need a refilling of compassion, and more guts. Don't let me cop out. I want to be as compassionate and involved as You were, Lord. Amen

"...To him who knows to do good and does not do it, to him it is sin."

James 4:17

August 27

Today is yours!

It is unique! Wonderfully personalized.

Nobody in the world has one just like it nor will anyone ever have one just like it.

Today holds the record of your past, and the potential for your future.

You can fill today with calm beauty and exciting experiences or ruin it with fruitless worry.

If the failures of the past enter your mind or threatening thoughts of the future, you don't have to dwell on them.

Nothing can steal this day from you if you refuse to allow it. So, thank God for today, and trust Him for tomorrow.

Why not make today your time to evaluate your spiritual state, and take whatever action is needed? If you haven't yet embraced Jesus as Lord and Savior you can do it now, by inviting Him into your heart.

If you are already a believer you can ask for a renewal of your spirit, a refilling of His Spirit. You can grow today. And rejoice while you are growing.

Dear Lord, thank You for this wonderful day. Don't let me spoil it because of a shortsighted faith or a miserable attitude. Let me savor every minute of it. I won't be overwhelmed by trivia, nor will I be overawed by obstacles.

You have made me a winner Lord. By Your grace and strength I can do anything I need to do. And I thank You. Amen

"This is the day which the Lord has made; We will rejoice and be glad in it."
Psalm 118:24

August 28

They played the same joke on every new engineer. Each newcomer was given the "impossible" task of developing a process for frosting lightbulbs on the inside.

An engineer, Marvin Pipkin, newly assigned at General Electric, was given the project.

Everyone noted the time and date and waited for the fun to begin.

But Mr. Pipkin took the task seriously. Not knowing that it was impossible, he went ahead and did it. He also discovered a way to etch the glass with soft, rounded pits which gave the bulbs added strength and effected a maximum diffusion of the light.

Isn't it great that no one told Mr. Pipkin that he had been assigned the impossible, that it was a company joke?

Our words can set barriers or open doors. Examples:

"You'll never amount to anything," or

"Keep working at it. You can make it."

Don't let anyone talk you out of the greatness you can experience today. God is on your side! Have you forgotten that? You and He are an overwhelming majority. He *loves you, man* (and woman).

Also, don't slip, and talk someone else out of her (or his) great day. Amen

"...With God all things are possible."
Matthew 19:26

Heavenly Father I need to be reminded daily of Your great love and mighty power. You have promised to be with me today. And tomorrow. Don't ever let me forget it, Lord. Amen

August 29

It has been several years since I buried my best friend, Chaplain Jim White, in the cemetery of the Minden, Louisiana, Presbyterian Church. It was about the hardest thing I ever had to do, harder even than giving the eulogy at my Dad's funeral.

At my Dad's funeral, I was free to grieve. My family members and I could hug, and cry, together.

At Jim's funeral, I had to be in charge, strong; to help the family deal with their grief. I really should have been sitting with them, grieving with them, on the first pew.

The term, burden of command, took on new meaning for me. That is a military term, but it means simply to be responsible for the welfare and behavior of others. At Jim's grave I felt the burden of responsibility.

So today I pray especially for those of you who feel the heavy burden of responsibility. I pray, too, for those of you who have lost, or are losing, a best friend. May God bless you abundantly.

How many friends do you have? Hundreds? Dozens? I am not talking about acquaintances.

My hunch is that most of us don't have more than five or six best friends. The ones with whom we can be our *true selves*. And if best friend means being able to discuss a shameful act that we have done, and kept hidden, we are blessed if we have more than one.

Be sure to tend to your friendship today. Amen

"Ointment and perfume delight the heart, and the sweetness of a...friend does so by hearty counsel."
Proverbs 27:9

Lord, I am rich because I have friends. Help me to be as good a friend to others as You have been to me. Amen

August 30

Today let's have compassion on the poor pitcher.

All athletes play under stress. They know that if their performance is marginal they will be yanked. Whether they are in football, basketball, or soccer. Tennis players must be highly stressed, too. But no one is more visible than the pitcher.

He knows that there are others in the bullpen, or warming up on the sidelines, who can take his place quickly. He has to deliver. Throw strikes. Avoid walks. And the camera catches his every move. He had better not scratch the wrong place, or pick his nose.

In the Parable of the Talents Jesus told the story of the master giving his three servants talents to use and multiply. (Read about it in Matthew 25:14-30.) To one servant the master gave five talents and he gained five more. To another he gave two and that servant gained two more.

One servant was given only one talent. He was so afraid of returning empty handed that he buried the talent in the ground for safety. Then he had the audacity to tell the master that at least he hadn't lost it.

The unprofitable servant's sentence was severe, "Cast the unprofitable servant into the outer darkness. There will be weeping and gnashing of teeth."

What this parable means to me is that *Christ expects something of us.*

Are you making a profit for Christ? Or are you a mere consumer in the Kingdom? What are you doing with the gifts that He gave you? Are you bringing back more than you received? Don't forget the bullpen.

"...To everyone who has, more will be given, and he will have abundance; but from him who does not have, even what he has will be taken away."
Matthew 25:29

August 31

An eight-year-old boy had a little sister, age 6, who was dying of leukemia.

The boy was told that a blood transfusion would save his sister's life, and without one she would die. His parents asked his permission to test his blood type to see if it was compatible with his sister's. He gave permission and sure enough their blood types matched.

When his parents asked if he was willing to donate a pint of blood they emphasized that his sister would die without a transfusion. Still, he hesitated, and asked if he could think on it and let them know the next day. They said sure, and the next day the boy gave his permission.

He was strapped onto a gurney beside his sister. He watched silently as the blood dripped into her vein.

The doctor came by a few minutes later to check on how the boy was doing. The boy opened his eyes, and asked, "How soon do I start to die?"

Pure love. Unvarnished, unpretended, real, true. Isn't that one of the traits that Jesus saw in children that made Him love and value them so? He told His disciples that they would have to humble themselves and become like a little child to enter the Kingdom of Heaven.

In the Scriptures love is always an action, never just a feeling? Jesus summarized the ten commandants into two: love God with all of your heart, and love your neighbor as yourself. Now I can command an action, but I can't command a feeling. People confuse love and like. You like apple pie, but you love your neighbor. That's the difference in feeling and acting.

"Beloved, let us love one another, for love is of God; and everyone who loves is born of God and knows God."
1 John 4:7

September 1

Notre Dame was behind the University of Southern California 7-17 at the half. Their unbeaten string and a possible national championship were on the line.

During half time, Coach Lou Holz was interviewed just prior to resumption of play. "What went on in the locker room, Coach?" the reporter asked. "We had a gut check," answered Holz.

Notre Dame came back in the second half to win 28-24.

Have you had a spiritual gut check lately? The Scriptures abound with illustrations.

As a young Hebrew slave in Babylon, Daniel "Purposed in his heart that he would not defile himself with the portion of the King's meat" (Daniel 1:8 KJV). That resolve served him well, especially in the lion's den.

Jesus, facing tomorrow's cross, and in great agony of spirit, asked that the cup be taken away, but then said, "Not my will, but Thy will be done" (Luke 22:24 KJV). That severe dedication to God's will and purpose enabled Him to endure the sufferings and death that purchased our redemption.

Lord, I'm not talking about gaining weight. I need another kind of gut check. I find it too easy to back off when I ought to be pushing for justice. I run out of compassion too quickly. I often am easier on myself than I am on others.

Whenever I would fall away from serving You because of hardship, fatigue, or embarrassment, bless me with your power and grace. Give me a gut check, Lord, and fill me with Your Holy Spirit. Amen.

"I pray that out of His glorious riches He may strengthen you with power through His Spirit *in your inner being.*"

Ephesians 3:16 (NIV)

September 2

I hurried to reach the door before she did so that I could open it for her. After all, being raised a "Southern Gentleman" I knew what my duty was.

The door didn't cooperate. It was a double door, and I was trying to open the wrong side. She apparently knew more about that doorway than I did. She easily pulled the other door open, and held it open for me to enter, smiling sweetly all of the time. And me outweighing her by sixty pounds! What could I do? I said, "Thank you."

That happened many years ago, during the heated national debate about the Equal Opportunity Amendment. Even though the amendment failed, I believe that a consensus has been reached by the American people that women must be recognized as equal with men. Period. (We men had better hope that the opposite sex will settle for equality.)

If the equality issue is settled, then, shouldn't we be moving on to the next dimension of the relationship between the genders? It does take "two to tango," but, more importantly, it takes two to make a *partnership*.

It is the Apostle Paul, unfortunately vilified by some as the original male chauvinist pig, who raises the issue to the level of Scripture. Neither sex can exist without the other. Both male and female come from God. Both exist to live their lives to His glory.

Paul writes,

"Nevertheless, neither is man independent of woman, nor woman independent of man, in the Lord. For as the woman was from the man, even so the man also is through the woman, but all things come from God."
1 Corinthians 11:11,12

Dear Lord, cleanse from our minds and hearts the political agendas that we bring to discussions of gender. Help us to view each other as Jesus taught.

September 3

A speaker held up a $20 bill and asked, "Who wants this $20 bill?" Hands went up all over the audience.

He crumpled the $20 bill in his fist. "Now who wants it?" Again the hands went up.

Next he ground the $20 bill into the floor under his shoe. Then he lifted it up, all crumpled and dirty. "I suppose no one wants it now," he said, "But let's have a show of hands anyway." Again, all of the hands went up.

Did you get the point? Nothing he did to the bill diminished its value. There is a difference between value and appearance.

I saw a father take his son into his arms. He cradled him to his heart while tears slipped down his cheeks. The boy had a terrible disease that attacks young children and twists their bodies so that they usually die in their early teens. The boy was unable to talk. Only his eyes could respond to his father's loving embrace. And his heart! The father was too choked to speak. Their tears talked to each other. The boy was about as crumpled as one can be, but his father couldn't have loved him more.

Have you been crumpled by a cruel fate? Have life experiences ground you into the dirt? Are you troubled by a sense of worthlessness? Perhaps you are using the wrong measure of worth.

How valuable are you to God? lie answered that by giving His "only begotten son" to die on a cruel cross for you. That son, our Savior, loved you enough to die on that cross for you. There can be no greater value put on you than that Christ died for you.

St. Peter wrote that your trials:

"These have come so that your faith...of greater worth than gold, which perishes even though refined by fire...may be proved genuine...."
1 Peter 1:7 NIV

September 4

Which of the following are you?
A fugitive is someone who is running from home.
A *vagabond* is a person who has no home.
A *stranger* is a man or woman away from home.
A *pilgrim* is a traveler on his or her way home.

If you answered none of the above I beg to differ. That is, if you are a Christian. With apologizes to fans of John Wayne (include me), "You're a pilgrim, pilgrim."

When I was young most of the people I knew lived in poverty, by today's standards. They worked literally from daylight to dark. Physical, back breaking work. Sun leathered skin. Tired muscles. Weary minds and hearts. They dreamed of heaven as a place of plenty, and rest.

My pastor, a wonderful man whose education was mostly from life experiences, preached often about Heaven. He wasn't joking about lying down in the shade of the Tree of Life, reaching up and picking a delicious fruit, taking off his shoes, and cooling his feet in the River of Life.

Who thinks about heaven today? We are too well off. Who needs heaven when we have full refrigerators, state of the art medical care, large incomes, nice cars, and assured futures? The world may have changed, but the Word of God hasn't.

"These all died in faith, not having received the promises, but having seen them from afar off were assured of them, and confessed that they were strangers and *pilgrims* on the earth. For those who say such things declare openly that they seek a homeland...they desire a better, that is a heavenly country...."
Hebrews 11:13-16

How are you doing, Pilgrim?

September 5

(A note to you who give devotional talks on occasions. The following outline can be used for a brief devotional. I have used it many times. And I am sure that I have copied bits from others. It is particularly helpful when you are called upon unexpectedly. Just type it on a 3 by 5 card and keep it in your coat pocket.)

Which is the great text? And why is it great?

Of course you know the answer, John 3:16. The King James Version is probably the best known and most beloved.

"For God" - The great creator.
"So loved" - The great initiative.
"The world" - The great number.
"That He gave" - The great act.
"His only begotten Son" - The great gift.
"That whosoever" - The great invitation.
"Believeth" - The great simplicity.
"In Him" - The great person.
"Should not perish" - The great escape.
"But have" - The great surety.
"Everlasting" - The great forever.
"Life" - The great possession.

John 3:16

Dear Lord, thank You for loving me. I can't fathom why You even bothered. Yet I am overwhelmed by Your love, Your mighty act of redemption. Thank You. Bless me.

And dear Lord, bless every reader of this page, and all of their family members too.

Amen

September 6

The richest man in the world, Croesus, once asked the wisest man in the world, "What is God?"

The wise man asked for a day to answer. Then another day. Finally, after several days he admitted that he couldn't answer the question. And that the longer he thought on the question the more difficult it became.

What the wisest of the world can't know through their own pursuits, the humblest Christians know through the simple act of believing.

Tertullian, an early church father, said that, "The most ignorant mechanic, among the Christians knows God, and is able to make Him known to others."

If you want to know who God is? Look at Jesus. Do you want to know how God thinks? Listen to Jesus. Do you want to know how God feels? Pay attention to Jesus.

Ask Jesus about the poor, the prisoner, the hungry, the naked. Ask Jesus about the meaning of honesty, justice, mercy, and charity.

There is a saying in the South that someone is a "spittin' image of his dad." Meaning that the person is so much like his dad that he could have been spit out of his mouth.

Think of Jesus as a photograph of God, in that His portrayal of the Father is accurate.

"I and My Father are one."
John 10:30

"...He who sees Me sees Him who sent me...I have not spoken on My own authority; but the Father who sent me gave Me a command, what I should say and what I should speak."
John 12:45,49

Lord, I want to have others see Jesus in me just as Jesus showed us how the Father is. Well, I need all of the help I can get. So help me Lord to be more like Jesus. Amen

September 7

According to a poll a few years ago the six spiritual needs in America are:

1. To believe that life has meaning and purpose.
2. A sense of community and deeper relationships.
3. To be appreciated and respected.
4. To be listened to, and heard.
5. To feel that ones faith is growing.
6. Practical help in developing a mature faith.

When I read the poll results I thought "church." And I wasn't even a pastor at that time.

It is in the faith community, the church, that one finds purpose and meaning for life. That there is more than the cynic's plaintive rhyme, "The worms crawl in and the worms crawl out; they eat you up and they spit you out...."

Check out almost any large congregation today and you will find numerous initiatives, groups, and programs designed to foster a sense of community and deeper relationships.

Where better to be listened to, and heard than a Bible study group? And how better to allow your faith to grow than by participating in an outreach program.

"For as we have many members in one body, but all the members do not have the same function, so we, being many, are one body in Christ, and individually members of one another. Having then gifts differing according to the grace that is given to us, let us use them...."
Romans 12:4-6

Lord, You give meaning and purpose to my life. Help me to be Your instrument in bringing the Gospel to others. Amen

See you in church Sunday.

September 8

The sermon was about "Holding the Ropes."

During a raging flood a farmer happened to fall into the swollen river and was immediately carried away by its force. He was quickly being swept downstream.

A neighbor saw what happened, got into his truck, and raced down river to the next little village. As he drove into the village he blew his horn for attention and shouted, "Everyone get a rope and run to the bridge."

They did. He lined them up on the bridge two feet apart. Each person dangling a rope over the side. As the struggling farmer was swept under the bridge he was able to grab a rope and was rescued.

William Carey, a great American pioneer missionary, said to his supporters, "I will go down, but you must hold the ropes."

Are you holding a rope? Ropes?

This devotion is about getting the saving news, the Gospel of the Lord Jesus Christ, to the *whole* world, to the millions that are being swept into eternity not having heard nor embraced the Gospel.

Every Christian has a responsibility to reach them. If you can't go you have to send someone else. Jesus didn't cut you any slack. There are hundreds of missionary families waiting now for enough support to allow them to go in your place. Will you help? Check it out.

"Go therefore and make disciples of all the nations, baptizing them in the name of the Father and the Son and of the Holy Spirit."
Matthew 28:19

September 9

The idea was preposterous.

How could I claim to have been called into the Christian ministry? My family had not distinguished itself by its young people becoming preachers. Not by a long ways.

My Dad had told me tales of his father's moonshine stills.

At the age of nine he had used horse and buggy to deliver the shine to loggers in the Withlacoochee river swamp in central Florida. Dad had been pretty wild as a young man. And there were dark rumors that one of his siblings may have committed murder.

As I was debating the call in my mind I was reminded that God chooses ordinary people to do his work, and they usually are reluctant.

Moses protested, "O my Lord, I am not eloquent...but I am slow of speech and slow of tongue" (Exodus 4:10).

Jeremiah claimed that he was too young, "Ah, Lord God! Behold I cannot speak, for I am a youth" (Jeremiah 1:6).

It's great to be humble, but don't use reticence as an excuse to not heed the call of God. Your protestations of inadequacies may be a cop-out. God knows you better than you know yourself.

So, if you are wondering if God can use you as a preacher, teacher, witness, carpenter, policeman, soldier, spouse, ditch digger, or whatever, listen up:

"...You see your calling, brethren, that *not many wise* according to the flesh, not many *mighty*, not many *noble*, *are called*. But God has chosen the foolish things of the world to put to shame the wise, and God has chosen the weak things of the world to put to shame the things which are mighty."

1 Corinthians 1:26,27

September 10

Big is not necessarily an indicator of importance.

This is being written shortly after a Super Bowl and during the Winter Olympics at Nagano, Japan. There is no intent in this devotion to make light of the great athletes, nor their sports.

The question is what makes something great? Is it money, sports, entertainment, fun, publicity, numbers?

To be great something must be life changing.

There was no crowd at Jesus' birth. No satellite communications, no renowned visitors, no speeches, no dedications. Yet it was the greatest event in human history.

More personally. When a bitter, hostile, and angry person is changed by the power of Christ it is a great event. When a selfish, self-righteous, and uncaring person is made new by the grace of God it is a great event. As is when a drunk stays dry, a drugger lives clean, and a thief gets a job.

The truly great event is a *single* human's encounter with the Almighty God: when Jesus creates a new heart, and the Holy Spirit empowers new behavior. There may be people around but it is always a *profoundly private* experience.

Can you remember it happening? Are you still waiting? Or are you rejoicing?

"And *you* He *made alive*, who were dead in trespasses and sins, in which you once walked according to the course of this world...but God, who is rich in mercy, because of His great love...raised us up together, and made us sit together in the heavenly places in Christ Jesus."
Ephesians 2:1-6

Lord, I know that you have made me alive. So why do I feel so sluggish spiritually? Today I will make it a point to read the Scriptures more carefully, pray more sincerely, and share my faith with at least one other person. Then won't I feel better about myself, Lord? Amen

September 11

Do you like silence? Some people seem to be threatened by it. Every minute has to be filled with sounds, with noise.

Even as I type this on my word processor I am listening to Christian music on CDs. Wouldn't this book be a mess if I liked different music, such as acid rock?

The chairperson of an administrative board in a local church always began meetings, not with a formal prayer, but with fifteen minutes of silence.

Members were expected to pray silently, either at their seats, or at the altar. Later, during the meeting, when a member spoke, her remarks were followed by silence. No one rushed in immediately to have his say. Instead they waited, reflected, listening for the voice of God.

Just as nature abhors a vacuum, many people dread silence.

Is the reason that we are always talking that we are afraid to listen? What if God should speak to us while we are silent? We would then have to obey. No more excuse. So, we keep talking, and wonder why we never hear from God.

Isn't it a question of the Lordship of Christ?

Doesn't it all boil down to who is in charge of our lives? We know that if He requires a certain obedience we have to obey, if He is to be Lord. So we drown Him out. Don't let Him speak. What we don't know we can't be responsible for. Correct?

"To everything there is a season...*a time to keep silence*, and a time to speak."
Ecclesiastes 3:1,7

Lord, I spend my hours acting as though I can know You through *doing* stuff. I forget that you told me that I can know that You are God when I am still. I'm not good at still, Lord. Teach me.

Amen

September 12

I couldn't bear to take Gene's name out of our address book.

While traveling around the world for over thirty years in the Army Chaplaincy, my wife, Shirley, and I have met thousands of people. Hundreds of whom we considered friends.

When our assignments separated us we usually would write occasionally, then less regularly, and then only at Christmas. Finally, we would stop exchanging mail altogether, and leave them out of our next address book.

I first met Chaplain (Father) Eugene A. Garvens when we were fellow students at the Chaplain School. He was a crusty old priest with absolute disdain for red tape and saw most military requirements as harassment. However, he loved people totally. I never knew a more caring pastor, or faithful friend.

Gene had no family so he created one.

Shirley and I, and our kids, were part of Gene's family. He was often at our house, and always having us to his. He showed his love for us in many ways, and he felt like a brother to me. When he finally had to go into an old priest's home we talked regularly on the phone. Shirley and I were also able to visit him once.

Then one day I called and the phone had been disconnected. Father Gene had "passed." He had been in our address book a long time. Now?

There is a book where our names are safe:

"He who overcomes shall be clothed in white garments, and *I will not blot out his name from the Book of Life....*"
Revelation 3:5

Lord, I thank You for Gene; Jim, Elijah, Al, and Jerry. And Mom and Dad, too. They are out of my book, Lord, but not out of my heart. Thank you for their love and friendship. Amen

September 13

A pastor told the story of an elderly lady who went into her insurance office with a tattered life insurance policy in her hand.

"I can't afford to make these payments anymore. I'm just going to have to give this policy back."

The agent urged her to try to keep the policy, "You've been paying on this many years. It would be a shame to have to let it go now. Couldn't the beneficiary pay the premiums for you?"

"Oh, I'm the beneficiary," she said.

It was a policy on her husband who had been dead for three years. She had been paying the premiums needlessly, not understanding that they had been canceled and that she was due a large sum of money.

A lot of people are like that in their relationship to Christ.

They act like they still have to pay the premiums. They pay in fear, guilt, shame, and sometimes, despair.

Christ made the final payment on our *policy*. Through His suffering, death, and resurrection those of us who trust in Him are forgiven.

And when God forgives us through Christ He does so without conditions. We are forgiven, free; with a new, fresh, start. The past is just that, *past*.

So stop paying on what has already been paid in full.

"In Him we have redemption through His blood, the forgiveness of sins, according to the riches of His grace."
Ephesians 1:7

Wow! I'm paid up. You are too, if you trust the Lord Jesus as Savior.

Thanks for picking up the tab, Lord.

Amen

September 14

I now believe in Santa Claus. Mine was an angel.

We had an accident on a Sunday Morning while turning into the church parking lot. Shirley was driving, turning left, and didn't see the truck coming toward her. In the split second before the accident she braked and swerved left. At the same instant the oncoming driver braked and swerved right.

There was considerable damage to the cars but no one was injured. If the drivers had reacted a second later we would have been broadsided and I could have been severely injured or killed. We were blessed.

The driver of the wrecker was big and rugged, and soft-spoken. To my wife he said, "Ma'am, Jesus loves you." He took care of every detail of getting the car to the garage. While doing so he told me about his church.

As he was about to leave me I asked his name. I believe that he said, "Norvan." But he told me that his co-workers call him *Santa Claus* because they think he looks like him. As he drove away he called out to me, "Just remember that Jesus loves you."

Now, why do I say that my Santa Claus was an angel? The Biblical definition of an angel is one sent from God, a messenger. Norvan was certainly sent to us from God. And what a message he brought.

Of course I do believe that there are celestial beings, angels, different from humans, that do the bidding of God. But you can be an angel, too. When you allow yourself to be *sent from,* and a *messenger of,* God.

Be an angel today. Someone needs to hear that Jesus loves him or her.

"Do not forget to entertain strangers, for by so doing some have unwittingly entertained angels."
Hebrews 13:2

September 15

Do you ever feel like giving up? Just quitting?

Wouldn't it be sad if you were about to succeed in a cherished goal but gave up, not knowing that you had just about made it?

A young, free-lance artist tried his best to sell his sketches to a number of newspapers. He was turned down by all of them.

One editor went so far as to tell him that he had no talent. But the young artist had faith in his ability and continued trying to sell his work.

Finally, he got a job making drawings for church publicity material. He rented a mice-infested garage for a work studio and continued to draw, hoping that someone would buy his sketches. One particular mouse caught his attention and must have inspired his cartoon character.

With the creation of Mickey Mouse, Walt Disney was on his way.

A country preacher said that there are two ways to get to the top: climb an oak tree, or sit on an acorn.

I don't like the proverb, "If at first you don't succeed, try, try again." It is often a formula for defeat.

It is great to be persistent, but some trails are dead ends. Try this, instead, "If at first you don't succeed, try a different way?"

Faith is the enabler. It enables you to persevere. Whether it is to keep knocking on a closed door or to take a completely different path, one "less chosen."

"He will render to every man according to his works: to those who by patience in well-doing seek for glory and honor and immortality, He will give eternal life."
Romans 2:6,7 (RSV)

September 16

Are you a water walker?

The disciples were on a boat in the middle of the Sea of Galilee when they saw what appeared to be a ghost walking toward them. As the "ghost" drew nearer they recognized that it was Jesus.

He told them to not fear.

Now most folks would have been content to exchange a few pleasantries. Maybe offer Jesus a ride back to the shore. Not Peter.

Peter cried out, "Lord, if it is You, command me to come to You on the water." Jesus said, "Come."

Peter stepped over the side of the boat, and apparently was walking okay until he noticed the waves. Then he began to sink. "Lord, save me," Peter cried.

Jesus immediately reached out His hand to Peter and caught him. Now here is the point that a lot of folks miss: Peter *walked* backed to the boat. He didn't swim. And the winds didn't cease until Peter and Jesus got to the boat. He walked beside Jesus, holding on to Jesus' hand.

You, too, can walk on your water. The water of doubt. Of fear. Of depression. Of failure.

You can face your fierce winds too. You can walk through them and not be blown away. The winds of trouble and strife. Of fatigue. Of suffering. Of disease.

You can walk on anything, through anything, as long as you are walking beside Jesus. As long as He holds your hand.

Probably with a smile, Jesus asked Peter,

"O you of little faith, why did you doubt?"
Matthew 14:31

Good question.

September 17

One candidate for president called another candidate a hypocrite. And it made the front pages. Folks hate hypocrites.

Shakespeare didn't like them either, "O, what may man within him hide, though angel on the outward side."

So, what is a hypocrite?

According to *Webster's Encyclopedic Unabridged Dictionary of the English Language* a hypocrite is "A person who *pretends* to have virtues, moral or religious beliefs, principles, etc., that he or she *does not actually possess*, especially a person whose actions belie stated beliefs."

The popular definition of a hypocrite is different, and *wrong*. It says that hypocrites are "People who don't live up to my standards."

By that definition, I am a hypocrite if I don't live up to your standards. And you are one if you don't live up to my standards.

Hypocrites are *pretenders*. When a person is striving to live out the claims of Jesus, but fails, and admits the failure, she is not a hypocrite.

The real hypocrites are those who sit outside and criticize those who enter. They feign moral superiority. They say, "I am not doing right, but at least I am not in the church not doing right."

Don't let them keep you from joining a good church and striving to be the best Christian you can be, even if you occasionally fail in your trying.

"Woe to you...hypocrites..."
Matthew 23:14

Please don't let some good go without doing today because you are afraid that someone will notice, remember one of your faults, and call you a hypocrite.

Better still, develop duck feathers spiritually so that stuff will roll off. Don't let your service to our Lord be measured by your fears of what others will think. Amen

September 18

A man who raised sheep kept losing them to his neighbors' dogs. What could he do? Fences? Barbed wire? Lawsuit? Shotgun?

None of the above.

Instead he gave a lamb, as a pet, to each neighbor's child. In no time at all the dogs were penned or on a leash.

Perhaps that is what is meant by *turning the other cheek*?

I should be good at this sort of thing, being a preacher. But, I'm not. When someone wrongs me, I want to get even. Getting back can be very satisfying. And it can be quick.

Following Jesus' teachings doesn't always bring quick solutions. Nor are the solutions always what we would personally hope. Our heart may be right, but the other person's may not be.

The Christian faith is not about winning at someone else's expense. It is about doing right.

It's a question of who keeps score.

When I follow my own human impulse to return hurt for hurt, I am running my own tab. When I do what I know is right, regardless of the consequences, I am letting God be the bookkeeper. It then becomes His doings, not mine.

Hello God!

So, it is not about my winning a struggle with an enemy. It is about my winning the struggle with myself.

"Do not be overcome by evil, but overcome evil with good."
Romans 12:21

Lord, You know that I am a counter. Help me to let You keep the scores. Amen

September 19

An Associated Press article told a great story of compassion and sacrifice.

For several months after a killer hurricane, Red Cross officials received an envelope of change each week for the hurricane victims. By the time officials discovered the identity of the anonymous donor, he had contributed a total of $17.00. I won't give his name, but he is a mentally handicapped man living on a Social Security income.

"I'm glad to humbly do good to help the poor and help end suffering," the man said. "I just wanted to be generous and help out. I have my troubles, too, and some of those used to be pretty bad. But I am a Christian now, and I try to be kind."

Giving is as much a part of worship as praising God, praying, reading responsively, and singing.

During over thirty years of conducting worship services in the Army I always took up a collection. Even under combat situations. If giving is an act of worship what right did I have to deny that worship opportunity to soldiers just because they were at war? Especially with them facing injury or death? The Chaplain Fund didn't need money. But the soldiers needed to give.

Do you have a plan that you follow in practicing your stewardship? Are you giving to support the ministry of the Gospel both at home and abroad?

Don't determine the amount of your gift to God by what is left over after everything else is paid. He loved you extravagantly.

It is a mark of our maturing as adults when we can say a quiet amen to what Jesus said, as printed below.

"...Remember the words of the Lord Jesus, that He said, 'It is more blessed to give than to receive.' "
Acts 20:35

September 20

A mother asked her seven-year-old son to polish her shoes.

When the boy finished the shoes he had done such a fine job that his mother rewarded him with a quarter. Later, when she put the shoes on, she felt something in one shoe. She removed the shoe and discovered a wad of paper with a quarter inside. On the paper, in a child's scrawl, were these words:

"You can keep the quarter. I done it for love."

I used to try to get home to see Momma on Mother's Day. After one particular trip I called to check on her and she said it had been the best visit we had since Dad died. It must have been the tape recording.

Mom had agreed to let me tape her responses to questions about genealogy and family history. It turned out to be great fun, especially when I threw in some extra curricular questions, such as "When did you and Dad first kiss?" and "Tell me about the birth of each of your children."

Mom really got into it, almost as though she were re-living events from her life. We laughed and there were a few tears. I wished that I had taped her thirty years earlier, and Dad too. What a blessing, and what a delightful treasure that one and one-half hour tape has become.

So, this morning, as you begin another day, pause a few moments and thank God for loving parents and for the strength and support of family.

And buy a tape recorder if you don't have one.

"Her children rise up and call her blessed...a woman who fears the Lord, she shall be praised."
Proverbs 31:28-30

Attention all grown children with living parents: Interview them on tape. Capture the history, the joy and the pain. Do it now while they are well, and lucid. You will thank me for reminding you.

September 21

(Following is a paraphrase of John 4:31-42. It is the story of Jesus speaking with the Samaritan woman at Jacob's well.)

"Morning, Miss. How about a drink of water?"

"Isn't it a bit odd for you, a Jew, to be asking something from a Samaritan? Even speaking with a Samaritan? A woman, at that?"

"If you knew who I am you could ask and I would give you living water."

"Aren't you something. You don't even have a bucket. Living water? Do you think you are greater than our fathers? Of Jacob?"

"Drink that water and you will get thirsty again. Drink the water I can give you and you will never thirst again."

"Okay. Give me some."

"First, go get your husband."

"I don't have one."

"But you have had five husbands, and are living with a guy now."

"Oh, so you are a prophet, then. Well tell me. In which mountain must we worship? Who is right, you Jews, or us Samaritans?"

"Neither mountain, actually. It isn't about mountains. It is about true worship. You see, true worship must be from the heart, with great sincerity and honesty. That's the kind of worship God seeks." *Hello God!*

Did you catch it? Seizing on a religious slogan to excuse an ethnic prejudice? Have you ever done that?

What about using the claim of religious conviction to mask a mean parochialism? "Oh, I can't have fellowship with you. You were baptized wrong." Stop it. Stop arguing about the right mountain, and worship God in Spirit with a merciful heart.

"God is Spirit, and those who worship Him must worship in spirit and truth." John 4:24

I'll take a drink of that water, Lord. Amen

September 22

Have scientists found the secret to how life came to earth?

They say that there are nearly one hundred complex organic chemicals in space that play a part in living cells. These chemicals *may* have bound to icy dust grains and evolved into RNA molecules capable of reproducing themselves. The molecules *could* have arrived on earth in comets, asteroids, and/or meteorites that bombarded the earth four billion years ago.

They say that the DNA molecule *evolved*, with its genetic code, about 3.6 billion years ago, and thus life emerged on the planet.

The arrogance of many scientists! Why must they exclude theologians from the search for the origin of life?

Upon reflection, however, I marveled at their *great faith*. Listen in:

Question: "Doctor scientist, where did humans come from?"

Answer: "They evolved from things that evolved from matter."

Question: "Where did matter come from?"

Answer: "It always existed."

I personally and firmly believe that the great God who loved the world through Jesus of Nazareth created the heavens and the earth. Since He is all-powerful, He may have done it in seven literal, i.e. human days. My point is that He did it.

Now I ask you: isn't it more reasonable to believe in a creator who called matter into existence than to believe that matter always existed? And if there were an evolutionary process isn't it easier to believe that God guided it and not mere chance?

The all-powerful creator loves you. Amen

"In the beginning God created the heavens and the earth."   Genesis 1:1

September 23

I always wanted a Gibson guitar. I either could never afford to buy one, or couldn't make myself part with the large sum of money necessary to buy one.

So imagine how covetous I was when, in the museum of a great entertainer, I saw four Gibson guitars encased in glass. Four of the world's best guitars. Not being used. On display.

A man in Italy was discovered living with very little furniture, but had 246 exquisite violins in his home. In the bottom drawer of a rickety bureau was a Stradivarius.

Because of the owners' devotion to the great musical instruments the world was denied the joy of hearing the instruments played.

Are you doing a similar thing? Are you keeping the music of Heaven, the Gospel of Jesus Christ, locked up behind the door of your heart?

The Gospel was given to us to be shared. No one has the right to keep it from the world.

Most folks who fail to witness seem to think that they aren't skilled enough, that only professionally trained persons can be trusted to share the Gospel. Not so. Every Christian can tell what God has done in his or her life.

Witnessing is as natural to a Christian as singing is to a bird. Don't try too hard. Don't try to sound fancy, professional. Just be yourself. Let the love of God flow naturally. Then what God promised to David will happen to you.

"...Open your mouth wide, and I will fill it."
Psalms 81:10

Lord, I don't want to be like the Gibson guitar wasting in the glass case. Dust me off. Tune me. Play me. Amen

September 24

The song asks, "What's ya gonna do when the well runs dry?"

Flash back to the prophet Elijah. He had been *hiding out* to escape the angry Queen's wrath. God had been using ravens to bring him bread and meat twice daily.

Then the brook from which he had been drinking dried up.

Hello God!

What are you going to do when your well runs dry?

What are you going to do when heaven seems to have turned into brass? When it feels like God has abandoned you? When a relationship fails? A friend betrays? When you can not find your way? When you are *empty*?

Elijah didn't dig in the dry creek bed. Nor should you dig among the sand and rocks of a dried up theological dogma. Sometimes the answer is to move on.

God has a word for you. A *personal* one. (There are no group plans in God's assurance program.) And God has the resources to make His plan for you work. You are wonderfully made and loved by God.

God is speaking to you. Are you listening? Maybe you have the volume turned down too low.

God's word for you may be a change in directions. New surroundings. New and more enriching and enabling worship experiences.

"...The word of the Lord came to him (*Elijah*), saying, 'Arise, go to Zarepath...and dwell there. See, I have commanded a widow there to provide for you'."
1 Kings 17:8,9

Lord, my well is nearly dry. I am listening. Amen

September 25

A little girl was lost.

It happened in late afternoon on a severely cold winter day in a Northern town. She had been playing in the backyard. One minute her mother looked and the little girl was there. Minutes later the little girl was gone.

The police were called. Time was critically important. It was killing cold. A radio message went out for volunteers. A hundred people responded. They searched frantically. All night.

At first light the mayor called everyone together. "We will join hands," he said, "and sweep every inch of the area until we find her." Sure enough the plan worked.

The father raced to where his little girl was, picked her up, and cradled her in his arms.

She was frozen to death.

With tears freezing on his face the father cried, "Why didn't we join hands sooner?"

I am afraid that when many of us meet Jesus we won't be complimented on how theologically correct we were, how orthodox, how exclusive.

Rather, He may point to the lost souls fallen into hell and ask, "Why didn't you join hands?"

Hello God!

"...We, being many, are one bread and one body; for we all partake of that one bread."
1 Corinthians 10:17

Are you a Methodist Christian who won't fellowship with Baptists? Or too Catholic to connect with Pentecostals? Too proud as a Presbyterian? Well, knock it off already. God is watching. Amen

September 26

No sea in the Holy City, the New Jerusalem! Well, who would have expected a sea in a city?

But no temple! Now that's a stretch.

No First Baptist Church with services at 8:30 and 10:45 A.M., and 6:00 P.M.? No Aldersgate Methodist Church with mothers' day out? Or First Presbyterian Church with marvelous bells echoing throughout the city? No extended services at Victory Revival Center?

None. There will be no *need* for a temple (or church).

The temple was built as a house of God. It was established as a place to meet God, to experience His presence.

God *fills* Heaven. His presence in Heaven will be real, and total, to a degree that we can't fathom in our human understanding.

He is with you today. Whatever your trials. Whatever your illness. Whatever the source of your sadness. God is with you. Write it down.

Hello God!

But you will be *in Him* in Heaven. (I hesitate to use that terminology for fear of being misunderstood, but ponder on it.)

"I saw no temple in it, for the Lord God Almighty and the Lamb are its temple."
Revelation 21:22

Lord, You'll have to help me with this. I know that Your Spirit is *in me* now. Won't I, in a wonderfully new and profound way, be *in You* in Heaven? Help me to comprehend that profound possibility with my spiritual understanding.

In the meantime, Lord, I need you to help me with the here and now. My faith tells me things that my mind finds hard to accept. I am connecting through faith Lord, not sight, touch, or sound. Amen

September 27

What kind of day are you having?

If you feel forsaken, under siege, or pressed upon, I want to remind you that God is with you today. Look around for Him. If you listen carefully you will hear Him speak through ordinary things.

Once I was questioning how God could possibly be working for my good in something that didn't make a bit of human sense. He "spoke" to me through a blue bird.

The bird had gotten down our chimney and was entrapped behind its screen. When I tried to catch him he escaped into the open part of our house. Back and forth he flew. In several efforts to escape he crashed into the picture window, then recovered, and kept flying around inside the house. I finally caught him with my minnow net. When I released him at the front door he probably thought that he had escaped death, rather than that he had been rescued.

Do you see my point yet? My very acts that would eventually save the bird brought terror to him.

When it seems that God is working against you, pause to understand that He really is working to save you. The things that seem wrong now, in our limited understanding, may be wise in the mind of God. He sees the whole picture and works for our good.

God is there, today, doing things in your life that will count for eternity. They don't have to make human sense to be for your good.

So, don't worry about the future. He holds your future in His hands. He wrote the plan.

You can trust Him, because He has said,

"I am the Alpha and the Omega, the beginning and the end...."

Revelation 22:13

September 28

No one ever sins in isolation. Someone else is always, inevitably, involved; often hurt.

How else can I understand that frightful passage in Exodus 20:5 "...I the Lord your God, am a jealous God, visiting the iniquity of the fathers on the children to the third and fourth generations of those who hate me?"

The passage tells me that when a man sins he establishes a context in which others must live. He creates an environment. He sets in motion a chain of events that follow naturally, if not sequentially.

When a woman prostitutes herself and lives openly in that shameful way, she shouldn't be surprised to see a daughter follow her example.

When a man floats in a world of substance abuse, gets his living by selling to others; he shouldn't be surprised to have a son follow.

I can't believe that the passage means that an innocent child incurs God's wrath directly and only because of the sins of another. That would go against the teachings of the New Testament as I understand them.

What a burden example can be.

I pray that you will bear up well under the challenge. Lead the way. Give others a good model after which they can pattern their lives. But be aware that God holds each of us responsible for his or her actions.

"So then each of us shall give account of himself to God."
Romans 14:12

Lord, this scares me. You know that I like to go through my days as though no one is watching, and like it doesn't matter what I do because it only effects me. Well, I know better. Please help me to do better. Help me to live this day as though I knew I was going to meet You at bedtime. Amen

September 29

It isn't nice to call someone a dog. Then why did Jesus do it?

A Canaanite woman asked Jesus to heal her daughter. (I paraphrase the following.)

"It just isn't right," Jesus said, "to take the children's bread and give it to dogs."

"That's true, Lord," she persisted. "I'm a puppy dog, a pet, so can I please have some crumbs that fall from the children's table?"

She had caught His choice of words. He hadn't used *kunis*, the word for street dogs, mangy curs, gentile dogs. Instead He used the word *kunarois*, the word for beloved household pets.

Surely His eyes sparkled. She had caught his humor. He granted her request and complimented her faith.

What was it with that woman? *Faith.* First, it was a faith that could grow. She moved from addressing Him as Son of David to calling Him Lord.

Second, it was a faith that wouldn't give up. She didn't have the luxury of quitting. Her daughter was in critical condition. He was her only hope.

Third, her faith was enhanced by a cheerful disposition. She let repeated opportunities for taking offense slip by. Something within her allowed her to understand that Jesus' remark about dogs was a friendly response. And this quality saved the day for her daughter.

How many blessings have you missed because you are too hot under the collar? To quick on the trigger?

"...O woman, great is your faith! Let it be to you as you desire...."
Matthew 15:28

And also to you dear reader. Amen

September 30

There is a story about four people named Everybody, Somebody, Anybody, and Nobody.

There was an important job to be done in the church. Everybody was asked to do it.

But Everybody was sure that Somebody would do it. Anybody could have done it.

But Nobody did it.

Somebody got angry about that because it was Everybody's job. Everybody thought Anybody could do it. But, Nobody realized that Everybody wouldn't do it.

It ended up that Everybody blamed Somebody when Nobody did what Anybody could have done.

And the work of ministry was left undone.

What do you *do* for Jesus? What role or task in the church have you accepted as your own? And do with diligence and faithfulness?

If you are unemployed in the vineyard you aren't pleasing God. And there is something that everyone, even the most challenged, can do.

This joke made the rounds during WWI. A Blind man was inducted and told that his condition wouldn't preclude his pumping water from the unit well.

A man was inducted who had no arms. He was told to go over to where the blind man was pumping water and tell him when the bucket was full. (I still remember my Dad laughing as he told the joke.) Forgive the joke, but get the point.

You may think that you are so without talent that there is nothing for you to do in the kingdom. Well, you are wrong. There is something for everybody to do. You just have to find it. Isn't Jesus talking to you when He urges:

"...Son (daughters too), go, work today in my vineyard?"
Matthew 21:28

I'm working Lord. Let me be refreshed constantly by Your word and spirit. Amen

October 1

During this writing a national debate is occurring over the role of morality in government.

Does it matter if Representative X, Senator Y, or President Z commits adultery, tells lies, or sells influence, so long as he or she is doing a good job?

Anyway, isn't it all relative? Shouldn't we all be a little more broadminded?

Well, not in the laboratory. If it isn't two parts hydrogen and one part oxygen it isn't ever going to be water. Even though it may be liquid, clear, and tasteless.

Not in the garage. If the engine's rings must fit within a hundredth of an inch there can be no variation, or the motor will overheat and burn up.

Not in mathematics. Neither geometry, calculus, nor trigonometry allows for flexibility in rules and standards.

Certainly not in the pharmacy.

And what about space travel? All specifications must be exact. If they are a person can go into space and come back safely. If not, tragedy. No room for relativism there.

So, when your preacher lays it out straight, understand that he is concerned for your eternal soul. Something much more important and valuable than the examples above. Don't expect him to be very broadminded about eternity.

"Enter by the narrow gate; for wide is the gate and broad is the way that leads to destruction, and there are many who go in by it."
Matthew 7:13

Lord, I like the boulevards. Narrow streets and paths cramp my style. I have a lot to learn about following you. I want to be a good student. Bless me, Lord. Amen

October 2

How do you look to God?

If God were looking for a person to be special and do special things would He choose you?

When God sent the prophet Samuel to the house of Jesse to choose a king for Israel, Samuel was quite impressed with Jesse's sons.

Samuel liked the tall one but God said no. Abinadad was passed over. Shammah, too. Then Jesse had seven of his sons stand before Samuel. The Lord had not chosen them.

"Are these all of your boys?" Samuel asked.

"Well, no. The youngest lad is out there with the sheep," answered Jesse.

"Send for him."

Finally, when young David stood before Samuel the Lord said, "This is the one." Samuel anointed David on the spot. And the Spirit of the Lord came upon David.

Jesse must have thought David too young, too small, to be considered by Samuel. There is a lesson here.

Don't judge people by what you see on the outside.

I remember the scrawniest, most smart aleck, boy in my Bible College class. He was always mouthing off. Always rubbing people (at least me) in the wrong way. He seemed to carry a chip on his shoulder all of the time. He went on to become a great missionary, and today heads his denomination's outreach to the Muslim world. Today he is in my top ten best friends list.

"...Man looks at the outward appearance, but God looks at the heart."
1 Samuel 16:7

Lord, keep blessing Your servant and my friend Ron Peck. Prosper his ministry and keep him and his family well. Amen

October 3

A horseback ride to Heaven?

At Jerusalem's Dome of the Rock is the very stone from which, according to Muslims, Mohammed rode horseback to heaven. Believers claim to be able to see the imprint of the horse's hooves on the rock.

Devout Muslims believe that a prayer said there is worth more than a thousand prayers elsewhere.

(It is not my intention to be disrespectful of the Muslim religion.)

Jesus taught that the place of prayer is not significant. He really beat up on the Scribes and Pharisees that prayed on the street corners, dressed in ostentatious ecclesiastical garb.

Rather, Jesus taught us to seek a quiet place where we may pray undisturbed and without distraction. From telephones, televisions, radios, doorbells, even family members.

It's not wrong to pray in public.

Paul prayed in public (Acts 22:17). Jesus prayed with and for His disciples (John 17:9). Isaiah and King Hezekiah prayed together (2 Chronicles 32:20). Many early believers gathered together in prayer (Acts 12:12). Sick folks are instructed to seek out the elders of the church for prayer (James 5:14).

However, the great truth is that prayer is between you and God, and not primarily for the hearing of others.

"...When you pray, go into your room, and when you have shut your door, pray to your Father who is in the secret place; and your Father who sees in secret will reward you openly."

Matthew 6:6

October 4

The best thing God can do for you sometimes is to not answer your prayer.

I should note here that I believe God answers all prayers. It is just that sometimes the answer isn't what we wanted. So, when I talk today about unanswered prayers I really mean prayers where God refuses to grant specific requests.

Surely Moses prayed and yearned to be able to lead Israel into their Promised Land. God didn't permit it.

Because of an earlier disobedience by Moses God allowed him to see, but not enter, the land. Then He buried Moses in a valley in the land of Moab.

But look at Moses centuries later. On a high mountain, in the Promised Land. With Jesus. He appeared on the Mount of Transfiguration and talked with Jesus (Matthew 17).

The mighty prophet Elijah prayed to die. God wouldn't let him. He already had a fiery (shining) chariot and a whirlwind reserved to bring Elijah to Heaven.

Oh yes, Elijah was also with Jesus at that meeting on the mountain.

Preachers teach that God answers all prayers. Okay. But the answer isn't always *yes*. He sometimes says *no*. God may say no because He knows that what you are asking for would harm you.

He sometimes says no because he has *something better* for you than what you are praying for. He sometimes answers neither yes nor no. Sometimes the answer is *later*.

"The eyes of the Lord are on the righteous, and His ears are open to their cry."
Psalm 34:15

October 5

Good lessons from a bad person? Jesus apparently thought so. Read about it in Luke 16:1-13.

In Jesus' parable of how the unjust steward survived we learn some valuable lessons.

You, as a child of God should be wiser than the people of this world. Didn't Jesus mean that when He said that we should be as wise as serpents and as harmless as doves?

It is not humility to be dumb about finance and budgeting. Business. It is stupidity.

A second lesson is that you should view material possessions as a means, not an end.

Jesus taught us to "Lay up for yourselves treasures in heaven, where neither moth nor rust destroys and where thieves do not break in and steal" (Matthew 6:20).

A rabbi had this saying. "The rich help the poor in this world, but the poor help the rich in the world to come."

A gift in Jesus' name to the poor and needy is an investment in Heaven. Jesus made it clear. You can't serve God with all of your heart and be enslaved by material things.

A third lesson from the parable is that little habits reveal big attitudes.

You may proclaim lofty ideals and preach a hard line, but if you cheat in little things people will always figure you out. And God doesn't need to. He already knows.

"...Who then is that faithful and wise steward, whom his master will make ruler over his household, to give them their portion of food in due season? Blessed is that servant whom his master will find so doing when he comes."
Luke 12:42,43

Lord, it is more fun to receive than to give. Yet I know from Your words that in giving I receive a larger blessing. Help me to get it right, Lord. Amen

October 6

What a guy! Eating at the home of a leper while being visited by a woman of the street. (No offense is meant to the Jesus I love and serve.)

It was the home of Simon the Leper. Table settings were configured so that diners reclined on their left shoulder while eating with their right hand. So the legs would be extended and the feet visible, and reachable.

Customarily a servant would have brought water, without being told by the host, and washed the dusty, sandaled feet of any guest. No one had done that for Jesus. Was it a subtle put down for an itinerate Rabbi with strong moral preachments? Or was it a host so enamored by having a guest, thronged by the masses, that he simply forgot basic hostly manners?

A woman came in off the streets. She knelt at Jesus' feet and wept so bitterly that her tears flowed onto His feet. She washed His feet with her tears and dried His feet with her hair.

Then she broke open a bottle of costly perfume and poured all of it over His head. It was customary to sprinkle drops of perfume over the head of a guest. But it was only for royalty, or an extremely important person, that the bottle was broken and its entire contents poured over anyone's head.

So what is my point in of all this?

True love is always extravagant. If love is miserly, measured, or conditional, it is not true love. Search the Scriptures. Look at your own experiences. Don't you agree? If you are still in doubt, read John 3:16.

So how does your behavior reflect your love of God? Your spouse? Family? Is your love extravagant?

"As the Father loved me, I also have loved you; abide in my love."
John 15:9

October 7

We know about the beginning. God created (Genesis 1). We also know about the ending (Revelation 22). Christ will establish the Kingdom of God universally.

But what about the middle? Is our God, who is the God of the beginning and ending, also the God of the middle?

The middle is your now. Your long in-between.

The middle may bring cancer eating away at a spouse. A parent suffering from debilitating pain. A child seeking nirvana through substance abuse.

The middle may bring a shattering divorce. Or a pink slip from a supervisor. It may bring a cold emptiness where warm spiritual life once flourished.

Has the rush, clutter, and clamor of a materialistic culture dulled your sensitivity to God in your life? Have you let your pain become an excuse for relaxing spiritual discipline? Are you faithful in reading the Scriptures and praying?

Are you drawing strength from your faith?

God is with you for the long haul. Through the lean times. In and past the suffering. Until there is healing.

Paul's admonition to the Christians at Philippi is good for you today.

"I thank my God upon every remembrance of you...being confident of this very thing, that He who has begun a good work in you will complete it until the day of Jesus Christ."
Philippians 1:3,6

Lord, You are the God of the beginning and ending, but also of the middle. Bless those who struggle. Ease the pain. Smooth the rough places. Help them to hold on, and never give up! Amen

October 8

When Mahatma Gandhi was a 24-year-old attorney in South Africa, he purchased a first class ticket and boarded the train. Another man (white? whiter?) had him thrown off.

Years later, Gandhi said that being thrown off the train was the most creative experience of his life.

Wouldn't Ms. Rosa Parks agree?

Another story comes from a German jail cell.

A young pastor, Dietrick Bonhoeffer, was imprisoned by the Nazis for behavior that they considered treasonable. He wrote prolifically, and his writings are still used in seminaries. Prior to his execution at Berchtesgaden, he wrote, "Much as I long to be out of here, I don't believe a single day will be wasted."

My best friend died after a long and painful struggle with cancer. He was a county judge who loved the Lord and took advantage of every opportunity to tell of God's love and saving grace. To my human mind it doesn't add up. It seems such a waste.

Yet Holy Scripture agrees with Bonhoeffer.

Nothing is ever wasted!

Even the most tragic suffering can work to a spiritual good when we turn to God (CF Romans 8:28). Even the most hurtful things call our attention to God, instruct us, and provide an opportunity for fellowship with the Lord Jesus.

Saint Paul suffered much. He was beaten, imprisoned, and eventually executed for his faith. So Paul could write about his desire to

"...Know Him...and the fellowship of His sufferings...."
Philippians 3:10

Dear Lord, bless all who are battling cancer, and other painful and debilitating diseases. Heal Your people Lord. You are the Great Physician. Amen

October 9

Are you salty?

I am not asking if you are a sailor.

In the time of Jesus salt was used as a preservative.

If you are about my age (don't ask) you are well aware of that usage. Fish, hams, and other food items were preserved with salt. They still are in some places of the world.

Another basic use of salt is to flavor.

When asked to describe salt by his teacher a little boy answered, "Salt is what ruins the stew when you leave it out." A dear friend, when told by his doctor that he could not have any salt, seasoned everything with syrup. Ugh. Can you imagine collards seasoned with syrup?

In Jesus' day outdoor ovens were built upon tiles placed over a bed of salt. The salt added to and retained the heat. Over time, when the strength of the salt dissipated, it was replaced with new salt. The old salt was thrown along the streets and roads. People walked on it.

So I ask again. Are you salty?

Is your presence a leavening influence in your neighborhood? Do folks refrain from telling dirty, racist, or sexist jokes in your presence? Does your behavior add a good flavor to the activities of those around you? On the job? At the club? The bowling alley?

Are you, by your spiritual experience and Christian behavior, making a difference? How tragic if you have to answer no.

"You are the salt of the earth; but if the salt loses its flavor, how shall it be seasoned? It is then good for nothing but to be thrown out and trampled underfoot by men."
Matthew 5:13

October 10

It was the ugliest American flag I had ever seen hanging in a place of honor. I was in the office of then lieutenant colonel (later Brigadier General) Herb Lloyd.

When I asked about the tattered flag on his office wall he told me a great war story. North Vietnamese regulars had decimated his outfit. Only Herb and his radio operator remained alive. They called for rescue.

A warrant officer pilot attempted to rescue them but the chopper drew hostile fire on the first effort. On his second try, the pilot was able to get them out. Herb grabbed the flag from where it had been hanging in their bunker and took it with him on the chopper. Shrapnel that filled the air during the fierce fighting had shred it. Herb has kept the flag ever since then.

A few days later Herb received a letter from his sister. She wrote about visiting their mother and finding her asleep on the front steps. When Herb's sister woke their mother Mrs. Lloyd said, "Honey, I'm so worried about Herb. I've been praying as hard as I could for days. And in the last several hours, I just sat on the doorsteps so I could concentrate better."

When Herb checked the date and time difference, he learned that *his mother's praying had coincided exactly with the time of his greatest peril.*

Prayer is such a blessing. And what a blessing to have a loving family member praying for you. But what about your praying?

Are you praying like you should?

If indeed there is power in prayer and you are an intercessor you are performing spiritual service. If, on the other hand, you are failing to pray as you should you are failing God, those without Christ, the sick and needy, and your family. The Scriptures are strong in this regard.

"Rejoice always, *pray without ceasing.*"
1 Thessalonians 5:16,17

October 11

Are you bright? I mean do you shine brightly?

We lived in a beautiful part of Virginia that was well forested. We could travel along a road at night and come upon a town completely by surprise. The trees hid the town from us until we rounded a curve.

However, in the open sky country of Texas, where we lived twice, we could see a town at night, twenty miles away. If you travel west from Belton on highway 190 you will top a hill where you can see all the way to Killeen. The countryside is lit up with the lights from homes and communities.

Jesus said that Christians are like cities on hilltops. Highly visible. Shining!

He also said how foolish it would be to light a lamp and then cover it with a basket.

One snowy night I had to drive down Ober Salzburg, the mountain at Berchtesgaden, Germany. I feared the frozen roads, the banked snow, and the sharp curves.

But I had to drive down. How relieved I was to discover that the dangerous edges and curves had been marked by reflectors.

So, are you bright?

Does your representation of Christ illumine the community? Or serve as a warning, as does the light at a railroad crossing or school? Does your life reflect Jesus the light of the world? Does it guide others away from destructive paths, and to the Lord?

"You are the light of the world. A city that is set on a hill cannot be hidden. Nor do they light a lamp and put it under a basket, but on a lampstand, and it gives light to all...Let your light so shine before men, that they may see your good works and glorify your Father in Heaven."
Matthew 5:15,16

October 12

In his remarkable little book, *Illusions. The Adventures of a Reluctant Messiah,* one of Richard Bach's characters argues that friends will know you better in the first minute you meet than acquaintances will get to know you in a thousand years.

One of the things that set humankind apart from the rest of creation is the ability to develop close and lasting friendships.

You simply don't see it in the animal world, although there are rare and remarkable examples of attachments that survive the passing of time. Members of species do sometimes work together. There is the hunting pack that brings down a larger animal. And the species that bunch together for safety. However, even after mating and the birth of offspring most mates and their offspring go their separate ways.

Toward the end of His ministry, and after three and one-half years *on the road,* Jesus called His disciples together and said, "Boys, let's acknowledge a new reality. I no longer think of you as just servants. Let's be friends" (my paraphrase).

When I was standing at my Dad's open grave, someone put his arm around me and said, "I know what you are going through." He did, too. He had buried his own Dad. He just stood there with me. No clever words were spoken. No clumsy attempt at saying something memorable. There was no need. A friend's just being there was as eloquent as it can get.

Jesus' remark tells us something about Him, and us. Today, I ask you to thank God for friends. And be one.

"No longer do I call you servants, for a servant does not know what his master is doing; but I have called you friends, for all things that I heard from My Father I have made known to you."
John 15:15

Jesus, it seems so presumptuous for me to say that I want to be Your friend, but I do. I know that I am not worthy. Again, Lord, I thank You for the friends that have enriched my life so very much. I cherish each one. Amen

October 13

During the Vietnam War some young men took extraordinary steps to avoid the draft. One way was through bogus religious ordinations.

One diploma mill advertised ordinations for $15.

My chaplain buddy, Wayne Ballentine, sent in the name of one of his prize bulls, Argo B1, and a check. Sure enough a certificate arrived a few days later certifying that B. I. Argo was duly ordained in the Christian ministry. There was a note that said that for just $25 "Reverend" Argo could have a doctorate.

Wayne joked that he had the only ordained bull in the Army. I responded that I knew a few ordained bulls, and that some of them were colonels.

It was a lot of fun. Then I read about Jonah.

Where the English text says that God "prepared" a great fish to swallow Jonah the Hebrew word is *manah*, which means to *ordain*. God also ordained a gourd, a pesky worm, and a fiery east wind to get Jonah's attention and obedience.

Jonah had been told to go one place but went another. God pursued him, caused a great storm to frighten the sailors, and let Jonah be thrown overboard. Then the ordained fish swallowed Jonah and cast him ashore near where he was supposed to go.

What about you? Are you going in the right direction? Are you swallowed up in disobedience? Burned by the winds of adversity? It doesn't have to be.

God loves you. He may "ordain" a great fish when you are wayward. But He will forgive and strengthen you when you return to Him. Amen

"...The Lord prepared a great fish to swallow Jonah...."
Jonah 1:17

October 14

In one of my pastorates a lady often requested prayer for her voice.

In her prayer requests she always reiterated how hard it was to work outside, at night, in the cold. Then she would emphasize her physical need by clutching her throat. Her voice would give way completely as she sat down.

There's no telling the times I asked her how she was doing to have her answer, "Oh Brother Hunt, I can hardly talk." Nor could I count the times I prayed for her voice to be healed.

Well, one morning I was working in the back yard and heard her talking over the fence to a neighbor (she lived two doors down) in a loud, clear voice. I said to Shirley, "Honey, the Lord has healed Sister Jones (name changed). I'm going to walk over to her house and congratulate her."

Off I went. "How are you today, Sister Jones?" I asked. Clutching her throat, she whispered, "Oh Brother Hunt, I can hardly talk."

Are you arguing for *your* limitations? Do you need them? If so, isn't it a little sick? Shouldn't you be doing the opposite? If you argue for your limitations you will surely have them.

What do you *feed* your soul? Is it doubt? Weakness? Fear? Or is it faith in Jesus' promises? A positive outlook? An upbeat attitude?

The writer of Proverbs was indeed wise in this observation,

> **"... As he *thinks* in his heart, so is he...."**
> Proverbs 23:7

Lord, help me to give up the crutches and excuses that have kept me from being all that I can be for You. Let me think large thoughts. Let me dream big dreams. Help me to feed on Your Word and Spirit. Amen

October 15

This was in a news article.

An old woman in Stockholm, Sweden, died and lay undiscovered in her apartment for over three years.

During the whole period computers received her pension and paid her bills. Over 36 months, or 156 weeks, or 1,095 days; and no one knew. No one checked her out.

An impersonal society? Human interaction replaced by technical advancement?

Shirley and I were sitting in a restaurant next to two women and could not help overhearing their conversation. One remarked, "Well, at least God doesn't put me on hold."

We make a telephone call and get a machine. The machine then plays a list of options. The last option often is to hear the list of options again. I sometimes want to scream, "How do you get a live, warm, human being on the telephone?"

But why scream at a machine? You can't make it mad, hurt its feelings, or cause it to do differently than it does.

Then you go to church and hear about a *personal* God. One who loves you individually, and it is hard to fathom.

Well, believe it.

It is true. You must realize it today, now. So that the machines don't overwhelm you. You!

God knows you. He has feelings for you, personally. He loves you. Amen

"My sheep hear My voice, and *I know them*, and they follow me."
John 10:27

Lord, it sounds so presumptuous to talk about a personal relationship with you. But that was Your idea. So I accept, and thank You for it. Amen

October 16

When I took over the chapel in Kaiserslautern, Germany, in March of 1970, I was useless as a chaplain. Four moves in four years, the last one a year of combat, had drained me spiritually. I was empty.

The chapel that could seat 500 people had been averaging just over 50 per Sunday. Things were bad in the early 1970s: drugs, riots, and near anarchy in the barracks. I was in no shape, spiritually, to deal with it.

My preaching even bored me. I was as dry as shucks. The challenge of ministry in that setting and the job of building an effective religious program there, daunted me. I sought a transfer. No luck. I finally was forced to deal with the real issue, *me*. I realized that I was burned out.

I turned to prayer, and not as a military task.

The canned sermons, that I had been using, were woefully out of date. At a New Years Eve service I made only one resolution, to toss the old sermons. I would preach nothing "warmed over" in 1971. Everything would have to be discovered new. Fresh. Through prayer and study, spiritual discipline, my own spiritual condition improved.

My preaching caught fire. Within months the congregation doubled, and eventually increased five times over. A lot of good people helped, but if I hadn't taken care of the number one problem, me, it couldn't have happened.

Beware of burnout. If you are spiritually empty, dry, you can't minister effectively to others. You have to take something in to be able to keep giving something out.

Nor should you beat yourself over the head with guilt. It is not a sin to overwork yourself in the vineyard, but it isn't smart. It isn't smart because you will inevitably render yourself useless to the owner of the vineyard. God will still love and cherish you but of what use will your gifts and talents be?

"But you, beloved, *building yourselves up* on your most holy faith, praying in the Holy Spirit, keep yourselves in the love of God...."   Jude 20,21

October 17

For every mile of the Panama Canal 500 workers died.

The Canal was built to open a waterway between the Atlantic and Pacific Oceans. The fifty-mile long canal allows seafarers to sail through the nation of Panama and avoid the long trip around the tip of South America. But at what a price in human deaths.

Once there was a great chasm separating sinful humans from the holy God. It was a chasm cosmically larger than the isthmus that separated the two oceans. How could that gulf be spanned?

What would be the nature of that redemptive connection? And at what cost would it be made?

As the song says, they searched through Heaven to find a Savior. No mighty angel could suffice. It had to be the Son of God. There had to be a sacrifice. All of the gold in the whole world could not buy humanity's redemption. Only the Savior.

The connection took the shape of a cross.

The cross of Jesus reaches upward to the highest Heaven, to the heart of God. It reaches downward to the lowest hell, to the heart of man. Its arms stretch outward to the most remote, the darkest region, to the farthest soul.

What a blessed connection. What a wonderful Savior. Amen

"For it pleased the Father that in Him all the fullness should dwell, and by Him to reconcile all things to Himself, by Him...having made peace through the blood of His cross...And you, who once were alienated...now He has reconciled."
Colossians 1:19-21

Thank You, Lord, for reaching across the breach of our alienation. You have taken my hand in Yours. I am reconciled to God. Amen

October 18

Are you getting used to the dark?

While in college I had a job as night watchman in a citrus canning plant. I worked Saturday and Sunday nights. Since sudden bursts of light temporarily blind me I learned to move without flashlight most of the time. After a few minutes my eyes would adjust and I would be able to make my rounds.

It is like walking into a dark theater. If you are like me you have to stand inside the door a couple minutes before looking for your seat.

There is a more insidious darkness, *the darkness of evil*.

You see it on movie and television screens where the cultural elite display and promote a lifestyle of sex, drugs, and violence. It is seen in the philosophy that claims an absolute right to feel good. If it feels good, whatever it is, just do it.

The tragic result of this pervasive evil is seen in the pictures of abused spouses and children, and in blood spattered school playgrounds and classrooms.

Christians are called to stand apart. To be *in* but not *of* the world. It is our task to criticize a sick culture, to demand an accounting for the evil, to call attention to the darkness.

"For you were once in darkness, but now you are light in the Lord. *Walk as children of light.*

And have no fellowship with the unfruitful works of darkness, but rather expose them.

For it is shameful even to speak of those things which are done by them in secret.

But all things that are exposed are made manifest by the light, for whatever makes manifest is light."

Ephesians 5:8-13

October 19

A little boy had trouble pronouncing *worship*. He called it *wash-up*.

He had it right. In a profoundly little boy or little girl way.

Do we go to church to wash-up? Don't evil things and happenings surround us? Doesn't the dirt of everyday living cling to us?

Jesus explained it to His disciples in that remarkable foot-washing sequence. (Read the story in John 13.)

In New Testament times the host was responsible for the foot-washing courtesy. But they were in a neutral place, an upper room. It was nobody's home. Still, it was a servant's task. One of the disciples should have volunteered. But no one did. Jesus took the basin of water and the towel and proceeded to wash the disciple's feet.

Peter protested, "You shall never wash my feet." Jesus raised the stakes, "If I don't wash you, you have no part with me." Peter reached, "Lord, not my feet only, but also my hands and my head."

Hello God!

Jesus explained it, and I paraphrase, "When you are washed you are completely clean. You then only need to keep clean."

A Christian, cleansed by the blood of the Lamb of God, is spiritually ready for Heaven. But that Christian still needs to experience God's grace, to hear the reassurances of His love, to be instructed by the Scriptures, and to be honed in the spiritual exchanges with fellow Christians.

So, I have been cleansed, yet I am being cleansed.

"...You were washed...you were sanctified...you were justified in the name of the Lord Jesus and by the Spirit of our God."

1 Corinthians 6:11

October 20

Do you have "I" disease?

Listen to the rich young farmer: "I will pull down my barns and build greater, and I will store all my crops and my goods. And I will say to my soul, 'Soul, you have many goods laid up for many years; take your ease, eat, drink, and be merry.' " (Luke 12:13-21)

The man made three tragic assumptions.

First, he seemed to think that life was the sum of things.

How about you? There is a joke that the winner is the one who dies with the most toys. Are you a toy collector?

Second, he thought that his soul could be satisfied by natural pleasures.

How about you? What are you feeding your spirit? Someone said that there is a God-shaped vacuum in everyone that only Jesus can fill.

Lastly, he seemed to think it clever to ignore spiritual needs.

That attitude angered God.

The world has adopted a macho view of masculinity. The renaissance man of today is tough, amoral, fun loving, and party pleasuring. Doesn't that description also fit women?

What about you? Where are your priorities?

Are they to please God and serve Him? Or do you live to be thrilled, to feel good, to be comfortable, to be entertained?

"...God said to him, 'You fool!'...So is he who lays up treasure for himself and is not rich toward God."
Luke 12:20,21

Lord, don't let me come down with "I" disease. Amen

October 21

Stop the procession!

As Jesus approached the city of Nain He was met by a funeral procession for a young man. (Read about it in Luke 7:11-17.)

He saw the weeping mother and it hit Him in the gut. Literally. The English text says that He "had compassion." But the Greek is much stronger. A transliteration of the root word is splagschnon. It means bowels, entrails, intestines, or guts. He *splagchnoned.* He *compassioned.*

Now, there are other Greek words that the writer could have used. Such as words for kindness, pity, mercy, or sympathy. The choice of splagschnon was deliberate, to show great emotion; feelings arising from deep within Jesus.

Luke recorded for us a compassionate Christ. One who loves dearly and feels deeply.

Jesus raised the dead other times. One at the request of Jairus for his daughter (Mark 5:39), and once His dear friend, Lazarus (John 11:15).

At Nain no one asked Him to do anything. His action was prompted by pure and powerful compassion. Like a Savior who loved enough to die for us. Like a High Priest who makes intercession for us. And as a Friend who never forsakes us.

Know that Jesus. Serve Him. Be like Him.

I learned my first Scripture verse in the third grade. The teacher bribed us with prizes. I was too smart. I chose the Bible's shortest verse, which I now see as one of its most profound:

"Jesus wept."
John 11:35

By now you surely know that I believe that Jesus was a real man. Not a wimp. Real men sometimes cry. Amen

Sure Jesus is the Lord of Life. But what does that mean?

It means that He *was* life. That he *gave* life. That He was and *is* Life.

There is no record of anyone ever dying in Jesus' presence. Could that be why He delayed His return to Bethany (see John 11)? To wait for Lazarus to die? Because no one could die in the presence of the Living Christ?

How about when He was on the cross? He *gave up* the ghost; i.e. He yielded up His spirit. I don't believe He died early merely to end the pain of having his legs broken. Rather, it was a mercy to the thieves hanging on each side of Him.

How could they die as long as the Prince of Life lived between them?

There is no record of anyone ever *staying dead* in His presence. The example at Nain (see Luke 7) bears this out. A funeral procession could not pass the Lord of Life without an engagement. No corpse could stay dead in His presence.

If you have time to chew on more, read about the Old Testament saints rising with Him on Easter Sunday Morning (Matthew 27:52ff).

An Old Testament prophet (e.g. Elijah, 1 Kings 17:17-24) raised the dead with some physical effort. Jesus did it with a word. Others raised the dead by a power not their own, outside them, a spiritual force flowing *through* them. Jesus did it by the virtue that flowed *from* Him.

Are you fully alive in Christ? If not, let this day be a day of discovery. Of infilling. Of refilling of the life and power of Jesus through the indwelling Holy Spirit. Amen

"Jesus said to her, 'I am the resurrection and the life. He who believes in Me, though he may die, he shall live.' "
John 11:25

October 23

Will you be able to die with both eyes closed?

Shirley and I were having dinner with Dr. In Sik Kim and his wife Ha Ja. I had been helpful in his coming to the states to study in the 1960s. At our meeting Dr Kim headed his denomination's missionary outreach to the Pacific Rim.

He told of the emotional reunion with his mother. They had been separated in 1950 when North Korea invaded South Korea. Dr. Kim's father, and some family members, were able to escape to the South. However, Dr Kim's mother, and other family members, weren't able to escape the communist North.

In 1986, Dr. Kim was a member of a ten-person delegation invited to North Korea. He mentioned his mother, and the authorities found her. The two of them had a joyful, tearful reunion. Understandably. Imagine 35 years of not knowing if either was alive.

As he prepared to leave North Korea, and his mother, In sik encouraged her to have faith and trust God. "If I am not able to see you again on earth I will see you in Heaven," he promised.

His mother hugged him one last time and said, "Now I can die with both eyes closed." In Sik explained that she was repeating an old Korean saying. It meant that she wouldn't have to keep one eye open, wondering if he would make it to Heaven.

Today I hope that you will remember and cling to the promises that God has made to and your family.

"...The mercy of the Lord is from everlasting to everlasting on those who fear Him, and His righteousness to children's children, to such as keep His covenant, and to those who remember His commandments to do them."
Psalm 103:17

Lord, bless families that have been torn apart. Comfort the distressed and hurting ones. Enrich their lives with Your divine presence. Amen

October 24

Five hoecakes and two perch. Enough for a miracle? To make one a hero? To feed over 5,000 people? Actually, 5,000 men, plus women and children.

When a crowd had followed Jesus and were hungry, He invited them to eat. But what? Philip argued that it couldn't be done. That even 200-denari worth of bread wouldn't be enough to feed the crowd.

However, Andrew worked the crowd, and found a lad with a lunch.

"Hey kid, what's in the brown bag?" (Andrew)

"Five barley hoecakes and two sardines." (The lad)

"Jesus needs food to feed these people. Are you willing to share?"

"Sure."

"Okay, come with me."

"Where to?"

"To Jesus."

"You're kidding, right?"

The boy had a ringside view. Watching the food multiply as it was broken and blessed by Jesus. *You can be blessed and multiplied too. Just place yourself in Jesus' hands.*

(By the way, you make a hoecake by mixing flour as if you are preparing biscuits. Then you pat out a pone about half an inch thick and cook it in a greased frying pan on top of the stove. Makes me hungry thinking about it.)

So what was the "recipe" for this miracle? (1) The presence of Jesus; (2) The industry of an Andrew; and (3) A lad's lunch.

"...Jesus took the loaves, and...distributed them ...and likewise the fish, as much as they wanted."
John 6:11

October 25

A Chinese pastor asked a young convert if it was true that he had been a Christian for three months.

"Yes, it is blessedly true," answered the new Christian.

"And how many have you led to Christ?" asked the pastor.

"Oh," exclaimed the convert, "I am only a learner. I never owned a complete New Testament until recently."

"Do you use candles in your home?" the pastor probed.

"Yes," answered the convert.

"Do you expect the candle to shine only after it has burned part of the way down?" the pastor continued.

"No, as soon as it is lit," replied the new convert.

Zinzendorf, the founder of the great Moravian Missionary Movement asked a brother if he could go as a missionary to Greenland. The man answered yes. Zinzendorf then asked if he could go tomorrow. The man answered, "I can go tomorrow if the cobbler is finished with my shoes."

There are many wonderful programs available in churches today to help you witness for Christ, to help you gain confidence and learn skills. Take advantage of all that you can.

But remember that the best, the most effective, witness of all is simply telling what Christ has done for you. No one can deny what has happened to you personally.

You can give this simple and profoundly powerful witness now. Do it today. Amen

"(The blind man) **answered...'One thing I know: that though I was blind, now I see.'** "

John 9:25

Lord, how can it be so difficult for me to witness since Your redemptive love has blessed me so? Help me to never be too afraid to tell the simple and wonderful story of Your grace in my life. Amen

October 26

Live in a city? Forever?

The marvelous last two chapters of Revelation describe in great detail what the Holy City, the New Jerusalem, will be like. I am intrigued by *what won't be in the city.*

No sea. Strange mention. Who would have imagined, anyway, that there would be a sea in a city?

Jewish thought, contemporary to New Testament times, drew from the mindset of other ancient people who feared the sea.

In Babylonian mythology the sea was the dwelling place of Tiamat, the dragon of chaos.

Egyptians viewed the sea as the power that swallowed up the Nile, leaving the land dry and sterile.

It's pleasant to imagine (better to experience!) a peaceful walk on the beach on a warm day.

But think of the ravages of an angry sea. One that produces El Ninos, hurricanes, typhoons, and tornadoes. One that swallows people, destroys beaches, and eats homes.

If your heart is troubled today, if your spirit is in turmoil, if you yearn for a day when there will be no more turbulence; it's coming.

May you know that calmness and assurance today, and tomorrow. In this life. If you are a Christian you will know it in eternity.

"...I saw a new heaven and a new earth...there was no more...sea...death...sorrow...pain...for the former things have passed away. "
Revelation 21:1-4

Lord, you know that I am a country boy. But if I have to live in a city forever to be with You I am willing. Save my place, Lord. Amen

October 27

Hunting was a necessity, not a sport, for my family. Things were tough in the late 1930s and early 1940s.

I used to take my single shot 22 caliber rifle, a handful of 22 short rounds, and my homemade headlight (made from a cut-off flashlight) and try to kill a rabbit or two for the next day's food. I would shine the rabbit's eye, take aim, and hopefully, bag a meal.

The spiders were a problem. Their eyes shone, too. I had to differentiate between their eye, that shone white and a rabbit's eye, which shone reddish. (Only one eye of a rabbit or a spider shines at a time.)

I hunted on 80 acres of dairy land behind our house. Animal carcasses were drug to the lower part of the pasture to rot and/or be devoured by creatures. There was lots of grass for rabbits. There were other animals, too. One night I was throwing the dish water off the back porch and a panther screamed at the edge of our yard.

Hunting out, with the house behind me, was easy. But hunting on the way back to the house, with the dark pasture behind me, was scary. I never got a rabbit walking back toward the house. Too much time looking over my shoulder.

Those fears were unwarranted. They came out of a child's imagination. But fear is not a benign thing. It is a killer.

"The wicked flee when no one pursues." (Proverbs 28:1)

If you live in fear, if your superstitions dictate your behavior, you are falling short of the full victory that is your birthright as a child of God. You don't have to live in fear. Don't do it anymore. Amen

"There is no fear in love; but perfect love casts out fear, because fear involves torment...."
1 John 4:18

October 28

My buddy, Chaplain Raymond Caulder tells this story.

While Napoleon was visiting his troops he met a soldier who had lost an arm. On his uniform he proudly wore the coveted Legion of Honor.

"Where did you lose your arm?" Napoleon asked.

"At Austerlitz, sir," came the sharp reply.

"And for that you received the Legion of Honor?"

"Yes sir. It is but a small token to pay for the decoration."

"You must be," Napoleon continued, "the kind of man who regrets he did not lose both arms for his country."

"What then would have been my reward?"

"Then," the great general replied, "I would have awarded you a *double* Legion of Honor."

With that the proud fighter drew his sword and immediately cut off his other arm.

Did you catch on? That was a joke. Speakers use that story to illustrate that one mustn't believe everything one hears. How could a one armed man draw his sword and cut off his only arm? Gullible!

Almost every week there is news of some weird religious claim. Some new messiah. Someone who knows the exact date that the world will end.

The good news of Jesus Christ, while wonderful in its scope and power, is not complicated. It requires no magic portents or formulas. It is simply that God loves you, and Jesus died to save you. Believe that with all of your heart and treat the next occult manifesto with skepticism.

"Beloved, do not believe every spirit, but test the spirits, whether they are of God; because many false prophets have gone out into the world. By this you know the Spirit of God: Every spirit that confesses that Jesus Christ has come in the flesh is of God."
1 John 4:1

October 29

You have a part to play in receiving what you need from God.

I was reading again the story of the healing of the blind man (John 9). The one on whose eyes Jesus put clay mixed with spit. Great story, lots of angles to pursue. What struck me was Jesus telling the man to go wash.

Why? To get the mud off? Oh sure, but I doubt that Jesus went around telling people who needed a bath to take a shower.

The blind man had a part to play in his healing.

So did the crippled man. Remember the story of Jesus healing the man who had lain by the Pool of Bethesda for 38 years, waiting for the troubling of the waters? Jesus healed the man, then told him to get up, clean up his area, and get on his way.

The crippled man first seemed to blame *God*, "waiting on an angel;" then he laid blame on his *family*, "I have nobody;" then it was the *system*, "someone steps in ahead of me." Maybe I am being unfair to the poor man.

But the point is valid. He did have a part to play. And so do you.

You can keep a positive attitude, eat healthily, exercise, nourish your spirit through prayer and Bible study, and do a dozen other things that you can think of for yourself. Or you can let yourself go and blame it all on God.

I once heard a preacher say that we ought to pray like everything depends on God, but work like everything depends on us. Well, maybe. As long as we understand that we are saved by faith in Jesus, not by our good works. Yet, works are important.

"Now may the God of peace...make you complete in every good work to do His will...."
Hebrews 13:20,21

October 30

Stop The World I Want To Get Off. That was the name of a play a few years back. It's also the way I feel sometimes.

Things are moving too fast.

Look at the United Nations. Do you know how many members there are? And their present and former names?

Look at science. It seems that only a few years ago Newton was discovering gravity. Then someone split the atom. Isn't someone now splicing genes?

And what about new ways of conception? In vitro. Frozen sperm. Surrogate mothers. What's happening to the world?

Then the preacher gets up and tells us that Jesus is the same. And you want to shout, "Thank God for that."

But how is Jesus the same? Well, it's not a static sameness, like a math or algebra formula. It's not a monotonous sameness like a boring relationship. Nor a dull sameness, like a closed mind.

Jesus is the same in His compassion. He began His ministry by stating that He was sent to preach the Gospel to the poor. See Him weep at Lazarus' tomb. Witness his compassion over the hungry multitude.

He also is the same in His demands for discipleship. He still says that if we love family or things more than Him we are not worthy of Him. He still requires us to take up our cross when we follow Him.

Jesus is still the same in His power to change lives. Mary Magdalene had seven devils in her but Jesus set her free. The resurrected Jesus changed a hardheaded Saul of Tarsus into an obedient Paul the Apostle.

"Jesus Christ is the same yesterday, today, and forever."

Hebrews 13:8

October 31

Happy Reformation Day.

In 1517 A. D. a young monk, burdened with the weight of his own sin, aghast at the selling of indulgences, and cramped by the rigid requirements of tradition, rediscovered some truths that changed church history.

Martin Luther was striving for personal salvation. He had no intention to start a new church, end the middle ages, begin modern times, or make Protestantism a chief propelling force in modern western civilization.

And it wasn't that the truths that Luther rediscovered were not already a part of the church. It was a matter of emphasis.

So, on this important day in Protestantism, let's look at those foundational truths.

Solo Scritura. Scripture only. The Scriptures are inspired by God and are an infallible guide for faith and practice.

Solo Fide. Only faith. Good works do not save a person. One does good works because she is a Christian. But one does not become a Christian by doing good works. Salvation is "by grace...through faith...not of works" (Ephesians 2:8,9).

Solo Gratia. Only grace. Keeping the Old Testament law doesn't save a person. It is through the unmerited favor of God (Grace) that he receives eternal life.

So, on this special day for me, a Protestant, I celebrate the great truths that undergird my rich tradition. I do so knowing that millions of devoted Christians, and many personal friends, don't agree with the emphasis I give them.

Isn't that the beauty, and strength, of the Christian Church! We differ in emphasis, but are united in one cardinal fact: Christ is Lord.

"Therefore being justified by faith, we have peace with God through our Lord Jesus Christ."
Romans 5:1

Thanksgiving Day

On a bleak day in December 1621, the Pilgrim fathers proclaimed a day of thanksgiving.

Weaker souls would have declared a day of mourning. One half of their number were buried in unmarked graves, leveled and planted over, to deceive the Indians.

That was *in your face thanksgiving*. It was a thanksgiving that evidenced a determined spirit that says, okay, I have taken your best shot, and I am still thankful to God.

Thanksgiving causes healing to take place in the *thanker* and the *thankee*.

When I taught sixth grade there was one student who was very disruptive. He had been held back and was then three years behind his age group. By size alone he dominated the other students. I did every thing I could think of to reach him, but never really knew for sure if I had succeeded.

However, when he saw that I could pass a football better than he could, he started giving me some respect. Over the year I actually grew to like him, and it appeared that he liked me.

On the last day of school he hung around until every other student had left the classroom. Then he walked quickly out of the room, dropping a crumpled note on my desk as he passed. On the note he had written, "Mr. Hunt, you have *hepped* me. Thanks." I sat there alone, in the empty classroom, and choked back tears.

Today, and every day in the coming year, give thanks to God for somebody or something that you are not pleased with. It will help you keep a sense of perspective. It will bring sweet healing to your soul.

Take your cue from Jesus, who, on the night in which He was betrayed and facing tomorrow's cross,

"(He)...Took the cup, and gave thanks...."
Matthew 26:27

Have a great Thanksgiving. And don't forget to *be thanks giving*. And *thanks living*. Amen

November 1

Happy All Saints Day.

A Protestant writing about a Catholic Holy Day is on shaky ground. But my heart is right, so here goes.

All Saints Day is a feast day for all of the saints who do not have a special feast day of their own. Originally in May, it was moved to the first day of November to coincide with the end of harvest. It was first called All Hallows for "All The Holy Ones."

The November date also provided a Christian definition for popular pagan and quasi-religious celebrations. On October 31, the last night of their year, the ancient Druids used to perform secret rights by candlelight to ward off evil powers. The pagan feast was called Hallows Eve, eventually Halloween.

In addition to the popular saints like Francis of Assisi, and Patrick, there are numerous others whose names are listed in the Church's canon. I never gave much credence to the intercession of saints. However, my Catholic friends make some good points.

And the passage in Hebrews 12:1 (RSV) intrigues me: "...Since we are surrounded by so great a cloud of witnesses...let us run ...the race that is set before us...." The verse follows immediately the great faith chapter, Hebrews 11, where Old Testament saints, known and unknown, are revered. If the believers who have passed on are somehow aware of our faith journey what are they doing about it? Watching us? Cheering us? *Praying for us*?

Historically, saints of the church have been people who did something, whose lives were characterized by selfless service. And they have been a true blessing. To me New Testament Scriptures teach that believers are already saints, not through their good works, but through their faith in Jesus as Lord and Savior.

"Now therefore you are no longer strangers and foreigners, but fellow citizens with the saints, and of the household of God." Ephesians 2:19

November 2

"Surprise! Surprise!" Remember Gomer Pyle?

I thought of that television series while reading the parable of how Jesus will judge the nations. (Read the account in Matthew 25:31-46) It seems that everyone there at the judgment is surprised.

In the parable Jesus first congratulated the good guys for feeding Him when He was hungry, giving Him water when He was thirsty, giving Him clothes when He was naked, and visiting Him when He was sick and in prison.

They were incredulous. When had they done such things for Jesus? His answer was, in effect, that He takes personally our behavior to the sick, ill clothed, thirsty, and imprisoned. To the poor. As if it were *literally* done to Him.

The bad guys were also surprised. Their behavior in failing to properly care for others was likewise a failure against Jesus.

Now, will you be surprised at the judgment? Will you be surprised hat there will even be a judgment where you will be held accountable for your actions?

Will you be surprised at *how* you will be judged? Not by your great successes on grand occasions? Not on the abundance of your gifts and talents? But by the day by day service that you give in Jesus' name.

There is a great lesson here. You can't treat Jesus well while treating others badly. He takes everything personally. Better take it seriously, for guess who will be the judge. The Son of Man.

"...Inasmuch as you did it to one of the least of these My brethren, you did it unto Me."
Matthew 25:40

This is a hard lesson for me, Lord. Some people are just so obnoxious that it is hard for me to see You in them. I am looking closer though, Lord, because I know that what makes them special is that You love them too.

November 3

Do you like solitude?

The Dictionary defines solitude as the state of being or living alone; seclusion; remoteness from habitation.

Thomas Merton wrote, "Solitude is not something you must hope for in the future. Rather, it is a deepening of the present."

I agree. To me solitude is the state of being at peace within myself. In my Christian life and experience it is the peace that Jesus brings to my soul. It is not dependent on quietness or the absence of others.

The Gospel writer, Luke, tells the story of two sisters, Mary and Martha. (Read it in Luke 10:38-42.) Martha was the keep-busy type. When Jesus was going to visit their home she would hurry around, tidying up the house, and then cook Jesus' favorite food.

Mary, on the other hand, would sit at Jesus' feet for hours, hanging on every word that He spoke.

Martha was angry with Mary for her behavior. She scolded Mary, and chided Jesus, for not caring that she had to do all of the work.

But Mary had it right. She may have been a woman that could lie down beside a pile of dirty clothes and take a nap, but she knew what was important. Busyness is not necessarily a sign of spiritual health.

I pray that your day won't be filled with such busyness that you can't experience the solitude that Jesus brings. That peaceful, restful, state of mind and soul where confidence in the providence of God evens out the rough spots and makes a day a joy to live.

"...I am not alone, because the Father is with me."
John 16:32

Are you still in bondage to old gods?

After the Children of Israel had been taken captive and dispersed into other lands the king of Assyria saw the need to resettle Samaria. He sent a priest along with the settlers to teach them about God.

But things didn't work out. Even though the people "feared the Lord," they still "served their own gods." (2 Kings 17:33)

What about you? Are you still serving other gods? They are too numerous to mention them all. But here are some examples, the god of:

Security?
Comfort?
Pleasure?
Sexual promiscuity?
Substance abuse?
Pride?

You can't give your best service to the Lord if your heart is set on other needs. If you are split between what your body enjoys and what your spirit tells you is wrong you are out of sync with Christ.

We are talking again about the lordship of Jesus.

I realize that part of the reason that I return again and again to this subject is my own lifelong struggle to be completely surrendered to Christ. I always want to hold a little back, to keep a secret space for myself.

It doesn't work. Never has and never will.

Pray with me:

Lord, help me to unlock the secret place, and let the Spirit of God fill my whole life. Let me keep no other gods. Amen

"You shall have no other gods before me."
Exodus 20:3

November 5

When you are in the Army you go when and where you are ordered.

During a four-year period of the Vietnam war I moved once a year. I should have been ready for it, though. I had been ordered to active duty on October 17, 1965, by telegram, with a reporting date of November 1.

The patriarch Abraham could have been in the Army, too. At least as far as having to move is concerned.

When God called Abraham to a new land he went. His only compass was the sun and stars. His only purpose to obey God.

A preacher might call what Abraham did *Marching Off The Map.*

His faith enabled Abraham to hear and see what others couldn't. It sustained him through his wanderings, and eventually brought him to the Promised Land.

When God promised him an heir Abraham believed. He was then 100 years old. Sarah was 90. Through their son came a nation, and the Messiah, the Lord Jesus Christ. My Savior.

Now let's talk about you.

Are you missing spiritual blessings and adventures because you are afraid?

Are you hanging back while others are forging ahead in Christ? How far have you progressed since becoming a Christian? Are you stale, blah? You don't have to be.

The Christian life is a walk. A journey. Be like Abraham, who, trusting God,

"...Went out, not knowing where he was going."
Hebrews 11:8

Lord, instead of charging off to new spiritual adventures I sometimes feel like Israel, wanting to linger at the mountain of blessing instead of going on into the promised land. Nudge me when I need it, Lord. Amen

November 6

Everyone has heard, from someone or other, about my new book, *Humility, And How I Obtained It.*

It's easier to be humble if you are honest about the realities:

However much you know, it is but a fraction of the sum total of knowledge.

However much you do, there will be much left undone.

When you depart this life, work and the world will continue.

Mother Teresa didn't set out as a young girl to obtain Sainthood. Instead, she sought lepers and other sick folks. People who had sores, who had lost the strength to care for themselves. Children without hugs. Cast-offs abandoned by the world.

Mother Teresa shunned the bright lights and beautiful people. Not from a false pride. She never claimed that she was better than others. Rather, she acted out a severe dedication to live out the challenges of Christ.

Sainthood found Mother Teresa.

So, are you humble? Proud? When you volunteer is it ever to do the dirty work? When you go somewhere do you seek out the front seat? Position yourself in front of the video camera? Sit down by someone popular?

Jesus taught that when you are invited you should go and sit in the lowest place.

When you take the humble position and the person that invited you sees where you are sitting, he may say that he intended for you to take the front row. Then you will feel honored. Wouldn't it be embarrassing if it happened the other way around?

"...Whoever exalts himself will be abased, and he who humbles himself will be exalted."
Luke 14:11

November 7

On a fog encased mountaintop in the Holy Land there was a most remarkable burst of light.

(I want us to view the transfiguration of Jesus against the Biblical truth that "...God is *light* and in Him is no darkness at all," 1 John 1:5).

According to the Gospel writer, Jesus' clothes became shining, exceedingly white, as snow, brighter than any launderer could whiten them. (Mark 9:2-9). Unearthly?

The shining wasn't on Jesus. It was from within Him.

When He burst forth from the tomb Jesus' appearance was like *lightening* (Matthew 28:3).

In the Holy City, the New Jerusalem, the city has no need of the sun or moon for the glory of God illuminates it "...And the Lamb is its *light*" (Revelation 21:23).

Now, what do you draw from the promise that when Jesus appears "...We shall be *like Him*, for we shall see Him as He is" (1 John 3:2)?

Hello God!

What about Daniel's statement that the wise (i.e. children of God) will *shine* like the brightness of the firmament (Daniel 12:3)? Or Jesus' own words, "Then the righteous will *shine forth* as the sun in the kingdom of their Father...." (Matthew 13:43)?

I've often wondered if the reason that Adam and Eve needed no clothing was that they were *creatures of light*. And that their nakedness showed when they sinned, and *lost their light*. That's a stretch, I know. But think of it.

I do believe that one day, when we get to Heaven, Christians will literally *shine*. But what about now? Are you shining yet?

"You are the light of the world...."
Matthew 5:14

November 8

Peter was jabbering away because, according to the Gospel writer, "He did not know what to say." (Mark 9:6)

Ever happen to you? You talk and talk because you have nothing to say?

(We are back on the Mountain of Transfiguration, where we left off recently. Read about it in Mark 9:2-9.)

When Moses and Elijah appeared with Jesus on the mountain Peter wanted to build tabernacles there, on the spot, one for each of them. He sounded like some board members and ministers that I have known: "Let's get this thing organized. We need to institutionalize it. Form an outreach committee. Create some agencies. Perpetuate it."

Peter got a quick lesson on the *pre-eminence of Christ*. A cloud covered them and a strong, clear, voice proclaimed, *This is My beloved Son, hear Him.*

Jesus is the measure of things.

Hello God!

Our theological conundrums are vacuous when they are not centered on Christ. Our denominational rules and polities are incompetent when they don't implement His will and teachings. Our doctrines are powerless when they don't flow from the well of His Lordship.

Jesus is also the measure of people. Thank God for Moses. Thank God for Elijah. Thank God for great prophets, popes, evangelists, theologians, and teachers.

But most of all thank God for Jesus. He is what *remains* after the clouds lift. Amen

"Suddenly...they saw no one anymore, but only Jesus...."
Mark 9:8

Lord, we both know that I am often like Peter, talking when I ought to be listening; coming up with wrong answers. Help me to pay better attention, so that I can see Your light, and be on the mountaintop with You. Amen

November 9

The early 1970s were rough times for the Army. Drug abuse. Anti-establishment attitudes. Disdain for authority.

I had an Army congregation in Kaiserslautern, Germany. The troop area. I struggled for ways to counter drug abuse. One way was to have speakers who had been addicted, but were now drug free through their faith in Christ, give their testimonies. I used many of them.

One Sunday Morning a young captain from the congregation informed me that he wouldn't be back. I had preached on *The Prodigal That Stayed Home*, from the story of the Prodigal Son (read about it in Luke 15:11-32). I had pointed out that you can stay home, keep the rules, work hard, but still be a prodigal.

And it's true. Some of the meanest people that I have ever seen appear outwardly to be very pious. (What I had meant to convey about the elder brother was that he had become stern, austere, harsh, and inflexible.)

But the captain had a point. He had been trying hard to live out his Christian faith, to do the right things, and had just become tired of my emphasis on reaching the far out crowd. How sad for him.

How sad for the elder brother, too. He had failed three ways:

He failed to comprehend the father's love.

He failed to maximize the benefits of the father's house.

He failed to maintain a constructive attitude, becoming mean and sour.

The elder brother had kept the faith, but missed the joy. Don't you dare make the same mistakes.

To the angry, elder, son, the loving father said,

"...Son, you are always with me, and all that I have is yours.

Luke 15:31

November 10

At the beginning of St. Paul's lofty letter to the Galatians he revealed that he went into Arabia before beginning his ministry.

Journey Into The Desert. Have you made the journey yet?

Everyone does you know, sooner or later. By *desert* I mean experiences of suffering, tragic happenings; periods of aloneness, where you are too far from the antennae, out of reach.

Periods in the desert can be most productive. The great songwriter, Ira Stanphil, wrote Gospel standards while experiencing a painful marriage.

Journeys into the desert can be life changing. Saul of Tarsus was an angry prosecutor, seeking to find and destroy members of the new Christian religion. After meeting Jesus on the road to Damascus, and after his time in the desert, he became known as the great Apostle Paul.

God comes to us in the deserts of our lives. Remember Moses? He was on the backside of the desert. God got his attention with a burning bush. Remember Elijah, and the still small voice? Same desert.

Jesus went into the desert, too. He was tempted there for forty days. Although hungry and weak, He resisted the devil the same way that you can, by knowing and quoting the Word of God. Afterward angels came and ministered to Him.

You may feel like you are in a desert today. It may be an excruciating illness, a profound sorrow, an ugly relationship, or a hundred other things.

Look around you. Listen for His footsteps. He will come to you. He knows about deserts. He will be with you, and sustain you, in yours.

"...I went to Arabia, and...Damascus...then after three years I went up to Jerusalem...."
Galatians 1:17,18

November 11

Happy Veterans Day.

I saw a bumper sticker the other day that read, "If you are free thank a veteran."

I am a fan of Rudyard Kipling. His delightful poem, *Tommy*, contrasts the way the British treat their soldiers in peace and war (Tommy is the British equivalent of the American G. I.) In wartime nothing is too good for the soldiers, but in peacetime they are sometimes treated as an embarrassment.

World War II soldiers came home heroes. And that they were.

My pals from Vietnam came home to harassment in the streets. I was told not to wear my uniform when traveling back to the States. We were warned that we might be harassed and spat upon. Many were.

But now a spirit of patriotism is back.

The dedication of the Vietnam Veterans Memorial on November 11, 1982, marked a turning point in the national attitude. Then came several more memorials, and I am not sure in what order: the Korean, the Women's, and the World War II Memorial.

So, today let us thank God for veterans and pray for them.

They are heroes among us. They are back from thousands of battles on land, on the sea, and in the air. They are our fathers and mothers, brothers and sisters, uncles and aunts, and our sons and daughters.

Oh Lord, bless mightily, with your sustaining power and grace, all of the American service men and women who have served our nation. We pray especially that you guard and protect all of those presently serving. Thank you for their sacrifice. And may peace fill the earth, and freedom flourish, as a result of their commitment. Amen.

"How the mighty have fallen in the midst of battle...."
2 Samuel 1:25

November 12

A mom and dad attended the graduation of their son from basic training. As the company marched by the reviewing stands, mom was heard to say, "Look, Dad, everyone is out of step but our boy."

There is a lot of pressure for you to get in step.

Like in the days of Noah, society is pleasure motivated. Like Jesus warned his disciples, too many are pre-occupied with possessions. As Paul predicted, people are self-centered, proud, boastful, insulting, and disobedient to parents.

Sex sells cars, clothing, even breakfast cereal. Feeling is the royal emotion, reigning over intellect, reason, and logic. If it feels good, well, do it. The siren song of the media is that to be cool you must get in step.

Against today's cultural, societal, and religious background the Christian is called upon to *get out of step*. That doesn't mean to be a crazy, a fanatic. Or to become a hermit. Not to practice weirdness for weirdness sake. Nevertheless, to get out of step.

You ask, "Why?" Because of who you are, a child of God. You have to be *in* the world but you must not be *of* it. Because of what you are doing.

I had a church member who used to end her testimony with, "Pray for me that my life may be my testimony." I wanted to yell, "It is, sister!" You are a light, a witness for Christ. Get out of step because of where you are going. You aren't heading where that other crowd is going.

There are several marvelous translations of Romans 12:2: "Do not be conformed to the patterns of the world" (NIV); "Do not conform yourself to the behavior and customs of the world" (TEV); I once translated the verse to say to "not be fashioned with" the world.

Of all the translations I like the Williams paraphrase best:

"Don't let the world around you squeeze you into its own mold."   Romans 12:2

In a vision a saintly old priest was first taken on a tour of Hell.

There his ears were immediately assaulted by a cacophony of screaming, wailing and complaining. The people were all seated at long tables. On the tables was a most delicious meal but the spoon handles attached to their hands were twice as long as their arms. They could catch the food in the spoons but they couldn't get the food to their mouths.

The cries of the starving denizens were so piercing that the old priest asked to be taken out of Hell.

In Heaven the people were also seated at long tables. There, too, the tables were covered with delicious food; again, the spoon handles were too long for human arms. However, there was no loud screaming, wailing, or complaining in Heaven. No one was hungry. *All of the people there were feeding each other.*

A godly Roman commander, in a vision, heard an angel calling his name, "Cornelius!" (Read about it in Acts 10.) Seeing the centurion's fear the angel put him at ease. "Your prayers and your alms have come up for a memorial before God."

How does your giving measure up? Is it ever noticed in Heaven?

Some thought it strange that I always took a collection from soldiers, even in combat, when I had a worship service with them.

The soldiers needed the blessing that comes from giving.

And so do you. You can't afford to be parsimonious. Amen

"There is one who scatters, yet increases more; And there is one who withholds more than is right, but it leads to poverty."

Proverbs 11:24

Lord; put a longer handle on my spoon. Amen

Jesus affirmed a most questionable woman.

Have you figured out yet that this woman who came in *off the street* into Simon's house and washed Jesus' feet with her tears was not well reputed?

It was brazen for her to walk into a stranger's house just because she heard that someone was there. Then to take over a servants chore. To act like she was a member of the household. What impudence.

Further, what she did had erotic overtones. She let her hair down in public. She handled a man's feet. She poured expensive perfume over a stranger's head.

Understand: I am not saying that she was intending to seduce Jesus.

She was just doing what she knew how to do. While others were scandalized by her behavior, Jesus saw the purity of her intentions. He defined her gift positively, accepting it, and affirming her in so doing.

The affirmation was redemptive. If you imagine, as I do, that this very woman may well have been the sister of Martha and Lazarus the plot really thickens.

Whether that is true or not we can take away from the story two valuable lessons.

The first is that Jesus looks into a person's heart. How often I have misjudged a person, formed unfair first impressions, because I could see only the surface.

The second is that it is important to seize the moment. What if the woman had listened to her fears? To others? To community mores? She may well have missed out on a most blessed experience, having Jesus accept and value her gift. And besides that, she made it into the New Testament. And look, we are still telling her story.

"...What this woman did will...be spoken of as a memorial to her."

Mark 14:9

November 15

What do you do when you fall flat?

Saul of Tarsus was a young rabbi with a bright future. (Read about it in Acts 9:1-9.) He hated the followers of Jesus; was determined to locate these latest heretics, chase them down, and destroy them. He knew that he was right. Had to be. He was doing it for God.

As he traveled he couldn't forget the words of the martyr Stephen. He had been at Stephen's stoning, had even watched the stoners' clothing for them. Stephen's preaching about Jesus nagged at his soul, causing him to be even more determined. Maybe there was something to what he had heard.

Then, boom!

Nearing Damascus he was confronted by Jesus in an explosion of light. Saul fell to the ground. I ask again, what do you do when you fall flat?

First, you ask how you got there. Saul was convinced that he was doing the will of God, but he had really been doing his own thing. He was operating out of his own prejudices.

Next, you accept a new vision. Saul had been so sure of himself. That he was right and the Christians were wrong. Now he learned that the very ones that he had been persecuting were God's special saints. He had to turn completely around. Accept the new reality.

But most importantly, you seek God's will. "Okay, Jesus, You know that I have been after Your followers. Thought I was doing the right thing, but know better, now."

"...Lord, what do You want me to do...?"
Acts 9:6

Lord, I often don't ask what You want me to do because I am afraid that You will tell me what I don't want to know. Help me to get past that selfishness, Lord, and be open and responsive to Your will for me. Amen

He had been earning a living from that field. Perhaps renting it. Maybe sharecropping.

One day his plow struck an object. He thought that it was just another rock. However, when he dug-up the object he discovered that it was a chest full of gold, gems, and rubies. (Read about it in Matthew 13:44.)

He knew that if the chest were his he would be rich.

He quickly re-buried the chest. He had to *own* the field. So, he *joyfully* sold everything that he had and bought the field. Who wouldn't be happy, selling junk to obtain treasure? Sounds like what happened when I gave my life to Christ.

The man found the treasure while going about his everyday duties.

Today I pray that you will find a treasure in your *field*.

Find a treasure in your job. Your family. Your neighborhood. Find a blessing that you have overlooked. It's easy to get into a rut, to see only the *forest*. But there are *trees* out there that are beautiful, blooming, colorful.

I have spoken a lot about happiness in this book. Everyone wants to be happy, but a lot of people don't know how. They seem to think that it comes from having things. The right friends. The best clothes. Or winning the lottery.

Happiness can't be bought or earned.

Happiness comes to you when you do your duty, serve the Lord, keep the golden rule, and live honestly.

So keep plowing your field. Sell your junk and buy real treasure. Embrace Jesus as Lord and Savior. Then you will know real happiness. Joy unspeakable. Amen

"...Happy are the people whose God is the Lord!"
Psalms 144:15

November 17

At a makeshift laboratory at Tuskegee Institute, Dr. George Washington Carver held a peanut in his hand and prayed, "Tell me, great Creator, why did you make the peanut?"

To the world's amazement he soon began to make things from the peanut: milk, cereal, soap, face cream, salad, vinegar, butter, paint, oil, dye, axle grease, shampoo, and a hundred other useful products.

His success greatly aided a nation too dependent on petroleum. And thousands of poor people were able to get jobs.

Early in my chaplaincy I helped a woman, the wife of a soldier in one of our units, work through some personal problems. On our last meeting she surprised me.

She brought her parents to meet me. They were both deaf, and had been since birth. Nevertheless they had mastered sign language, gotten a college education, held good jobs, and raised a child. I never saw anyone more proud of her parents.

In his sermon a pastor said that a lot of people ought to get up off their blessed assurances and get a job. I agree.

Are you looking at a peanut and seeing nothing more? Have you stopped dreaming?

Are you clinging to a handicap as an excuse? Have you given up? Are you satisfied with merely getting by?

It is wrong for you to live beneath your potential.

"...If you have *faith as a mustard seed*...."
Luke 17:6

I just have to pray, Lord, with the father who brought his son for healing: "Lord, I believe. Help my unbelief." Amen

November 18

A man was jogging through the neighborhood with his dog in tow.

The jogger's goal was pretty obvious, to have a good run. But the dog wasn't similarly motivated. He was interested in fire hydrants and trees, and the smorgasbord of sights, sounds, and odors.

We all have our agendas. But others impose their agendas on us too.

Shirley has expectations of me. So do my kids. The bishop has definite ideas about how I should behave and minister. When I was in the Army my Chiefs of Chaplains and Commanding Officers evaluated me according to their expectations.

My dear Dad's agenda for me was simple: to marry a local girl, live down the street, and raise grandchildren. He never did understand why I had to marry a girl from out of town, join the Army, and serve in faraway places. I know that he grieved because my family didn't live nearer.

Do you know God's agenda for you?

If you are planning marriage do you know if God approves of your choice of a mate?

If you are thinking of getting a divorce have you kept an open mind about it? Have you prayed honestly about it? Are you willing to stay married if God wants you to?

Are you seeking God's will about a vocation?

There are many wonderful pastors who are in ministry today as a second career. Meaning no offense, I wonder if God was calling earlier, but they were not listening.

"...Whoever does the will of My Father in heaven is My brother and sister and mother."
Matthew 12:50

November 19

Have you had your spiritual exam?

When I first joined the Army they required a physical exam every five years. As I grew older the frequency increased. It became three years, then two, and finally once a year.

Let's play doctor and give you a spiritual exam.

We start with your **ears**. Jesus said that His sheep know His voice and follow Him, and will not follow a stranger. He also condemned people who have ears to hear but don't. Do you hear well?

Next come the **eyes**. Are you seeing well? Jesus told the lukewarm Christians to "anoint your eyes with eye salve that you may see" (Rev 3:18).

Mouth and **throat**. What are you putting in and what comes out? How does your language sound? Any cursing or swearing? What about taking the name of the Lord in vain?

What about your **heart**? Is there hardness? You may see it in the way you view the lost, the needy; the people that are different from you. It can be seen in the way that you treat fellow Christians, even family.

We must check your **metabolism**. Are you eating the proper *food*, the "Bread of Life?" Are you getting your *rest*? The Scriptures teach that the believer has rest in Jesus, that he has ceased struggling and worrying, and learned to trust. Are you taking your *medicine*, the Word of God?

And, finally, are you getting enough *exercise*? If not, practice your faith.

It is a good time to get this checkup. Thanksgiving is near. Advent is just around the corner. Be ready. Stay healthy. Amen

"...Let a man examine himself...."
1 Corinthians 11:28

November 20

The beat is the thing. In some music the beat has become almost the only thing.

In the military the beat is the thing. When I was having trouble marching in the Chaplain Basic Course I was assigned a trainer. The young lieutenant informed me that, "The left foot hits the pavement when the bass drum sounds."

The beat is important in medicine. When the doctor puts the stethoscope to your chest the beat is THE thing.

Today your most difficult task may be to keep up the beat. To keep up your courage. Courage to live without your parents' help, to begin a new career, to witness for Christ, to live with a debilitating disease, or to face life after the death of a spouse.

There are times when you must force yourself to care for others.

The company that he keeps will corrupt a man who lives only by and for himself. The cross of Jesus, that reaches up to the highest heaven, and down into the lowest hell, also stretches outward, to the farthest, the darkest, and the most remote regions of the world.

There are times, when you are in God's will, that you have to hang on a little longer. The tide always changes. The great missionary, Adonirum Judson spent seven years in Burma before he won his first convert.

There are times that your faith may be fragile and has to be carefully nourished. Search and memorize the Scriptures. Pray. Keep company with other people of faith. Worship in church. Keep up the beat.

"...I run...not with uncertainty. Thus I fight: not as one who beats the air...I discipline my body and bring it into subjection...."
1 Corinthians 9:26,27

Lord, when I miss a beat, help me to hear more clearly the rhythm of Heaven. Amen

In the book, *Illusions. The Adventures of a Reluctant Messiah*, one of Richard Bach's characters observes that a person teaches best what he or she most needs to learn.

I wish I had understood that better when I was raising (or attempting to raise) my kids.

I was always after my oldest son about his not setting higher goals. My middle child, a daughter, upset me with her quickness to judge others. I was always trying to get my youngest son to be more rational in making choices.

I was trying to correct in my children deficiencies that I sensed, at least subconsciously, in myself.

Now that is not to say that my children didn't need parental instruction. But much energy was wasted as I aimed it in the wrong direction.

What inner motivation gives rise to the values *you* emphasize, the way *you* relate to others?

You are at your most mature self when you know who you really are and how you came to be that way; when you are dealing with reality, not fancy. When you are not knee jerking out of your own needs.

Inscribed on the Temple of Apollo at Delphi are two words: *Know Thyself.*

It's a mark of Christian maturity to know your inner motivations. But what is most important is to know the Lord.

"...I *know* whom I have believed and am persuaded that He is able to keep what I have committed to Him until that day."
2 Timothy 1:12

Lord, is the reason that I don't try to know myself better that I am afraid of what I will find? Help me to look honestly and deeply into my innermost self and give me the courage to deal with what is there. Amen

November 22

A little boy was asked by his teacher to describe salt. He answered, "Salt is what spoils the potatoes when you leave it out."

Thankfulness is like that. It spoils everything when you leave it out. It flavors every relationship and enhances every exchange when you include it.

I heard a respected pastor say that children who get under foot need praise. He further stated that giving thanks for something about which you really aren't happy releases God's power of healing into the situation.

It isn't always easy to be thankful for something for which you really aren't happy.

Take children for example. They can be very hurtful. In fact, the hurt by a son or daughter is the most painful hurt of all. And a praise a day doesn't always keep delinquency away. But don't you agree that the good pastor was on to something?

It is the time of the year to be thankful. The President will declare a certain Thursday as a holiday. The federal government will give its employees time off with pay. The Scriptures are filled with urgings to give thanks.

Remind yourself of the many ways that God has blessed you. As you count the ways your spirit will be humbled and thankful. You won't need my laundry list of things to be thankful for, either. And you will be blessed.

Dear Lord, from the deepest part of my heart, and with the sincerest effort of my mind, I thank you for loving and blessing me so. Amen.

"In *everything* give thanks; for this is the will of God in Christ Jesus for you."
2 Thessalonians 5:18

So, here's an easy quiz: how can you know that you are doing the will of God? The answer is in the text above. Don't forget, it says everything. Not just the pretty things, the easy things, the fun things. Everything! Go for it.

November 23

My commander at Sixth U.S. Army had asked me to furnish him a brief written devotion to begin each day. In fact, that request started a process that resulted in the writing of this book. (Thank you, LTG Bill Harrison.)

The problem was that training and travel requirements often made it necessary to write for a future date. So it was that I was writing the Thanksgiving devotion on Halloween day. It was 1990. Desert Shield was boiling. I feared that we could be at war by Thanksgiving. But I couldn't know.

So I wrote about courageous thanksgiving. Like that of St. Paul, who, after surviving a disastrous shipwreck, knelt on the beach and gave thanks to God.

Courageous thanksgiving is the kind that we give when things are bad. It is given because of who God is despite our personal circumstances, good or bad.

Giving thanks releases God's power of healing in our lives. It begins the process of recovery. Giving thanks acknowledges that man is not the ultimate measure of things, that there is a higher power, a divine plan. It is an admission of our humanity.

"In everything give thanks, for this is the will of God concerning you" (1 Thessalonians 6:18). The key to this text is the preposition. Paul didn't say give thanks *for* everything, but *in* everything.

In the midst of all human situations, in gladness or sorrow, in victory or defeat, in suffering or health, in *everything* give thanks. I know this may sound a little Pollyanna, but it is the only game in town. Nothing else works: neither anger, bitterness, nor recrimination.

"...Paul ...thanked God and took courage."
Acts 28:15

Lord, I don't want thanksgiving to be just a day, or a season. I want it to be the key in which my heart sings. Every day. All day long. Amen

November 24

Yesterday I wrote about Courageous Thanksgiving. Today I want to tell you how to do it.

Everyday, give thanks to God for something for which you aren't happy. This is important. It acknowledges the sovereignty of God. That He is wiser than you. It indicates that you recognize your dependence on His mercy and grace. That today isn't all that there is. That He can take care of tomorrow.

A young, divorced, mother and her son sat down to eat. It was Thanksgiving evening. There wasn't much on the table. She had worked a long day at the diner and was weary to the bone. She was so very depressed. She asked her son to ask the blessing. In his little boy way he said his usual prayer, then thanked God for wallpaper.

Wallpaper? A ray of light! She realized how far down she had let herself slide. That she still had much to be thankful for. Her son. Their health. Her job. Wallpaper.

Giving thanks releases the power of God into the situation. It is an act of will. An exercise of faith. It is not just meek acceptance. Fatalism. Rather, it is an expression of faith that envisions a brighter future, and clings to it with tenacious determination.

So, how are you doing these days? Are you down to thanking God for wallpaper? Then go ahead.

It's better than sitting in the dark and moaning, or wasting your breath whining. Go on. Give thanks to God, as the Scriptures instruct you to, and let the responsibility be His.

"Continue earnestly in prayer, being *vigilant in it with thanksgiving.*"
Colossians 4:2

Lord, I am thanking You for this great house you have blessed me with. But I am not forgetting wallpaper. Amen

November 25

Give thanks for something that is beyond your understanding. (This devotion follows the theme of the last two days, *Courageous Thanksgiving*.)

One of the greatest Thanksgiving hymns came from the pen of Martin Rinkert. He was the only minister to survive the terrible years in Eilenburg, Saxony. From 1620-1648, pastor Rinkert's parish was ravaged four times by invading armies.

Then the plague came. For a whole year Rinkert conducted as many as fifty funerals a day. Nearly 4000 burials, one of which was his wife.

The villagers never thanked him. Yet he wrote the song that we sing every Thanksgiving:

Now thank we all our God,
With hearts and hands and voices;
Who wondrous things hath done,
In whom His world rejoices.

Giving thanks to God, even (especially!) in bad times, acknowledges that He is in charge. That it is His world. His plan. His responsibility. And that we are but His people.

It is the human response that is the most positive, and the most remedial, in finding spiritual and physical healing.

The best advice I can give you today, if you are a Christian struggling with your faith, is to take a few minutes to give thanks to God. You will find personal release, and discover God's power at work in your life.

"...Let the peace of God rule in your hearts, to which also you were called in one body, and *be thankful*."
Colossians 3:15

November 26

It is true that the Pilgrim fathers, George Washington, Thomas Jefferson, and others celebrated a day of thanksgiving.

However, it was Sarah Hale who probably did more to persuade the government to establish a national day of thanksgiving.

Mrs. Hale began writing letters and calling on leaders in 1825. Finally President Lincoln accepted Mrs. Hale's suggestion, in 1863, and proclaimed the fourth Thursday of November the "National Thanksgiving Day."

It is good to have a special day to give thanks to God for His many blessings. But it is better to form the habit of giving thanks every day.

After being robbed, the great Biblical expositor, Matthew Henry, wrote:

"Let me be thankful, first, because I never was robbed before. Second, because although they took my purse, they did not take my life. Third, because when they took my all it was not much. Fourth, because it was I who was robbed, and not I who robbed."

Over the years I have developed a simple prayer that I use for practically any occasion, and sometimes when there is no special occasion at all. It is two sentences long.

Pray this prayer with me. After each sentence pause and reflect appropriately. Let's do it:

Dear Lord, thank You for all of the ways that you have blessed me. Bless me all of the ways that I need. Amen

"Enter into His gates with thanksgiving, and into His courts with praise. Be thankful to Him, and bless His name."

Psalm 100:4

November 27

Randy Travis had a hit song entitled, *On The Other Hand.*

The song's sentiment is something like this. On one hand I probably would enjoy having something going with you. But on the other hand? Well, on the other hand there's a golden band (a wedding ring) so I can't do it.

Jesus used the *one-hand/other hand* technique when He contrasted what He came to do with what the devil does.

What the devil is good at is highlighted in the daily headlines.

You see thievery, murder, destruction, rape, battery, all kinds of mischief; you name it and it is there. Little children beaten to death by parents. Spouses killed by spouses. Parents killed by their own children. It boggles the mind.

What a contrast Jesus brings.

In the midst of turmoil, tragedy, heartbreak, and suffering He brings life. Life in its broadest and deepest meaning. Spiritual health. Peace of mind. Fulfillment.

Don't think that you are being selfish when you seek and expect to receive God's best.

In fact, according to the beloved Apostle John, God wants you to have it: "Beloved, I pray that you may prosper in all things and be in health, just as your soul prospers" (3 John 2).

Today you should drink deeply from the cup of salvation. Don't be a spiritual pauper. Your Father is rich and powerful. Amen

"The thief does not come except to steal, and to kill, and to destroy. *(On the other hand)* I have come that they may have life, and that they may have it more abundantly."
John 10:10

Thank You Lord that I am on the "other" hand, and not on the hand of the one that comes to kill and destroy. Amen

November 28

What does it mean to be honest? Are you?

A janitor in Los Angeles picked up a canvas bag containing $240,000 in ten and twenty-dollar bills. He could have kept the money. In fact, many people ridiculed him for not keeping it. His kids were taunted mercilessly.

His explanation? "It wasn't our money, so we gave it back. How could anybody do otherwise and have peace of mind?" To him the $10,000 reward and a clear conscience added up to a lot more than $240,000.

"To thine own self be true, and it must follow, as the night the day, thou canst not then be false to any man." (Shakespeare)

I am committed to absolute honestly, but it is not always easy to know what is right anymore. Do you disagree? Well, what about that quarter you find in the pay telephone? It would cost more than that, plus your time, to return it to the Phone Company. If you put the quarter in your pocket are you stealing? If you leave it in the slot are you cheating the company?

The rapid pace of technological changes constantly challenges us to know, to understand, and to do, what is right. If we who are the light of the world and the salt of the earth can't live honestly who can?

Suppose someone says that you did something that you didn't do. You can be sure of yourself if your life's motto is to always do the right thing. You don't have to remember if you did it. You only have to know that it wouldn't have been the right thing to do.

I haven't always been able to live up to such a high standard, but I am not willing to use advanced technology or the next innovation as an excuse for not trying.

"...All who act dishonestly, are an abomination to the Lord your God.
Deuteronomy 25:16 (RSV)

November 29

After a conversation with Robert Ingersoll, an agnostic famous for his speeches and books against the Bible, General Lew Wallace decided to write a book to disprove that Jesus Christ ever lived.

For years Lew Wallace combed the libraries of the United States and Europe collecting material. He was eager to prove that what the New Testament says about Jesus is a fraud.

But as he began to write he had a change of heart. It became clear to him that Jesus was just as real a person as Socrates, Plato, Caesar, and other ancient men.

Conviction became certainty. He fell to his knees and prayed for the first time in his life. He asked God to reveal Himself, forgive his sins, and help him become a follower of Christ.

Light broke across his soul. He woke his wife to tell her that he had received Jesus as his Lord and Savior. She had prayed ever since he started writing that he would *find* Jesus while he wrote about Him.

But what to do with the materials he had gathered for the book?

He wrote *Ben Hur*. Using the same materials, but now from the position of faith, he wrote a tale of the Christ, and it was an all time best seller. Have you read it? Did you see the movie? Charlton Heston and everyone?

The story of Lew Wallace's conversion to Christ is an example of the *power of the Gospel*.

When the story of Jesus is told people are changed, saved. I must tell it. You must tell it. It is the greatest story ever told. Amen.

"...In Christ Jesus I have begotten you through the Gospel."

2 Corinthians 4:15

November 30

You have heard statements like these: "She was always in her sister's shadow." Or, "He never escaped his dad's shadow."

What kind of shadow are you casting? And over whom?

If you study the New Testament references about the Apostle Peter you get some stark contrasts.

Look at Peter on the mountain, a witness to the transfiguration of Jesus. What shadow does he cast? Jesus burst forth, shining from light emanating from inside Him. Peter stuttered and stumbled. "Lord, we can build tabernacles for everybody," I paraphrase. (Big crowds, big collections, and big importance: The shadow of a confused, perhaps selfish, Christian?)

Then look at Peter the night Jesus was arrested. He was standing outside, by the fire, when a young girl recognized him. She told those standing nearby that Peter had been with Jesus. Said it had to be true, because even his speech betrayed him. Peter denied it vehemently, cursing to make his point. (Fear driven, lying, cursing: The shadow of a sinning Christian?)

Then there is Peter after Pentecost, a fearless Apostle and powerful preacher. Crowds. Healings. People lined up in the street to have his shadow fall across them. The shadow of a successful Christian!

Which shadow are you casting? Selfish? Sinful? Or is the shadow of a true servant of Christ? And who is feeling your shadow? Let us pray for more of the Spirit, for that surely made the difference in Peter.

"...They brought the sick out into the streets...that at least *the shadow of Peter* passing by might fall on some of them."
Acts 5:15,16

Lord, I don't want my shadow to bring disrepute to those around me, who love me. I don't want to deny you. Help me to so live my life that those near me can find shade. Amen

Advent

Happy First Sunday in Advent!

He was the caretaker of a beautiful castle garden in Germany. One day a stranger asked him how long he had worked there. "Over 40 years," the caretaker replied.

The stranger then asked how many times the owner had visited. "Never," the caretaker answered.

Next the stranger asked how he knew what the owner wanted him to do. "He told me what to do when he gave me my commission," responded the caretaker.

"You've kept this garden so beautiful one would think that you expected the owner to arrive soon," the stranger remarked.

"I expect him today," the caretaker said.

That's the message of Advent.

The coming of the Messiah caught the world, even the religious community, by surprise. Don't let Christ's Second Coming catch you unprepared.

In Advent we look back to the coming of Christ into the world, and the great salvation that He wrought. We also look forward to His return to the earth to establish His kingdom.

Expect Him today!

"Take heed, watch and pray; for you do not know when the time is."
Mark 13:33

Dear Lord, I am cluttered with the noises and symbols of this wonderful season. I love it, but it can be overwhelming. Please bless me with good spiritual hearing, and keen insight, so that I won't miss the true message of Advent. Amen

Hanukkah

Happy Hanukkah!

In 167 BC a Syrian officer brought an unnamed Jew to the temple in Jerusalem and made him offer a sacrifice to Zeus on the holy altar. A priest named Mattathias witnessed the event, slew them both, called on the Jewish faithful to follow him, and then fled to the hills.

Mattathias and his sons organized the people for war, defeated the Syrian Army, and secured the city. The Syrian ordinances were repealed and the temple was cleansed so true worship could resume. (The deuterocanonical books of 1st and 2nd Maccabees record the events.)

Modern Jews remember this great event as the Feast of Dedication or Hanukkah (also spelled Chanukah). It is also known as the Feast of Lights and is marked by the lighting of eight candles. Jewish faithful around the world will observe this feast by lighting a candle today and continuing to do so for eight days.

Jesus attended the Feast of Dedication during His ministry (John 10:22). For over two thousand years the tradition has continued.

As a Christian I share the joy of my Jewish brothers and sisters, and notice the coincidence in the timing of Hanukkah with another wonderful event much associated with light that comes the 25th of December.

I thank God for the Jews. I thank them for obeying the call of God to be a chosen people. I pray for Jews everywhere, and the Jewish state.

No Christian can ever please God and hate Jews.

I appreciate that my Savior was a Jew, *The Light of the World.*

Shine in my heart today, oh Christ. Brighten my mind and lighten my path. Make me to know joy and gladness. Fill my day with the brilliance of Your glory. Amen

"In Him was life, and the life was the light of men."
John 1:4

December 1

What is the urgency in spiritual readiness?

It seems like preachers like to scare people. Be ready for the end of the world. The return of Christ.

On October 17, 1965, I was called out of teaching a Sunday School class to receive a telegram from the Department of the Army. It was read to me over the telephone. I was ordered to active duty in the Army and required to report not later than November 1.

I was able to make the reporting date because the call didn't catch me by surprise. I had known that I was going to be called up. I just didn't know when. So I got ready, doing all of the things I could do without actually giving the church notice of my leaving. Then I *stayed ready*.

That, my friends, is the message of Advent. Don't let His coming catch you unaware, not ready, like a thief in the night.

A poor boy and a rich girl fell in love. But her parents were adamant in their disapproval of their plans to marry. So they decided to wait five years. Grow a little more. Surely her parents would change their minds when he returned in better financial condition. He went away, worked hard, saved his money, and built a home. She enjoyed parties with her friends.

After the five years he returned for his bride. When he arrived at her home there were cars and lights and lots of people. He walked around to the back yard and there she was, in another man's arms. He didn't say a word. Just got in his car and left, and she never knew that he had come.

It's Advent. This is the time to think of and work toward spiritual readiness. How are you doing? Making any progress?

"...What I say to you, I say to all: Watch!"
Mark 13:37

December 2

For years their leader had warned of the coming apocalypse. It finally came. But only for them.

Shirley and I had driven to the site where the Branch Davidians had lived near Waco, Texas. It was just days after the siege had ended. All that remained was charred rubble that had been bulldozed into piles. Signs warned of contamination.

The pastures along the roadside were green. Cattle grazed peacefully. The corn was getting tall. Birds sang.

If it hadn't been for hawkers peddling T-shirts with *We Aren't Coming Out* emblazoned on them we could have missed that the Davidians had ever been there.

The blessed season of Advent is upon us.

We look back on Christ's first coming and learn that we must be prepared for His return to the earth. The prayer of Advent is, "So come, Lord Jesus."

All of the liturgies, sermons, and songs combine to teach us to be ready. However, Holy Scripture and common sense also teach us to be cautious.

"...If anyone says to you, 'Look, there is the Christ!' or 'There!' do not believe it.

For false christs and false prophets will arise and show great signs and wonders, so as to deceive, if possible, even the elect."
Matthew 24:23,24

Lord, the song of a false messiah can be so sweet. So enticing. It allows me to retain my old biases. It permits me to be comfortable with my paranoia. It lets me feel that I belong while concealing the loss of my selfness.

Guard my mind and heart, Lord. Don't let me be enticed by the siren sound of a spiritual Lorelei. Bless me in this Advent season, Lord. Amen

December 3

Who are you? It depends on whom you ask.

To some scientists you are a higher animal.

To some behaviorists you are a puppet.

To some psychiatrists you are a pile of secrets.

To some idealists you are a struggle between heaven and earth.

To the Internal Revenue Service you are a number.

To the businessman you are a customer.

To the mailman you are an address.

To the manufacturer you are a consumer.

Some say that you are what you think. Others say that you are what you eat. Still others say that you are what you achieve.

There is great wisdom in knowing yourself. Your idiosyncrasies. Those inner proclivities. The hidden weaknesses. The unrealized strengths. When you truly know yourself it doesn't really matter how others know you.

What is most important is what you are to God.

To God you are a human being that He loved so much that He sent His Son to die for you on the cross.

If you trust in Jesus as Lord and Savior, you are a child of God. There is no higher relationship. No greater honor.

So who are you? You are someone that God loves. Amen

Dear Lord, I know that I can't ever be worthy of Your love, but I do want to please You. You have blessed me immensely. I am rich in your grace. Thank you Lord. Thank you. Thank you. Amen

"We love Him because He first loved us."
1 John 4:19

December 4

Bethlehem is a magic word for Christians. The Bethlehem star has been a subject of much scholarly inquiry.

Was it Halley's Comet that shone brightly in 11 BC? Or the conjunction of Saturn and Jupiter in 7 BC? Or was it the "Dog Star," Mesori Sirius that rose at sunrise and shone with extraordinary brilliance during 5-2 BC? Mesori means "birth of a prince," so the Magi could easily have understood it to signal the birth of a great king.

Perhaps it was a special star, created for such a purpose, hung out to shine by divine command, to mark the birth of the world's savior. I can believe that.

And why Bethlehem, an obscure village in an occupied land, of no political importance?

I would have chosen a different spot: Rome, the center of world government; Athens, the cultural and academic magnet; Alexandria, rich in centuries of history and commerce; or London, already a growing city, on the edge of the future.

In Biblical history Bethlehem is significant. Jacob was buried there (Genesis 35:19, 20). Ruth lived there when she met Boaz (Ruth 2:1). Most of all it was king David's town (1 Samuel 20:6).

Bethlehem was the promised site: "...O Bethlehem Ephrathah... from you shall come forth... one who is to be ruler in Israel, whose origin is from old, from ancient days" (Micah 5:2 RSV).

Micah's prophecy came hundreds of years before the birth of Jesus in Bethlehem. Yet it came true. During this precious season of Advent you can know that the promise of the Scriptures will be fulfilled. Christ will come again. What encouragement. What a great hope. Blessed Advent!

May the brightness of Bethlehem shine in your eyes. And mine. God bless Bethlehem, and us. Amen

"When they saw the star, they rejoiced with exceedingly great joy."
Matthew 2:10

December 5

What a blessed time of the year! Jingle bells and Christmas music everywhere. It seems that everyone is wishing me a merry Christmas. Okay, but let's not rush. Let's savor the moments.

When the magi sought the young child they traveled without compass. Nor did they have an atlas with a highlighted route to follow. They searched for a king whose birth had been signaled by a star. Finally they drew near Bethlehem.

"Where is He?" they asked.

We do well to ask the same question during this Christmas season. Where is Jesus in all of this? Isn't He obscured by commercialism? Kids must have a terrible time separating Santa Claus and Jesus.

I watched a Christmas parade in a small southern town. In the Bible belt! Not a single float had a religious theme.

Where is Jesus in the home? Is He heard of only in a child's table grace? Has the family altar been replaced by the television?

When I was a kid and we all lived in the old house my mother had a plaque on the wall that read:

Christ is the head of this house,
The unseen guest at every meal;
The silent listener to every conversation.

I may not be able to do away with the commercialism around Christmas, or, as they say, put Christ back into Christmas. Nor can I make His will and teachings the center of international commerce and jurisprudence. But there is one thing I can do, one place I can control--my heart.

Dear Christmas Baby, be Lord in my life, and King of my heart. Amen

"...Where is He who has been born King of the Jews...?"
Matthew 2:2

December 6

He was the most embarrassed man that I ever saw.

He had stood up in the church and prophesied that Jesus would come back to the earth within six months. When I met him it was about two weeks after the six months had expired.

What he had done was all over town. He was a laughing stock. But he had gotten part of it right. The part that Christ *is* coming back. He just had the timing wrong.

In this Advent season, this blessed now, we rejoice that the Son of God came into the world and became our Savior. That is one part of Advent. The other part is that He will come again.

The key is to be ready.

His first coming caught the world by surprise. Even (especially!) the religious leaders. They had their own ideas about the Messiah. He would be a mighty warrior and loose the bonds of Rome.

The Scribes and Pharisees weren't ready for a suffering servant.

It is in His return that He will come in great power and glory.

Are you ready for Christ's return? If He called today to tell you that He was on His way would you need more time to get ready? An hour? A day? Week? Month?

Are you sure that you even want Him to return?

"Therefore you also be ready, for the Son of Man is coming at an hour you do not expect."
Luke 12:40

What worries me, Lord, is that I am living so well, have so much, and am so very comfortable, that I seldom think of Your return to the earth. I really appreciate Your rich blessings on me. Just don't let them turn my head from looking for and expecting Your return. Amen.

December 7

This is Pearl Harbor Day. Do you know the significance of this day in our Nation's history? It was on this day in 1941 that the attack on American military installations in Hawaii occurred.

The Japanese attack came just six days short of my ninth birthday. I heard about it at school the next day. The principal took a radio into the auditorium and had us all assemble to hear President Roosevelt declare war on Japan.

Military strength and readiness is a proper subject for Christians. If you don't think it's a moral issue explain how the world would be better if we hadn't taken Hitler on. And how better off the Pacific Nations and Asia would be under Japanese hegemony.

Readiness is a crucial spiritual issue. It is the essential message of Advent. Christ's first coming caught the world by surprise. While here on the earth He constantly warned His followers to watch and pray. If He comes today will you be ready? What about tomorrow?

This is a blessed season. Christmas lights illuminate our nights. Seasonal music enriches the sounds of our lives. I hope that you will get caught up in the magic of it. Despite the commercialism, the songs of the season tell us that God came into the world in the person of a baby.

Just as America had to reexamine its strategies after Pearl Harbor I pray that you will also take stock of your spiritual status.

Advent is a great time to draw near to the one who drew near to us at Bethlehem. The way to have Christmas all year long is to have the Christ of Christmas enriching your life in your daily walk and talk with Him. Go for it. Be ready. Stay ready.

"...As the lightning comes from the east and flashes to the west, so also will the coming of the Son of Man be."
Matthew 24:27

December 8

It is said that when Somerset Maugham gave a lecture on fiction writing he made the point that all fiction is based on four subjects: religion, high society, sex, and mystery.

He then asked the students to write short stories including those four subjects. He sat down to do a bit of quiet reading, but within a couple of minutes one student turned in his story.

"You've already written your story?" Asked Maugham.

"Yes sir," answered the student.

"And it has all the four elements in it?" Persisted Maugham.

"Yes sir," said the student.

"Very well," said Maugham, with a sneer, "Then read it to the class."

"'My God,' cried the duchess. 'I'm pregnant, who did it?'" he read.

The pages of the Bible, the world's most popular book, are filled with stories of religion, high society, sex, and mystery. But much more.

Of course the Bible is about religion.

The Bible is holy history, a book of redemption. But it is rich with stories about kings (e.g. Solomon, Herod) and Queens (e.g. Jezebel and Esther). There is a lot of sex in the Bible, too. The stories of David and Bathsheba (2 Samuel 12) and Sampson and Delilah (Judges 16) are raunchy.

There is mystery, too. When will Christ return to the earth? This wonderful season, Advent, is about being ready to meet Him.

And Advent highlights the greatest mystery of all, the Incarnation. I can't explain it, how a virgin could conceive a son by the Holy Ghost. And how He could be fully God and fully man. I don't understand it, but I glory in it.

Snow, bells, lights, sleigh rides, busy shoppers, and carols; all of it is great. But guess who is the reason for the season.

"...The Word became flesh and dwelt among us, and we beheld His glory...." John 1:14

December 9

When I buried my dear friend, Chaplain Jim White, I learned lessons important for Advent.

When I arrived at Jim's home I began to look through his files, to see if he had left instructions. His *stuff* was together. One learns organization during a career in the Army.

Jim had a file for everything: insurance, allotments and pay, property and investments, wills, and so forth. His living will instructed that every effort be made to donate his organs, and that heroic measures would not be taken if he should become vegetative.

But he had not planned for the quail eggs.

Jim had rigged an incubator and was hatching quail eggs in his office. He raised quail commercially for sale to restaurants and airlines. Quail eggs (all eggs?) have to be turned daily in order for them to hatch. By the time someone noticed the incubator it had been four days.

Jim was a good and honest person, and certainly ready to meet the Lord. His death left a great lesson in preparedness, but also in the frailty of human plans.

Advent reminds us that the world was not ready for the coming of the Messiah. Both religionists and scientists were caught off guard.

In Advent we also remember that the second coming of Christ will be like a thief in the night. Are you ready? You may have done the big-ticket items, but what about the quail eggs?

Hello God!

"Therefore you also be ready, for the Son of Man is coming at an hour when you do not expect Him."
Matthew 24:44

Lord, don't let me forget the quail eggs, the little things. As I evaluate my spiritual well being during Advent, and prepare my heart for Christmas, help me to be thorough. Amen.

December 10

The following account is how a kindergarten teacher attempted to explain the omnipresence of God.

"Is God in your bedroom?" She asked?

"Yes."

"Is God in your kitchen?"

"Yes."

"Is God in the den with you when you play Nintendo?"

"Yes," The children responded, giggling.

The teacher then said that God can also be found outside the home. "God is even in the Best Value grocery store," she said.

"Which aisle?" One little girl asked immediately.

The omnipresence of God. What does it mean?

Must we understand it in a scientifically literal sense, as though He can be captured in a jar? Hardly. From the Scriptures we understand that God is everywhere that He chooses to be, and in what measure or form that He wishes.

The Jews saw the glory of God in pillars of fire or smoke in their wilderness wanderings. The Hebrew word behind "glory" is *Kabod*, often translated weight, or heaviness. It's a stretch, but think of God appearing above them in a concentration of His presence to warm them by night (fire) or cool them by day (smoke).

It's Advent, and our thoughts turn to the incarnation.

It boggles my mind to try to understand how God became man, in the person of Jesus Christ. Saint Paul painted the reality beautifully in his letter to the Philippians. Scholars believe that the portion in Chapter 2 may have been a hymn of the early church.

Follow, as Paul recounts how Christ Jesus,

"Who, being in very nature God, something to be grasped, but made Himself nothing, taking the very nature of a servant, being made in human likeness...humbled Himself, and became obedient to death...."

Philippians 2:6-8 NIV

December 11

We tried hard to get into the Christmas spirit in the Canal Zone. The problem was the climate. It was hot.

It is hot all of the time in Panama. It is hot and wet 8 or 9 months of the year and hot and dry 3 or 4 months of the year. Christmas comes in the hot and dry, and windy, period.

We were determined to have a great Christmas Eve despite climactic realities. Prior to leaving the candlelight communion service I instructed the congregation to carry their candles outside, still burning. We were going to gather at the manger and conclude the service by candlelight. The candles blew out the moment we stepped outside.

Adding to my sense of frustration was that I had heard that the youth of the chapel were complaining about having to do the live nativity scene. It wasn't even live. Not all of it. The animals were plastic, and the baby doll.

I had drifted into a kind of morose funk, and I felt that the congregation was just about as unhappy as I was. Might as well go sing to a plastic baby Jesus and get this thing over with. A wonderful surprise awaited us.

When we arrived at the manger there was a *live* baby lying in it. He appeared to be newborn. I was amazed. I didn't know how he had gotten there. But I wasn't going to miss a blessing. We sang Silent Night with all of our hearts, many of us with a teary catch in our throats. That still is my most memorable Christmas Eve.

(We learned later that a young couple had been walking by the chapel, just before we departed the sanctuary, and had put their newborn baby in the manger in place of the plastic doll. Caught in the rush, they waited until the ceremony was over to retrieve the infant.)

"...This will be the sign to you: You will find a Babe wrapped in swaddling cloths, lying in a manger."
Luke 2:12

December 12

Carl Sagan referred to planet earth as a "pale, blue dot." He was describing a picture taken by a voyager spacecraft from 3.7 billion miles out in space.

"The earth is a very small stage in a vast cosmic arena," Sagan wrote. "What is the glory and triumph of the greatest conquerors and builders of Empires? They were the momentary masters of a fraction of the blue dot. There is no better technological demonstration of the folly of human conceits than the distant image of our tiny world."

I agree with Sagan on the "folly of human conceits." But to the larger question, "What makes the earth special?" there has to be a scriptural, a theological, answer.

What makes earth special is that it is filled with people that God loves.

God loves better than humans do. It is easier for me to love humanity than it is for me to love some humans. I would have difficulty loving some of history's despots. Loving generically is sentiment, not real love.

God loves humans as a group and also as individuals. He loved Hitler.

I wish I had the ability to help you see how much God loves you. You are very special. As you go through this day please walk and talk like someone special, a dearly beloved child of God. You are, you know.

"...Because of His great love for us...it is by His grace you have been saved."
Ephesians 2:4,5

Lord, how You could be concerned with a "pale, blue dot" is beyond my comprehension. I am overwhelmed even more to realize that on that small dot of a planet, in the universe yet unmeasured, You can know and love me, specifically.

Thank You for Your love, Lord. And thank You for giving Your life that I might be saved from wrath to come, and have a home with You in Heaven. Amen

December 13

It was said of a Scottish pastor that he was "Invisible for six days a week and incomprehensible the seventh."

In the Chaplaincy we talked a lot about the "ministry of presence." I never liked the term. It seems to me the very height of arrogance to presume or claim that my just being somewhere is ministry. But it is.

Commanders often understand it better than chaplains do: "I want you out there, with the troops, chaplain." I had one commander that put so much emphasis on my being in the motor pool (vehicle repair and storage area) that I set up a field table there one day a week and did counseling and sermon preparation. He thought it was great.

One of my great disappointments was that because of a disease of the spine I had to stop running with the troops. Chaplains build goodwill doing that.

Did you know that one of the names that God calls Himself (there are seven in the Scriptures) is Jehovah-Shammah, "the Lord is there?" The theological term is *omnipresence*, the everywhere presence of God.

There was a *ministry of presence* to shepherds in a tiny village named Bethlehem nearly 2,000 years ago. The angels sang praise to God and heralded a baby's birth. The incarnation, or enfleshment, of God in human form is the greatest miracle, profoundest mystery, and most precious grace of all times.

The every-where-present God is with you today! As always! The God who lit up the skies of Bethlehem can brighten your life today. Happy Advent!

"Where can I go from Your Spirit? Or where can I flee from Your presence? If I ascend into heaven, You are there; if I make my bed in hell, behold, You are there."
Psalm 139:7,8

Congratulations to all of you who, like me, were born on this date. I wish you a very **Happy Birthday!** Bless you.

December 14

Your hands tell a lot about you. Your spiritual hands.

When I went into a state prison to visit an inmate they stamped my hand. The stamp would only be visible under a special kind of light. If there was trouble in the prison and I was taken as a hostage they would shine the light on my hand to help in my identification.

How do your hands look to God? Are they dirtied from involvement with the needy? The down and out? Are they callused from the hard work of the Kingdom? Are they soft, tender? From non-use?

On a recent cold day I reached into my jacket with a gloved hand and learned a spiritual lesson: the danger of insulation.

While wearing my gloves I am protected from sharp edges. And the cold or heat does not discomfort me. But I can't use this word processor. Or play my mandolin.

Are you sensitive to the needs around you? To the voice of God? To the requirements for Christian discipleship? Beware of calluses of the spirit.

The hands of Jesus are prominent in the Scriptures. They help to identify Him. How else do you think the Emmaus disciples recognized Him in the breaking of the bread? They saw the nail holes. (Read about it in Luke 24:13-27.)

Zechariah prophesied that the Messiah would have wounds in His hands (13:6). In heaven Jesus is seen as a lamb *slain* (Revelation 5:6).

Advent, the season when we realize how very much God has done for us, is a good time to ask what we have done for Him. And for others. Look at your spiritual hands and they will tell you what you need to know.

"...He *showed them His hands*...Then the disciples were glad when they saw the Lord."
John 20:20

Lord, do I dare show You my hands?

December 15

He was the saddest soldier I ever saw.

While stationed at Camp Casey, Korea, a soldier came to me for counseling. He wanted me to tell him what to do. He simply couldn't bear having to decide between his two families.

He had left a wife and three children at home during his thirteen-month tour in Korea. While in Korea he had lived with a Korean woman who bore him a daughter. He wept as he told me that he loved both his families. To keep one he would lose the other. And he had to return to the states in less than ten days. "What can I do, chaplain?"

Where is King Solomon when you need him? Two women claimed the same infant as their child. Solomon offered to cut the baby in two and give each woman half. The true mother said no, that the other woman could have the child. Of course Solomon then knew who the true mother was, and handed the baby to her.

I tried to help the soldier see how the law defines his predicament. Then I led him through the Scriptures, pointing out what the Bible teaches. We prayed together and I asked God to help him to know and do the right thing. I never did find out what he decided to do.

There is a hard truth here. No action is without its consequence. What may seem only fun and temporary today remains in your account. It may come back to haunt you tomorrow, or next year.

Advent, this blessed season when we contemplate the Lord's return to earth to bring judgment, is a good time to evaluate your attitudes and behavior. Is what you are planning to do tonight pleasing to God? This weekend? Will you regret it someday? Then don't do it. Amen

"He that sows iniquity will reap sorrow...."
Proverbs 22:8

December 16

A great sculptor was asked about his ability to carve such a perfect statue of a lion when he had no model. "Well," the sculptor answered, "I just carve away anything that doesn't look like a lion."

In his letter to the Ephesians St. Paul states that the devil "Works in the sons of disobedience" (2:2).

You only have to check the daily headlines to see his work.

How successful has the devil's working been in your life?

Is pleasure your consuming goal? Do you react violently when wronged? Do you hate? Do you harbor anger in your heart? Are you self disciplined? Do you worship regularly? What about your language? Your secret thoughts?

Because of His great love for you God *is* working in your life. His hammer and chisel sometimes hurts.

The failing of a cherished goal may be necessary to cause you to seek God's will for your life.

It may be that you have to be knocked flat on your back before you will look up.

You may have to lose a job to understand your utter dependence on God.

This is a time of preparation. Advent, the time when we remember that God sent His Son into the world, is the time when we prepare our hearts for His return.

Bear the hammer's blows, and the chisel's cut. Grow. Pray that God will keep chiseling until there is nothing left that "Doesn't look like a lion."

"...It is God who works in you both to will and do His good pleasure."
Philippians 2:13

Lord, there is still too much of me that doesn't look like a "lion." Keep whittling on me, Lord. But I hope that it doesn't hurt too much. Amen

December 17

When the first astronaut landed on the moon the American President exclaimed, "The planting of human feet on the moon is the greatest moment in human history."

Soon afterward Dr. Billy Graham challenged the President's remark. "With all due respect," he said, "The greatest moment in human history was when the infinite and eternal God set foot on the earth in Jesus of Nazareth."

The mystery of the Incarnation intrigues me during this blessed Christmas season.

That God's Son would come into this world and give His life for our sins is beyond my comprehension. The Psalmist struggled similarly, "What is man that You are mindful of him...?" (Psalm 8:4)

Years ago I read that a scientist had broken down the human body's components—hydrogen, oxygen, calcium, and other minerals—and placed its value at $1.98. Inflation surely has raised the price but the question remains.

Why are humans so valuable to God? I don't honestly know. But I do want you to realize that you are of incomprehensible value to God.

You will be buffeted today by the stress of many pressures. People and events may test you. Throughout this day please pause to reflect that God loves you. Carry that thought with you throughout this whole wonderful month.

"He who did not spare His own Son, but *gave Him up for us all*--how will He not also, along with Him, graciously give us all things?"
Romans 8:32 (NIV)

Dear Lord, Almighty God, it rattles my mind to consider what You have done for me. I am not worthy, Lord. At my best moment I fall short of deserving Your bountiful mercies and unlimited Grace. But thank You anyway, Lord. Amen

December 18

The smell of new mown hay!

Is that how you imagine the place where the baby Jesus lay? A clean, sanitary place? Where clean, sanitary animals lived at night and in inclement weather?

We can't know for sure whether the manger was in a man made stable or in a cave on the hillside where animals were kept. However, there is one thing that we can be certain of. The place smelled like a stable. It surely stank. Anyplace where animals live, urinate, and defecate stinks.

There is a great lesson here. He was not born in a palace, where only nobility could hear; or in a rich man's home, where the poor would be unwelcome.

He breathed His first breath in a stable.

Hello God!

He came into a world of sin and alienation, wars and sufferings, and poverty and disease.

He comes into the messiness of our lives. Into the poverty, racism, cocaine babies, battered wives, substance abuse, and homeless children. Into our guilt and shame.

He is with us among the frightening creatures in our lives.

He searches through the muck and mire of our barnyards. None of us is so far away that His love won't reach us. Nor is any of us is so far down that His power can't lift us. Yes, He is the Lord of the boardroom and marketplace, but He is also the Lord of the stable.

"...They...found Mary and Joseph, and the Babe *lying in a manger.*"
Luke 2:16

Lord, surely my righteousness must smell more like a barnyard than a floral shop to You. Thank You that Your righteousness has been imputed to me. Amen

Do you have a mental filing cabinet of people who have wronged you?

Remembering the slights? The hurtful deeds? Slanderous words? Emotional injuries? From an insulting neighbor? A rebellious child? A nagging spouse? An abusive boss? How do you deal with it?

Do you look for ways to get even? We are in rebellion against God when we seek vengeance. Vengeance is His. We are in rebellion against God when we don't forgive. Forgiveness is His, but it flows through us. No one has a right to try to withhold it.

Do you want to be right or reconciled? Repay hurt with hurt and remain estranged. Forgive and be forgiven. Forgiveness is the critical factor in reconciliation. It is the most blessed gift that you can give another.

Forgiveness and healing go together. You experience healing when you forgive, and so does the person that you forgive. Forgiveness also brings peace to your conscience. Because when you forgive you turn the situation and the person over to God.

You say, "But I don't feel like forgiving." You don't have to feel like it. It is an act of the will. Feeling comes later, after forgiving. It is true psychologically that when you act positively, and continue the action, the feelings follow.

The number seven, in Scripture, is symbolic of completeness, totality. With that in mind, read on.

"...Peter came to Him and said, 'Lord, how often shall my brother sin against me, and I forgive him? Up to seven times?' Jesus said to him, 'I do not say to you, up to seven times, but up to *seventy times seven*.' "
Matthew 18:21,22

Lord, I would rather get even than forgive. Because I know that when I forgive You expect me to forget. I prefer remembering and plotting. That is wrong. Forgive me. Help me to be faithful to forgive and quick to forget. Amen

December 20

Have you sung, or hummed, any medieval hymns lately? You probably have, although you may not have known it.

O Come, O Come, Emmanuel is a Christian hymn from that period of the church's history. It was sung then as a series of antiphons, which are short musical statements. Each antiphon greeted the anticipated Messiah with one of the titles ascribed to Him.

There are five verses in the hymn, each one addressing Messiah by a different title. In addition to Emmanuel other titles are Wisdom, The Lord of Might, The Rod of Jesse, Day Spring, and The Key of David.

Just as faithful Jews anticipated the coming of the Messiah Christians anticipate His return. It is during Advent, a period beginning four Sundays before Christmas, that church liturgies deal with the great themes of preparation, readiness, and watchfulness.

It is a time for you to examine your heart, confess your sins, and draw closer to God.

Emmanuel means "God with us." Do you feel Him with you? Have you left Him somewhere? Or simply lost the sense of His presence in the busyness of your daily routine?

He has not forgotten you. As the refrain goes,

> *Rejoice, rejoice,*
> *Emmanuel!*
> *Shall come to thee,*
> *O Israel.*

"Behold, a virgin shall be with child, and bear a Son, and they shall call His name Immanuel, which is translated, 'God with us.' "

Matthew 1:23

December 21

Where does a person get time to write over 6,500 hymns? While doing itinerant ministry on horseback? And founding a church?

Of course I am referring to John Wesley. You have probably been singing one of his songs during this Advent, *Come, Thou Long-Expected Jesus*. The song was published in 1744 in a collection of poems for use in Nativity services. Rowland H. Prichard wrote the melody around 1830.

For centuries the world awaited the coming of the Messiah.

Again we wait, knowing that Christ has promised to return to the earth. Advent is not a time for just waiting. It is a time for watchfulness, for anticipation; for preparation.

Let us sing a prayer. Joining in with all of the saints throughout the ages, let us pray:

Come, Thou long-expected Jesus,
Born to set Thy people free;
From our fears and sins release us,
Let us find our rest in Thee.

Born Thy people to deliver,
Born a child and yet a king;
Born to reign in us forever,
Now Thy gracious Kingdom bring.

You will hear a lot of music today. There will be Jingle Bells, Winter Wonder Lands, Red Nosed Reindeers, and Frosty Snowmen.

But don't ever forget that the reason for this wonderful season is that precious baby that was born in Bethlehem. Move closer to Him, today. Amen

"I will shake all nations, and the desire of all nations shall come...."
Haggai 2:7, (KJV)

December 22

The feeling of anticipation is growing. And I am not talking about how many shopping days remain.

A star is moving toward Bethlehem, Kind David's hometown. We are beckoned. The prophet Micah prophesied 700 years before that something strange and wonderful would happen in Bethlehem:

"But you, Bethlehem Ephrathah, though you are little among the thousands of Judah, yet out of you shall come forth to Me the one to be ruler in Israel, whose goings forth have been from of old, from everlasting" (5:2).

We are also drawn to Bethlehem by the words of a great hymn, *O Come, All Ye Faithful*:

O Come, all ye faithful, joyful and triumphant,
Come ye, O come ye to Bethlehem;
Come; let us adore Him...Christ the Lord.

We are on a spiritual journey. Our travel takes us to a manger in a stable.

Are you ready to meet the Savior? You must sing the whole song, "O Come, let us adore Him, *Christ the Lord.*"

Is He Lord in your life? You still have three days to get ready.

"...Let us now go to Bethlehem and see...(what) the Lord has made known to us."
Luke 2:15

Lord, I am straining to hear the true songs of Christmas. There are so many other sounds flooding the airways. People seem to want me to think more of Santa Claus than of the Baby Jesus. And they seem to want me to value getting instead of giving.

Whatever the tunes, Lord, it is the message that clangs the bells of Christmas.

Christ is Lord. Amen

December 23

Did you get the present for Jesus yet? I'm serious.

Don't you remember His parable of the Judgment of the Nations (the Sheep and the Goats) in Matthew 25? And how He took everything personally?

When you fed the hungry you fed ME.

When you gave drink to the thirsty you gave drink to ME.

When you took in a stranger you took in ME.

When you clothed the naked you clothed ME.

When you cared for the sick you cared for ME.

When you *visited the* prisoner *you visited ME.*

See what I mean? So I ask again, what are you getting Jesus for Christmas? Having trouble thinking of something for such an important person? Need some help? I have some suggestions, based on what we learned above.

If you have room in your home, and you have love to give, you can consider adopting a baby. How wonderful it is to be adopted. I visited an orphanage overseas that had over 500 children, all reaching out their arms to me. An adopted child can say, "My parents chose me."

You should include in your stewardship ministries that help the people Jesus mentioned in Matthew 25: prisoners, those needing food and drink, the sick, those needing clothing, and the "strangers."

You can obey Christ's words in two ways. You can go into the prisons personally and take the Gospel. You can work in a food kitchen. You can become a volunteer at a hospital or nursing home. You can buy or donate clothing to those who cannot afford proper clothing. Or, you can give to send others to do these things. You must do one or the other.

To me personally the strangers are those still beyond the reach of the Gospel. Missionary ministries. Both and home and abroad.

"When they...saw the young child...they...opened their treasures, (and) they presented gifts to Him...."
Matthew 2:9

December 24

It is a rough trip from Nazareth to Bethlehem; and me riding bareback on this donkey, and nine months pregnant. It's cold.

Joseph has to go to Bethlehem, his hometown, because of a decree by Caesar Augustus. I would rather stay home but my husband is afraid to leave me by myself. I'll do the best I can.

These Plains of Esdraelon are so beautiful, despite the season. My ancestor, King Saul was slain here. How nice that we chose this route.

I'm glad we stopped here in Shechem to rest. I wish I could find where Abraham and Jacob built their altars. Oh, I love this cool water from Jacob's well. How refreshing! I can almost hear Joshua calling on the people to "Choose for yourselves this day whom you will serve." Shechem is such an important place in our people's history. But we had better hurry.

We are resting again, this time in Bethel. The name means House of God, getting its name from the place where Jacob wrestled with the angel. I wonder if it was also Gabriel that visited him here. My angel!

The Baby is restless. I wonder if He senses where we are. Ouch!

Ramah is a beautiful village. Samuel is buried here. Wish we had time to visit his grave. But we must move on.

I can't wait to see Jerusalem. Just five more miles. The City of David is so huge. And the temple is there. I wish I felt more like sightseeing.

I feel this baby moving. I'm scared. It's getting dark. I need to lie down and rest. But we have to hurry on to Bethlehem.

Won't a nice bed feel wonderful!

"...She brought forth her firstborn Son, and wrapped Him in swaddling cloths, and laid Him in a manger, *because there was no room for them in the inn."*

Luke 2:7

Hello God!

December 25

Merry Christmas.

For days my grandson had been asking about Baby Jesus. He obviously was trying to sort out all of the sights, sounds, and songs of Christmas. And he seemed to be doing a pretty good job of it too.

On that Christmas Eve he was particularly attentive during the candlelight communion service. At two and one half years he was usually more interested in crawling under, or running up and down the pews, than sitting still.

Then when Joseph and Mary were spotlighted his attention was riveted on Baby Jesus in Mary's arms. He sat perfectly still for the whole fifteen minutes of the scene.

Later, when we were home, he crawled into my lap and asked, "Poppa, will Baby Jesus grow up?" Then it dawned on me. For him, Christmas was happening right then and there. It was real.

As a pastor and chaplain for over forty years Christmas has become rather perfunctory for me. A ministry task. I *do* like Christmas and I can do a great Christmas service. But honestly, it has become rather routine.

How I would love to experience Christmas as Zachary Ian Randall did that week.

Dear Lord, let the Christmas child be born anew in my heart today. Let it be like a new beginning. And let Him live and grow there until I can experience Him in the same profound simplicity as my grandson. I don't want this wonderful Christmas spirit to grow stale, Lord. Amen.

"...A little child shall lead them."
Isaiah 11:6

Lord, I don't want to just *do* Christmas, I want to *live* it: like my grandson, Lord, with eyes wide and faith simple. Let the Christmas Child grow in my heart until I can surely know that He is the Lord of my life.

December 26

James Montgomery was appointed editor of the Sheffield Register in London at age 21, and held the position 32 years.

The son of Moravian missionaries, who had been killed on the mission field, he championed several social causes. His writings on the abolition of slavery, and the condition of the poor and downtrodden, won him two imprisonments.

During the last fifteen years of his life Montgomery was blind. He was a prolific writer of hymns. The one by which he is most remembered is *Angels, From The Realms Of Glory.*

You will surely be singing this great hymn during this wonderful season. As you do I hope that you will notice how the writer addresses different entities. First the angels, then the shepherds, then the wise men, and last, today's believers.

I will quote only the last verse and the chorus:

Saints before the altar bending,
Watching long in hope and fear,
Suddenly the Lord, descending,
In His temple shall appear.

Come and worship,
Come and worship,
Worship Christ, the newborn King.

I pray that you will accept James Montgomery's invitation today (and always): Worship *Christ, the newborn King.* Amen

"And behold, an angel of the Lord stood before them, and the glory of the Lord shone around them, and they were greatly afraid."
Luke 2:9

Are you still singing Christmas Carols? Don't let the spirit fade. *Joy to the world, the Lord is come!*

December 27

Isn't this Christmas music great?

You don't hear it? Right, and isn't it a shame? Why must radio and television stations stop playing Christmas music at midnight on December 25?

Let's keep singing anyway. A most joyous Christmas hymn is *Joy To The World*. It captures the mood and message of the great passage of the Psalmist in Psalms 98:4-6:

> "Shout joyfully to the Lord, all the earth;
> Break forth in song, rejoice, and sing praises.
> Sing to the Lord with the harp,
> With the harp and the sound of a psalm,
> With trumpets and the sound of a horn;
> Shout joyfully before the Lord, the King."

The song first appeared in a hymnal by Isaac Watts in 1719. It was probably Lowell Mason who later set the hymn to music, influenced by Handel's *The Messiah*, which was first performed in 1742.

Let's sing a few bars:

Joy to the world, the Lord is come! Let earth receive her King;

Let ev'ry heart prepare Him room, and heav'n and earth sing.

Joy to the earth the Savior reigns. Let men their songs employ.

While fields and floods, rocks, hills and plains; repeat with sounding joy.

The child is born. Hallelujah! Let Him be born anew in your heart, and mine. Keep singing. Amen

"Then the angel said to them, 'Do not be afraid, for behold, I bring you good tidings of great joy which will be to all people'."

Luke 2:10

December 28

Oh, what a night, was the night that fell on Bethlehem,
Oh, what a song, the angel chorus came to sing;
Oh, what a Baby, to cause a Blessed Mother's smile,
Oh, what a gift, when God gave the Christmas Child.

(From the Christmas Cantata, *Following the Star*, by this author.)

I'm still singing. December the 25th has come and gone. But the joy of Christmas remains. What about you?

It was early in the 19th century. There was a problem in Tyrol, high in the majestic Alps. Christmas was near, but the organ was inoperable.

Father Joseph Mohr wrote a song that could be accompanied by guitar. The village schoolmaster, Franz Gruber, wrote the tune, and the song was ready for the Christmas Eve Mass. You guessed it, didn't you?

Silent Night is the most beautiful Christmas carol. Let's sing it:

Silent night! Holy night! All is calm, all is bright;
Round yon virgin mother and child, holy infant, so tender and mild;
Sleep in heavenly peace
Silent night! Holy night! Son of God, love's pure light;
Radiant beams from Thy holy face, with the dawn of redeeming grace,
Jesus, Lord at Thy birth.

It's now three days after Christmas. Three days after He was born the baby Jesus cried when hungry or needed changing, and suckled his mother. A normal, healthy child. What a lovely image.

It's easier to deal with a baby Savior than a grown Lord. But He grew. And so must you. Amen

"...There were in the same country shepherds living out in the fields, *keeping watch over their flock by night.*"
Luke 2:8

December 29

Don't lose the glow of Christmas. You can keep the blessing of Christmas in your heart if you keep singing.

Emily Elliott helps us to do that. She only intended to write a song to teach the truths of the Advent and Nativity of Jesus to her Sunday school children. However, the song she wrote is loved worldwide: *O Come to My Heart, Lord Jesus.*

Emily worked in St. Mark's Anglican Church in England, her father's church, during most of the last half of the 19th century. The song she gave us is filled with Gospel truth. Notice her effective use of contrast. We will use only 2 of the 5 verses.

Thou didst leave Thy throne and Thy kingly crown
When Thou camest to earth for me;
But in Bethlehem's home was there found no room,
For Thy holy Nativity.

The foxes found rest, and the birds their nest,
In the shade of the forest tree;
But Thy couch was the sod, O Thou Son of god,
In the deserts of Galilee.

Millions of people have sung the song's simple but eloquent refrain. How many began their Christian life realizing and personalizing the power of its invitation? Only God knows. Let's sing it together now as a prayer:

O Come to my heart, Lord Jesus. There is room in my heart for Thee. Amen

"...You know the grace of our Lord Jesus Christ, that though He was rich, yet for your sakes He became poor, that you through His poverty might become rich."

2 Corinthians 8:9

December 30

In these devotions after Christmas we have kept singing the songs. Before moving to New Years Eve, and a new emphasis, let's sing once more.

Go Tell It On The Mountain was first published in a songbook entitled *Folk Songs of the American Negro*, in 1907. It is a robust song, with clear rhyme and an active melody that ranges more than an octave. The song has been a blessing to all of God's people. Let's sing.

While shepherds kept their watching, o'er silent flocks by night; Behold, throughout the heavens there shone a holy light.

The shepherds feared and trembled when lo! above the earth; Rang out the angel chorus that hailed our Savior's birth.

Down in a lowly manger the humble Christ was born, and God sent us salvation that blessed Christmas morn.

Go tell it on the mountain, over the hills and every where. Go tell it on the mountain, that Jesus Christ is born.

What a song! Such profound simplicity. So rich in Gospel truth. And so challenging to us as Christians to tell the story of Christmas.

As this year dwindles down, and you look back on your spiritual journey, are you satisfied with your Christian witness? Have you told the story? Consistently? Has your behavior given validity to your words?

Dear Lord, help me to *tell it on the mountain.*

"You who bring good tidings to Zion, go up to a high mountain. You who bring good tidings to Jerusalem, lift up your voice with a shout, lift it up, do not be afraid; say to the towns of Judah, 'Here is your God'."
Isaiah 40:9 (NIV)

December 31

On this last day of the calendar year I need to know that you have clearly heard the Gospel in these devotions.

If you have been with me all year you know how sincerely I believe that the Gospel of Jesus Christ is the good news that sinners can be saved. Nevertheless, I want to spell it out for you, simply. If you aren't yet sure of your salvation here's what you should do.

First, you need to *admit* that you are a sinner. Being good is not good enough. Even moral men and women need God's forgiveness. While it is true that God knows if you are a sinner you still need to admit it. Put it into words, say, "God, I am a sinner."

Next, you need to *accept* God's forgiveness. You can do that because He has promised to forgive you when you ask Him to. He always does what He promises. Put it into words, say, "God, I accept your forgiveness."

Then, you need to *announce* that you have been saved. I don't mean grab a bullhorn and disrupt traffic. Simply tell others what God has done for you. You can't be a secret disciple and please God. It is when you tell others of God's saving act that you experience anew the joy of salvation. Put it into words, say, "Let me tell you what God has done for me."

Taking the steps that I outlined above only gets you through the door. You need more.

Find a good church and become a part of their congregation. There are blessings ahead that you can't now imagine. You will experience those blessings in cooperative fellowship with other Christians, and through the ministry of a pastor who faithfully preaches the Bible.

"If we say that we have no sin, we deceive ourselves, and the truth is not in us. *If we confess our sins*, He is faithful and just to *forgive us our sins* and to *cleanse us from all unrighteousness.*"
1 John 1:9

To order additional copies *of Hello God! a Daily Call to Faith and Worship*, send $17.00, plus $3.00 for postage and handling, to:

Henry Lamar Hunt
PO Box 463
Candler, FL 32111.

To order the author's second book, *Touching the Hand of Jesus,* send $12.50 plus $2.50 for postage and handling to the same address listed above.

Pay by check or money order.

You can also order both books on Floppy Disk. For *Hello God! a Daily Call to Faith and Worship*, send $12; and for *Touching the Hand of Jesus* send $10. Prices quoted for floppies include postage.

E-mail: CandlerSL@AOL.com
Telephone 352-687-1559
FAX: Call first to coordinate
http://www.authorsden.com/henrylamarhunt

The author enjoys hearing from readers and invites you to write him at the address above.